THE INDUSTRIAL ARCHAEOLOGY
OF DERBYSHIRE

THE INDUSTRIAL ARCHAEOLOGY
OF THE BRITISH ISLES

Series Editor: E. R. R. GREEN

Derbyshire, by Frank Nixon
The East Midlands, by David M. Smith
Lancashire, by Owen Ashmore
Scotland, by John Butt
Southern England, by Kenneth Hudson (2nd edition, revised)

ASSOCIATED VOLUMES

Bristol and its Region, by Angus Buchanan and Neil Cossons
Dartmoor, by Helen Harris
Gloucestershire Woollen Mills, by Jennifer Tann
Stone Blocks and Iron Rails, by Bertram Baxter
The Tamar Valley, by Frank Booker
Techniques of Industrial Archaeology, by J. P. M. Pannell

OTHER INDUSTRIAL HISTORY

Brindley at Wet Earth Colliery: An Engineering Study,
by A. G. Banks and R. B. Schofield
The British Iron and Steel Industry, by W. K. V. Gale
The Early Factory Masters, by Stanley D. Chapman
The Engineering Industry of the North of Ireland, by W. E. Coe

All these books are in uniform format

Frontispiece: *William Strutt, FRS 1756–1830, designer of the fireproof cotton mills of Derby, Belper and Milford*

The Industrial Archaeology of

DERBYSHIRE

FRANK NIXON

DAVID & CHARLES: NEWTON ABBOT

© FRANK NIXON 1969

Printed in Great Britain by
Latimer Trend & Company Limited Plymouth
for David & Charles (Publishers) Limited
South Devon House Railway Station
Newton Abbot Devon

Contents

5

List of Illustrations

PLATES

7

Plates not otherwise acknowledged are from the author's own collection

IN TEXT

Grateful acknowledgment is made to the individuals and organisations indicated for their kind permission to use the illustrations.

PART ONE

Preface

ON coming to live in Derbyshire twenty-five years ago the writer became interested in the signs of early industry which are everywhere to be seen. The first question which arose was 'what is it?' That answered, the sequence through who? and why? and how? and when? was inevitable.

The pursuit of answers to these questions has become a hobby of absorbing interest. It has led to excursions into little-known corners of the county, some of them of great and quiet beauty, to the formation of friendships with a large number of people who love the county, and to a deeper understanding of the writer's own profession through the study which it has entailed of the origins of processes and techniques.

The recent interest in industrial archaeology has come about through a realisation that many of the remaining relics of Britain's pioneering industrial enterprise are fast disappearing. The necessity to modernise industrial equipment, to widen roads and to build many more houses and factories, demands space that can no longer be left free for the preservation of the old and the obsolete.

Manifestly, there can be neither the hope nor the intention to preserve all of the industrial relics in which Derbyshire abounds. In order to succeed in preserving those most worthy it is essential to be selective. At the same time it is important that those in danger of destruction should be recorded, by photographic and written description. They provide valuable material for the study of the evolution of the technologies which they represent.

Although Derbyshire has been described as a poorly documented county, the search for information about its early industries has revealed an embarrassing wealth of data. In turn this has added to knowledge of the people who were involved—what manner of men they were, how they found their inspiration and their ideas, and how they solved the problems which confronted them.

The frequency with which Derbyshire installations are described in the old texts and encyclopaedias is token of the important part played by the county and its people during the last three centuries, throughout which Derbyshire men and Derbyshire enterprises have occupied a leading place in the world's industrial hierarchy. Many pioneers have found encouragement and appropriate circumstances in the county, and the consequence has been the establishment of enterprises, many approaching their centenary and some their bicentenary, which have long been renowned throughout the world.

To present a full and complete story would be a vast undertaking, requiring years of effort. This book can do no more than give a brief outline of the historical developments of the county's industries, illustrated by examples from the large number of relics which still remain to be seen. The county is so rich in industrial incident that each chapter could without difficulty be expanded into a complete book.

CHAPTER ONE

The County of Derby

IT can be no accident that the industries of a county with a total population little greater than that of Liverpool should have held for so long a leading position in the country, indeed in the world. From the production of lead and pottery by the Romans, to the aero engines and nuclear reactors of Rolls-Royce, Derbyshire has an exceptionally long and continuous history of pioneering industrial effort.

For a long time it was its natural advantages, its rich seams of lead ore, its ironstone beds and coalfields, its limestone, fluorspar, and gritstone, which attracted men whose exploitation of these resources posed demands for new technologies—the engineering developments which always follow mining. These established a reservoir of knowledge and abilities which later brought to Derbyshire a number of talented engineers, to draw upon the traditional expertise of its population and to build up a long succession of successful enterprises. The county's other natural advantage, the river Derwent, was to play an important part as a source of power in the early days of the expanding textile industry. The builders of the Old Silk Mill in Derby were succeeded by the cotton masters, the canal builders, the great iron founders and engineers, and the railway engineers—a clear and continuous story of evolution leading up to today's world-renowned firms.

Few counties can offer such a fertile field for the industrial archaeologist and historian, for with the exception of shipbuilding and tin and salt mining, Derbyshire has had at some time or other a finger in every industrial pie.

Situated practically in the centre of England, Derbyshire extends for 55 miles from north to south, and 35 miles from east to west. It has a total area of 643,572 acres, or a little over 1,000 square miles.

As Stephen Glover said in 1830, it is 'so diversified in geographical aspect, that it may be said to possess both high lands and low lands. The former are distinguished by their romantic scenery, their rocks and caverns, and for their mineral wealth; the latter differ little either in their appearance or in their produce from the fruitful districts of other British counties. In each of these, the labours of industry are eminently known, and it would be difficult to say whether the mountains or the plains are the wealthiest, or which owes the most either to the bounties of nature or the energies of art.'[1]

In Glover's time the county ranked fourth in the country's industrial output. Today it is fourteenth in rateable value, and the balance of wealth has been tipped heavily away from 'the mountains'. This is shown by the decline of such once important towns as Winster and Wirksworth and the rapid rise of others like Long Eaton.

The geological structure, which has been most thoroughly documented since the subject first aroused interest in the late eighteenth century, is predominantly of carboniferous age. The carboniferous rocks cover most of the county from the line Ashbourne–Wirksworth northwards (see map on page 20). They can be considered as consisting of three thick and distinct strata. At the base is carboniferous limestone, about 1,600 ft thick. Above this lie the shales and gritstones of the millstone grit series, with a thickness of about 2,200 ft, and above this again the coal measures, about 2,900 ft in thickness, near the base of which occur the seams of coal and ironstone.

Earth movements folded the limestone and forced it upwards. Denudation removed the coal measures and gritstones from the crests of the humps formed by this folding, exposing the thick massive beds of limestone in the 'Derbyshire dome' and producing the 'edges' of shale and gritstone surrounding the dome which are such a striking feature of the Derbyshire landscape. These are exemplified by the edges of Rushup, Stannage, Froggatt and Curbar. They culminate in the north in the 2,088 ft high Kinder Scout, with its thin capping of peat forming the bleak open moorland, intersected by groughs, the steep-sided trenches which make walking in these areas so arduous.

Page 17: (above) Tideslow Rake; (below) Lead-ore crusher, Odin Mine

Page 18: (above) *Tail of Hillcarr Sough*;
(below) *Yatestoop Sough, with Dr T. D. Ford providing the scale*

A good impression of the dome and the edges can be gained by looking north from Ball Cross, near Bakewell. The geological structure is indicated in the figure on page 21, which is based upon the historic cross-section published by White Watson, of Bakewell, in 1811.[2] The exposed limestones which constitute the dome are intersected by the deep narrow gorges of the Dove, the Wye and the Lathkill. Subsidiary foldings have produced smaller exposures of limestone at Ashover, Crich and Ticknall.

It was in the limestones that the rich deposits of lead ore were found. Earth movements caused fracturing of the hard brittle rocks, producing narrow fissures, sometimes several miles long. Following deep-seated volcanic disturbances, heavily mineralised solutions containing metallic and other compounds were injected into some of these fissures. On cooling, the metallic compounds were deposited, commonly as the sulphide of lead, or galena, usually as a narrow ribbon in the fissure, often flanked by gangue minerals, such as calcite, baryte and fluorspar, and some zinc blende. The main ore field stretched roughly south-eastwards from Castleton to Wirksworth. Smaller but still rich fields were located at Ashover and Crich. The same volcanic activity gave rise to intrusions of hard basaltic rocks, which are quarried locally.

Above the rocks of the millstone grit series lie the coal measures. Where the rich seams outcrop (see map, page 20) they are said to 'bassett', or 'bassett to day'. This bassetting of the coal seams, and of the ironstone beds which accompany them, made them easy of access, and this had an important influence upon the early working of coal and iron in the county. The line of bassetting ran roughly north–south and is well indicated by the places at which iron was first worked. The coal measures are partially exposed again in the southern part of the county, where they have formed the basis, with their accompanying clays, of the important earthenware industries of Swadlincote and Church Gresley.

Southwards from the carboniferous region the county is covered by rocks of the triassic period—bunter sands as seen clearly south of the

B

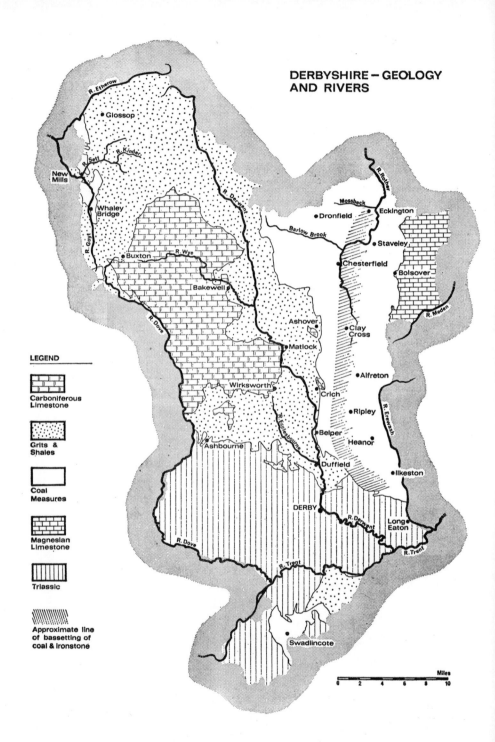

DERBYSHIRE – GEOLOGY AND RIVERS

R. Etherow

Glossop

R. Kinder
R. Sett
R. Uh

New Mills

R. Derwent

Whaley Bridge

R. Goyt

Buxton

R. Wye

Bakewell

R. Dove

Mossbeck

Dronfield

Eckington

Barlow Brook

Staveley

Chesterfield

Bolsover

R. Meden

Ashover

Clay Cross

Matlock

R. Rother

LEGEND

Carboniferous Limestone

Grits & Shales

Coal Measures

Magnesian Limestone

Triassic

Approximate line of bassetting of coal & ironstone

Wirksworth

Crich

R. Ecclesbourne

Ashbourne

Belper

Heanor

Duffield

Alfreton

Ripley

R. Erewash

Ilkeston

DERBY

R. Dove

R. Trent

R. Derwent

Long Eaton

R. Trent

Swadlincote

Miles
0 2 4 6 8 10

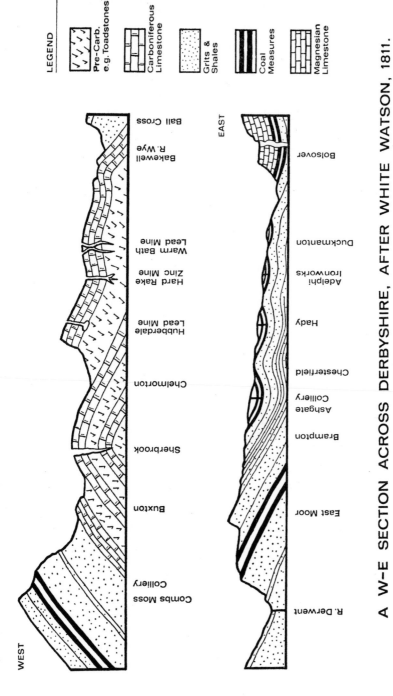

LEGEND

Pre-Carb. e.g. Toadstones

Carboniferous Limestone

Grits & Shales

Coal Measures

Magnesian Limestone

WEST

Combs Moss Colliery · Buxton · Sherbrook · Chelmorton · Hubberdale Lead Mine · Hard Rake Zinc Mine · Warm Bath Lead Mine · Bakewell R. Wye · Ball Cross

EAST

R. Derwent · East Moor · Brampton · Ashgate Colliery · Chesterfield · Hady · Adelphi Ironworks · Duckmanton · Bolsover

A W–E SECTION ACROSS DERBYSHIRE, AFTER WHITE WATSON, 1811.

The geological structure of Derbyshire

Ashbourne–Belper road, and at Sandiacre; keuper marls as exemplified by the red loam pits with their characteristic horizontal strata of pale-green loams, seen in and around Derby, with here and there deposits of gypsum.

The wide valleys of the Trent and the lower Derwent are covered with rich alluviums. This area is predominantly agricultural. At one time it was an important cheese-producing area. It is now a great source of milk, with a growing industry based upon dairy products. Along the eastern boundary of the county runs a narrow attenuated band of magnesian limestone, characterised by its warm golden colour.

Glacial drift covers local areas, and in deep pockets in the carboniferous limestone are rich deposits of siliceous clays. These are accidental in occurrence, and they form the raw material for refractory bricks for furnace-lining which are made at Friden and Brassington. The clays are often highly coloured, ranging in the same pit from creamy white through blue, orange and red to black.

The rivers and streams of the county, inconsiderable though many of them are, have played an important part in the early iron and textile industries as sources of power, for corn milling and for the fulling of cloth; for producing blast for the smelting, forging and rolling of iron; and for silk and cotton spinning. Stretches of the middle Derwent, the Barlow Brook, Mossbeck Brook and Sydnope Brook, once scenes of thriving industry, are now quiet retreats, the remaining signs of Glover's 'labours of industry', which help to locate the sites, being mainly their weirs and dams.

CHAPTER TWO

The Exploitation of Mineral Wealth

WORKING of the widely diversified mineral resources of the county persists after 2,000 years of continuous effort. Between the lead which attracted the Romans, and the large fluorspar and baryte plants of today, there have been many centuries of exploitation of iron, coal, limestone, gypsum, gritstone, brick-earth and clays.

The minerals have been important not only for the wealth they brought, some of which was applied to the development of other industrial enterprises, but also because of the demands which arose for better methods of winning, converting and distributing them. Mechanisation, drainage, smelting and communications posed problems which elicited responses of the greatest significance to later industrial developments.

Soughs, driven to drain the lead mines, encouraged the development of techniques—of surveying, levelling, and tunnelling—which were later to be used by the canal and railway builders. Water-powered methods of pumping out the water from lead and coal mines led on to the demand for greater power which was answered by the steam engine. The development of the steam engine created a demand for more iron, and for a better understanding of kinematics and mechanics which became the basis of engineering design. Eventually the application of steam power to locomotion made possible the development of the railways, which gave such impetus to the growth of industry.

THE WINNING OF LEAD

It is impossible to traverse the limestone zone of Derbyshire without seeing signs of lead mines, some of which are of great antiquity.

It is known that lead was being mined in quantity in Roman times: of the twenty-one pigs of lead of Derbyshire origin which have so far been discovered, nineteen are certainly of Roman date.[1] They had been cast between about AD 117 and the third century, and the importance of Derbyshire as a lead-mining area is indicated by the fact that only eighty pigs have been discovered in the whole country. Many of the local pigs bear Latin inscriptions, some containing the abbreviation LUT for Lutudarum, a place thought to have been in the vicinity of Winster, Wirksworth or Matlock. Six of them were found near Brough, on the Humber, four of them at Pulborough, Sussex. It is safe to surmise that they were en route to ports of embarkation for the continent. The typical weight was 184 lb, with a tolerance of ± 6 lb. Sixteen hundred years later Farey quoted the average weight of a Derbyshire pig of lead as 176¼ lb, showing a remarkable persistence of industrial practice.

It is thought that in Roman times this lead was smelted by a private concern, rather than by an imperial, or 'nationalised', organisation, as was usual in other parts of the country. There is implied evidence too that lead was being mined before the Roman invasion and there is the statement of Pliny the Elder (d AD 79) that 'In Britain lead is found near the surface of the earth in such abundance that a law is made to limit the quantity that shall be gotten.' Later, lead was worked by the Saxons, for in AD 714 Wirksworth mines—mentioned again in 835—were in the possession of the abbess of a nunnery at Repton. Domesday Book mentions three mines at Wirksworth, and one each at Crich, Ashford, Bakewell and Matlock. During the building of churches and castles in the twelfth century lead was in great demand for roofing, drainage pipes and troughs, for coffins and fonts, vats and cisterns, and some was exported to the continent. Peveril Castle was roofed with lead.

The early mines are difficult to trace amongst the disturbances of countless subsequent workings. Occasionally, however, the miner of more recent times, or the underground explorer, will have come across a level of smaller than usual cross-sectional area, a 'coffin level' shaped roughly to human form, still showing clearly the marks of a swinging pick. These are said to be the workings of 't'owd man', who may have been mining there at any time during the previous 1,000 years or more.

The mines of the seventeenth and eighteenth centuries can more safely be identified. There is a romantic appeal about this long-established industry which has attracted large numbers of researchers

'T'owd man', after the carving of a lead miner in Wirksworth church

and recorders. Hence there is far better documentation than in most other industries, and anyone wishing to learn more would be well advised to join the Peak District Mines Historical Society, to peruse its Bulletins, to read up the subject in Farey (who, surveying in 1807–9, listed 292 named mines in the county), and to consult the

Victoria County History, Stokes[2] and the recent authoritative work by
Dr Arthur Raistrick and Mr Bernard Jennings.[3] Much local information appears in the large number of articles published by Miss Nellie
Kirkham, whose detailed and painstaking work, particularly on the
soughs, is remarkable for its blend of historical research into records
with fieldwork both above and below ground.

Workings of the past three centuries are indicated in many places
by hummocks and hollows, now grassed over and absorbed into the
landscape, and by the ruins of small stone huts or 'coes'. The former,
once spoil heaps and filled-in shafts, are to be seen in profusion
around Wirksworth and Winster, Brassington, Carsington and many
other places. As the Hon John Byng recorded in 1790, 'All the county
is scoop'd by lead mines, and their levells: betwixt Winster and Elton
are the great lead mines of Port-Way.' In passing, it should be mentioned that these hollows, attractive as picnic spots sheltered from the
wind, are most unsafe. Often an abandoned shaft has been covered
merely by an old bedstead, or brushwood, which in the course of time
has become grown over. Shafts still left open provide a serious
hazard, particularly when hidden by snow.

More striking, for those who learn to recognise them and seek them
out, are the rake veins—long, narrow, deep workings, sunk from the
surface, as at Deep Rake on Longstone Edge (recently widened and
deepened out of recognition by the search for fluorspar), Dirtlow
Rake, Long Rake and Tideslow Rake (see plate, page 17). Some of
these date from the sixteenth and seventeenth centuries and earlier.

The coes, huts sturdily built by men who knew how to work in
hard stone, have survived in many places, especially in the neighbourhood of Winster and around the Yatestoop, Portaway and Placket
mines. In some cases these coes were built over the shafts. They
served as changing houses, where miners put on dry clothing after
their stint below ground, where they kept their tools, and where they
stored the ore which they had won until it could be taken away for
processing.

Many more signs of this early industry can be discovered by diligent search: these include stowes or stowces (ie hand winches), winding circles, crushing floors, washing floors, sough tails, cupolas, smelting flues, engine houses and meerstones. To recognise these, it is necessary to know a little about the methods which have been employed to win, crush, sort, measure, wash and smelt the ore.

Getting the Ore

Lead ore occurs in Derbyshire in three dispositions:

1. Rake veins—narrow fissures or crevices, in a near-vertical plane, running down through a series of rock strata, which have been mined to a depth often limited by water, and to a length of several miles. The sides of the crevices are usually lined with crystalline calcite, fluorspar, quartz or baryte, called collectively 'vein stuff' or 'gangue material', with the lead ore lying in the space between. Rakes are the commonest form in Derbyshire.

2. Pipe veins—the mineral filling of water-formed cavities between beds of limestone. They vary greatly in thickness, being thin where the water has merely opened out a bedding plane, and bellying out to fill what have been cave-like spaces. 'Leaders' of ore rising to the surface were eagerly followed in the hope of discovering a rich pipe. The ore in pipes was usually easy to work, consisting of large lumps embedded in soft ochre-ish material. The main drawback was that pipes were usually very wet.

3. Flat work—similar to pipe work, following the bedding planes between limestone strata, but usually not more than a few inches in thickness.

Since the time of Edward the Confessor and possibly earlier, the greater part of the Derbyshire lead-ore field has belonged to the Crown. The King's Field of the High Peak comprises a large part of the High Peak Hundred, and it includes the parishes of Castleton, Bradwell, Upper Haddon, Taddington, Monyash and the Hucklows. The King's Field of the Low Peak covers most of the Wapentake of Wirksworth, including the parishes of Aldwark, Ashbourne, Ballidon, Bonsall, Brassington, Cromford, Matlock, Wirksworth and Middleton, Wensley and Snitterton, and Middleton and Smerrill. Outside the immediate jurisdiction of the Crown are the 'Customary Liberties', where the mineral rights belonged to the landowner. Crich is a Liberty, as is Ashover; the Liberty of Ashford included the Longstones, Sheldon and Wardlow, and it has now been conjoined with the Liberties of Tideswell, Peak Forest and Hartington. Stoney Middleton and Eyam form a Liberty, and there are others.

Ancient laws applied throughout these areas, being varied somewhat outside the King's Field. Dating from 'a time whereof the memory of man runneth not to the contrary', these laws are thought by Hoover to be of Saxon origin.[4] They uphold the freedom of the individual to seek for and to get ore, subject only to the dues of lot and cope which he had to pay to the King or his lessee. In 1288 an Inquest held at Ashbourne heard the grievances of the miners, and reaffirmed their ancient rights. These were confirmed again in the sixteenth and seventeenth centuries, some of them becoming statute law in 1851 and 1852. In the King's Field, any man could dig for ore on any land, save under a church, in a churchyard, on the highway, in an orchard or in a garden. Stories are still current of people planting fruit trees overnight to keep out prospectors from their 'orchards'. Great Barmote courts were established at many places, including Monyash, Wirksworth and Ashford. The present Moot Hall at Wirksworth was built in 1814 to replace an earlier building of 1773. The court sits twice a year under the Barmaster, whose title stems from the Saxon Berghmeister.

In early times, 't'owd man' got his ore fairly easily by following veins down from the surface. Later he sank shafts, driving levels for a short distance along the vein until limited by lack of ventilation, when another shaft would be sunk farther on. Tideslow Rake, which was being worked in the seventeenth century, presents a graphic picture of this kind of activity (plate, page 17). The reputation of these early miners must have been high, for according to Pilkington 337 Derbyshire miners were taken from the Peak in about 1295 to work in the silver mines newly discovered at Combe Martin. To this day there are inhabitants of this Devon resort who claim kinship with Derbyshire visitors.

The mining was done by hand-pick, chisel and wedge, and by 'fire-setting'. This method dates at least from Roman times, being described by Pliny the Elder. A fire was built against the rock, and then water was dashed against the hot surface to crack it. It is not known with certainty when gunpowder was introduced from Germany: one story is that it was first used at the Ecton copper mine in the latter half of the seventeenth century. Examples of old tools—picks, wedges, augers and prickers for blasting—are still being found by underground explorers. Good collections can be seen in the museums at Derby, Buxton and Sheffield, and at Magpie Mine, Sheldon, the field headquarters of the Peak District Mines Historical Society.

The bowse, or ore combined with gangue, was raised to the surface in a wooden or iron bucket—a 'kibble'—by hand winch, or stowce. Until recently a ruined stowce lay on top of the upper shaft of the famous Yatestoop Mine, at Birchover, and there is another at Hopton.

A miner established his claim to a vein which he had discovered by

A kibble

placing a stowce on the spot. He would work the vein until he had
obtained a 'dish' of ore, which he would pay to the Barmaster, who
would then mark out on the ground the length of vein which the
miner would be allowed to work. This was measured in 'meers',
which varied from 29 yd in the Low Peak to 32 yd in the High Peak.
The miner would be allotted one meer on each side of the 'founder',
or original strike, and the lessee the third meer. Thereafter the finder
would be entitled to as many more meers as he wanted, provided that
he worked them. He had to mark his claim by placing a 'possession
stowce' at each end of each of his meers. These 'possessions', small
stowces which had to be made entirely of wood, 6 in square and 6 in
high, were required in large quantities. John Sommersett's Account
Book includes payments for miniature stowces made by him:

> 1836 The Erl of Newburgh (of Hassop Hall)
>   2 Duzen of Stoases 3/6 per duzen 7/–d.
> 1846 Thomas Broomhead & Coe, Gospel
>   4 dozen of Stoces 12/–d., 5 dozen of Stoces 15/–d.[5]

At many mines, 'whims' or horse-gins were used for raising the ore
and the flat circular enclosures can sometimes be recognised. Although they were more commonly used at coal mines, Ferber reported in 1776 that they were installed 'everywhere' at the lead mines
in Derbyshire.[6]

While the getting of the ore remained for a long time in the hands
of individuals or small groups working according to the old customs,
the disposal of the lead was in the hands of a small number of
merchants. With the development of better methods of smelting early
in the eighteenth century, these merchants became smelters. At the
same time many mines were becoming unworkable by the old
methods, because of water. Larger companies, notably the London
Lead Company and the Gregory Mine Partners, began to take up the
leases of numbers of small mines and to spend considerable sums
unwatering them, by driving soughs and by installing the new steam
pumps.

The wealth earned by the smelters was reinvested in these and other ventures. Their money and their initiative played an important part in the development of water power and of the steam engine. Their investment in the textile industry marks the beginning of the so-called Industrial Revolution, and they supported the demand for better communications which were such an important factor in the rapid growth of industry in general.

Crushing the Ore

The unwanted rock and gangue was knocked from the ore as far as possible by women, using a stubby hammer or 'bucker' weighing about 6 lb, a thick flat iron plate with a socket on one side for the handle. In 1776 Ferber thought this hand work extremely primitive as compared with contemporary German methods. During the next century the ore was often crushed by horse-power, using a crude version of a cider mill. A circular 'floor' of flat stones, set in a ring about 2 ft wide and 16–20 ft in diameter, had a centre post carrying on a pivot a long wooden beam on which was fixed a large stone roller, up to $1\frac{1}{2}$–2 ft wide and 6 ft diameter. This was trundled round by a horse, the ore being shovelled on to the floor ahead of the roller. Remains of several such crushers are to be seen, as at Eldon, Windmill and Odin. This last one has a cast-iron floor and a cast-iron rim for the roller (plate, page 17, and Gazetteer, Castleton). Some rollers have eight grooves across the periphery, for wooden wedges to hold the rim tight. The rollers are usually cylindrical, but that at Windmill is coned, to make for smoother turning.

In 1556 Burchard Cranich, a German, set up a lead-ore stamping mill in Duffield Frith. It had four iron-shod stamps, and a 16 ft diameter waterwheel (page 32), and its description tallies closely with that in Agricola's book of four years earlier.[7] The discovery of the site of this mill would provide an interesting archaeological exercise (see page 51). This machine appears to have gone out of use in Derbyshire, for when the engineer Francis Thompson saw a similar one in Cardiganshire 200 years later, in 1788, he was astonished and impressed, writing that it enabled one man and a boy to crush as much 'stuff' as '12 or 15 women can with broad-fased hammers or what we call buckers and hammers'[8]—the women referred to being the 'Hospital' or workhouse people at Ashover.

A—Mortar. B—Upright posts. C—Cross-beams. D—Stamps. E—Their heads. F—Axle (cam-shaft). G—Tooth of the stamp (tappet). H—Teeth of axle (cams).

Lead-ore crusher, as used in Duffield Frith, 1556. After Agricola

Washing the Ore

The crushed ore was separated from the unwanted matter by washing, one of the ancient rights of the miner being access to water for this purpose. Originally a hand-operated jigging machine was used— a wooden box with perforated bottom being jogged up and down in a tub of water, when the ore, being heavier, sank. The method was wasteful and in the 1560s an improvement was patented either by William Humphray (or Humfreys), founder of the Company of

VARIOUS MODES OF WASHING THE ORE.

JIGGING MACHINE

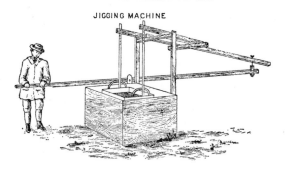

JIGGING MACHINE

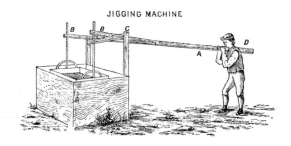

BUDDLING

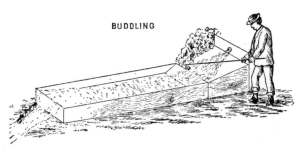

Jigging and buddling (A. H. Stokes, 1880)[2]

Mineral & Battery Works, or by Burchard Cranich, in which a wire sieve was substituted for the wooden box with its large holes.[9] William Furneys of Calver, however, who was eighty years old in 1615, claimed to have been the first to use sieves for washing ore, in 1575. Such disputes were not uncommon between Humphray and the German immigrants who had been granted privileges by the Crown on the one hand, and the native miners on the other.

The adoption of the wire sieve is interesting as providing an incentive for the manufacture of wire; another German, Christopher Schutz, a partner of Humphray, introduced wire-drawing methods which were put into use at Hathersage and Makeney.

The water which had been used for washing the ore became a slurry containing lead sulphide in fine form, much of which was lost, to the detriment of the fish in the rivers. Later, the ore was separated out by buddling—raking up against water flowing down an incline in the form of a tilted wooden trough, or a stone slope. The primitive washing methods, however, remained long in use, losing much lead. They were illustrated by de Loutherbourg in 1802, at a washing place on the Derwent at Matlock Bath. A later method introduced in the 1820s used a kind of Archimedean screw to move the slurry. These 'logs' as they are called, in wood or in metal, are fairly commonly seen on deserted sites. Later still a rocking tub was introduced, and one was to be seen still in use three years ago, by the run-in shaft of the famous Guy Mine at Alport. Remains of others are not rare.

With the great decline in lead mining during the nineteenth century, only a few small operators remained in business, saving the important exception of the Mill Close Mine Company. The small operators retained the methods of dressing and washing which had been used for over a century; Mr R. Marshall, born in 1874, described the methods used at the Wakebridge Mine, Crich, in the 1890s,[10] and these differed little from those mentioned above.

In direct line of descent from this early working is the current activity of 'Glebe Mines', now a subsidiary of Laporte Industries Ltd. At Cavendish Mill, Eyam, 'one of the most outstanding mineral

Page 35 : (above) Sickle grinders working on swinging 'horses' at Thos Staniforth & Co Ltd;
(below) Cold-blast iron furnaces at Morley Park, 1780 and 1818

Page 36: (left) Cast-iron window at St John's Church, Derby, 1827; (right) Cast-iron milepost by John Harrison, Derby

treatment plants in Europe', the now-valuable fluorspar and baryte are sorted and graded. These gangue minerals were once discarded, but today they are being mined at Lady Wash Mine and at Deep Rake on Longstone Edge.

Measuring the Ore

By whatever means the ore was separated, it had to be measured, to determine the 'lot', the levy due to the King or his lessee. Originally one-thirteenth of the ore won, this was often reduced on appeal to as little as one-twenty-fifth. The 'cope' was a duty, varying from 4d to 6d per load (nine dishes) of ore, payable to the Barmaster as a fee for measuring the ore. A standard measure was established, and a standard brass 'dish' dated 1513 still exists in the Moot Hall at Wirksworth. It is in fact a 'master reference', as wooden measures were usual in the field. Its internal measurements are 21·5 in × 5·3 in at the top, 20·7 in × 5·2 in at the bottom, 4·26 in deep. Its capacity is

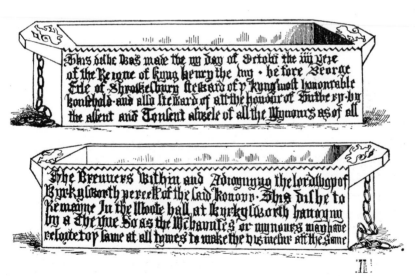

The lead-ore measuring dish, 1513, in the Moot Hall, Wirksworth

C

472 cu in, or a little over 14 pints Winchester dry measure. It bears the inscription:

> This dishe was made the iiij day of October the iiij year of the Reigne of Kyng Henry the viij before George Erle of Shrowesbury Steward of ye Kyngs most Honourable Household and also Steward of all the honour of Tutbery by the assent and consent as well of all the Mynours as of all the Brenners within and adioynying the Lordshyp of Wyrkysworth percell of the said Honour. This Dishe to Remayne In the Moote Hall at Wyrkysworth hanging by a cheyne so as the Merchauntes or mynours may have resorte to ye same at all tymes to make the trew mesur at the same.

Obviously this volumetric measurement of roughly graded ore was highly inaccurate and it is surprising that its use should have persisted for many centuries. It was not until 1803 that measuring by weight is known to have been introduced, at the Gregory Mine at Ashover, but according to Hooson[11] it was in use before 1745.

Based on the notion that lead ore 'grew and renewed itself in the vein', tithes were demanded of the miners, probably from the earliest days. They were strongly resented, and for long periods would lapse, to be reimposed by a strong incumbent. As a result of opposition they would be reduced, sometimes to one-twentieth or one-fortieth, while in Ashover, throughout the Hundred of Scarsdale, at Crich and some other places, no tithe was paid.

Smelting the Ore

For many centuries the lead ore was smelted in simple boles, crude hearths, perhaps 5 ft in diameter and 3–5 ft high, with openings to admit the wind for draught. Brushwood was the fuel used, and as large quantities were required the miners had traditional rights to adequate supplies. The boles were situated on the windward side of hills, and Cameron[12] has listed seventeen relevant Derbyshire place names, such as Bole Hill. Farey recognised sites of ancient boles, and about twelve years ago Miss Kirkham identified a few, but this is not easy today. Botanically-minded searchers, however, will be helped by

A—Burning pyre which is composed of lead ore with wood placed above it.
B—Workman throwing ore into another area.   C—Oven-shaped furnace.
D—Openings through which the smoke escapes.

A lead-smelting bole. After Agricola

Lousley's noting[13] that spring sandwort, *arenaria verna*, and alpine pennywort, *thlaspi calaminare*, favour lead-worked heaps between Wirksworth and Matlock. Farey makes one of his rare mistakes here in stating that the common harebell, *campanula rotundifolia*, is the identifying flower.

Improved methods of smelting, using bellows to raise the temperature, were introduced by the German miners in the Lake District. In 1565 William Humphray was granted letters patent for a small lead-smelting furnace using bellows, but it is possible that Burchard Cranich had introduced it, and used it earlier. 'Burchards furnise' was described in State Papers, Elizabeth, SP12, Vol 122, No 63, ie about 1570, and he claimed against Humphray that he had made much lead with a waterwheel (for blast) near Duffield in 1552–3.[14]

The furnace was rather like a blacksmith's forge, with a hollow basin for the lead. In 1729 J. Martyn described one such: 'The Furnace which I saw near *Wirksworth*, was very rude and simple, consisting only of some large rough Stones, placed in such a Manner as to form a square Cavity, into which the Ore and Coals are thrown *stratum super stratum*; two great *Bellows* continually blowing the Fire, being moved alternatively by Water.' The fuel was 'dried Sticks, which they call white Coal'. This furnace was the basis of the slag hearth and of the ore hearth, but, in contradistinction to development in the northcountry ore-fields, its use for primary smelting did not persist in Derbyshire. It was replaced by the reverberatory furnace probably because there was little 'clean' wood or peat for fuel, and coal had to be used. This reverberatory furnace was invented by Dr Edward Wright about 1690, to keep the fuel separate from the ore, and it was used by, amongst others, the Quaker Lead Company, at its works in Flint. The furnace was brought into Derbyshire, to Bower's Mill at Kelstedge near Ashover by the London Lead Company, from Flint, between 1734 and 1747. It is interesting that in the fourteenth–fifteenth century Thurston del Boure, a yeoman of Tideswell, made much money by smelting and merchanting lead.[15]

The reverberatory furnace was called, somewhat confusingly, a cupola. This word was used indiscriminately to describe the true reverberatory furnace; the whole smelting works, which might contain more than one furnace, as well as slag-hearths; and an iron remelting furnace, of the type which was also used, later, to smelt refractory lead slags. The reverberatory furnace had a fireplace at one end, a melting floor roughly 10 ft × 5 ft, an arched roof to 'reverberate' the heat of the fire, and a chimney. The remains of one are to be seen near the site of the Cromford Moor Mine, by Black Rocks, Wirksworth. This smelting works was operated by Wass & Co until about 1880.

In 1777, in order to abate the nuisance due to the spreading of the noxious furnace fumes, and to recover the valuable lead passed over in the smoke due to incomplete combustion, long flues were introduced. Smeaton had reported that the poisonous smokes might spread for 6 or 7 miles, as anyone who has seen the black smoke issuing from the lime works south of Buxton can well believe. In these flues the fumes condensed, to be scraped out periodically and re-smelted. The first was installed in Middleton Dale, and traces of one are still visible there. Another can be seen clearly rising straight up the hillside from what is now the Via Gellia Colour Works (see Gazetteer, under Bonsall). The 2½ in OS map indicates nearby a stream following a most unusual zigzag course down the steep hillside. An examination revealed that this is in fact the fallen-in ruins of a long condensing flue, marked blue incorrectly on the map. Long flues are more common in the North Yorkshire ore field.

Perhaps the most impressive remains of an important lead smelter are those at Alport-by-Youlgreave. Unfortunately they can be seen clearly only for a short period in the spring, when the trees are leafless, and when the westering sun is high enough to light up the stonework. Here is a great complex of flues, which rise to a square stone chimney, 15 ft square at the base. There appears to have been a round chimney at the west side of the 'collecting' box and an early photograph shows another, square, chimney on the opposite side. This smelting works was being operated by the Barker company in 1857.

The largest smelter in the county was situated at Lea. In 1807 it was operated by the Nightingale family, and later by Joseph Wass. For many years, until it closed down before world war II, this was the only smelter left in use in Derbyshire, and all the output of the highly productive Mill Close Mine was processed here. There were four Scotch hearths and two reverberatories, and formerly a Spanish slag cupola (similar to an iron cupola). A large brick condensing chamber, 'resembling a haystack', arrested much of the fume, and beyond this was a spiral (zigzag?) flue 600 yd long, and a short chimney stack.[16] According to Ure,[17] it had an unusual blast, consisting of two casks divided along a plane through a diameter, and partially filled with water. An oscillatory motion produced by waterwheel-driven cranks caused air to be expelled through nozzles.

The remains stood until 1948, but all that can be seen today is a noble heap of furnace ash which gleams whitely in the sun.

Unwatering the Mines

Many of the 'curious engines' brought into the country by the German lead miners in the sixteenth century were in fact means of pumping out water so that the veins could be worked to lower levels. They included rag pumps, chains of buckets, and piston pumps, illustrations of which have been reproduced often from Agricola's classic *De Re Metallica*, describing sixteenth-century mining methods. These pumps were usually driven by waterwheel, and must have helped men's thinking towards wider applications of water-power.

The mines were soon worked down to the limit of capacity of these machines, and to lower the water table still further 'soughs', or drainage tunnels, were driven from the nearest river to a point beneath the ore being sought. The contours of the county lent themselves to this type of drainage, and in consequence Derbyshire is particularly rich in what Farey called 'lasting Monuments of the spirit and perseverance of the Miners in this District'. Miss Nellie Kirkham's book describing the soughs, the men who constructed them, and the economic factors determining them, is eagerly awaited. In the meantime Mr J. H. Rieuwerts has compiled a list of more than 220 soughs in the county.[18]

The driving of soughs, often several miles long, was a costly busi-

A sixteenth-century method of pumping. After Agricola. A—shaft; B—bottom pump; C—first tank; D—second pump; E—second tank; F—third pump; G—trough; H—the iron set in the axle; I—first pump rod; K—second pump rod; L—third pump rod; M—first piston rod; N—second piston rod; O—third piston rod; P—little axles; Q—'claws'

ness and was a major factor in changing lead mining from an industry
for the small man to one in which entrepreneurs played an increasingly important part. Companies of adventurers would undertake the
work, recouping their costs by taking as payment a fraction of the
value of the lead uncovered. This fraction might be one-sixth plus
one-twelfth of the lead won from below the level.

Seeking sough outlets or 'tails' and tracing their routes is one of the
most interesting activities of the lead-mining historian. The most
important in the eighteenth century was the Hillcarr Sough, running
from the Derwent near Darley Dale, at an altitude of 320 ft OD,
south-westerly under the 1,050 ft high Stanton Moor, then roughly
north-easterly to beneath the mines at Alport-by-Youlgreave, a total
length of nearly 4 miles. It was begun in 1766, and by 1802 had
already cost £50,000 to drive. The outlet is a stone arch, about 6 ft
wide, with a ring in the keystone to moor the boat used by soughers
when clearing silt from the channel floor (plate, page 18). In 1962 an
exploration party was able to proceed for ¾ mile before being stopped
by an accumulation of silt and shale which nearly filled the channel.[19]

For part of its length, where it passes through shale, the sough is
lined with gritstone, and paved with flags.[20] Later, it traverses extremely hard and contorted limestone. There were docks inside where
boats loaded spoil and, later, ore, which was taken down to the river
at 1s 4d per load. It took three years to progress 3,000 ft, and not for
twenty-one years did the sough begin to show a profit. In addition to
the other difficulties, the soughers had to contend with 'ye Dampe'
when driving through the shale, and several men were badly burned
in explosions. But the sough's value is shown by the fact that it
lowered the water table below the reach of the pumps at Placket
Mine, and reduced the flow at Yatestoop Mine, respectively 1½ and
1 mile away. To drive such a level, 700 ft below the surface, requiring
air and spoil shafts several hundred feet deep, was a tremendous
achievement; the financial risk was certainly matched by the physical.

The oldest sough in the county of which there is any record, the
Longhead Sough, was driven in 1629–36, to unwater the Dove Gang

mines above Wirksworth. This work was begun by Sir Cornelius Vermuyden, the eminent Dutch drainage engineer. Also in this area is the Cromford Sough, which emerges behind the houses on the south side of the Black Rocks road at Cromford. Later, in 1771, this provided some of the water for Arkwright's cotton mill at Cromford. The sough had two waterwheels in it near Black Rocks, to raise water to its level.[21] Meerbrook Sough was begun in 1772. By 1811, £45,000 had been spent on driving it to Bole Hill; it was extended by a new company formed in 1840, and by 1846 had cost £70,000. It passes right under Wirksworth, and with its branches has a total length of about 5 miles. Today, some of its flow of 17,000,000 gallons per day is taken by the South Derbyshire Water Board, formerly the Ilkeston & Heanor Company, which first began to use the water in 1902. The outlet arch is one of the biggest in the county, about 10 ft wide and 7 ft high. The keystone bears the inscription 'F.H. 1772', for Francis Hurt of Alderwasley, the principal of the sough proprietors.

The soughs required bellows, fans and pipes for ventilation whilst they were being driven. There was, too, need for accurate surveying, to ensure that the ventilation and winding shafts intersected the level. To travel along a level of the Warren Car shaft of the Mill Close Mine, to its intersection with the Yatestoop Sough, which runs from near Birchover to the Derwent, and to see precisely at the intersection a third, vertical axis, an air shaft, gives one a due sense of respect for these miners. The plate on page 18 shows this point of intersection. The 2¼ mile sough was driven between 1742 and 1764 and cost £30,000. The sign of the nearby Square & Compasses inn is highly appropriate.

The great expense of driving soughs gave impetus to the development of water power for pumping. Smeaton increased the efficiency of waterwheels by his work on small-scale models to investigate the virtues of breast wheels and overshot wheels. A wheel 52 ft in diameter was erected at a point not yet finally identified, near the Mandale Mine on the river Lathkil.

The steam engine was another direct response to the need to unwater mines. It is probable that Newcomen's first engine was used at a coal mine near Willenhall in 1711–12, but the Derbyshire lead miners were quick to adopt the 'fire engines' as they were called, and before 1720 the first was installed at Yatestoop Mine; by 1730 three were at work there. As with soughs, the cost of these engines was beyond the means of the small man, another factor to encourage the formation of larger combines.

Lead mining thus played a vital part in the story of England's developing industry. It provided techniques which were later to make canal building possible; it developed water power and steam power; above all, it provided wealth and organisation which were to be put to good use later, in the financing of the canals, their ancillary tramroads, and the water- and steam-powered textile mills which marked the beginning of the great industrial expansion.

Later mining developments add little that will not be told in the chapter on the steam engine. The industry remained prosperous until the late nineteenth century, when the removal of tariffs on lead imported mainly from the rich mining field of Australia intensified competition and drove the small operator out of business.

The highly profitable Gregory Mine (over £100,000 profit was made during twenty-odd years of operation) closed down in 1803, but two enterprises are still remembered by many people. One of these is the Mill Close Mine, which was abandoned after many years of operation by the London Lead Company. Reopened in 1859 by E. M. Wass, it became the most productive mine in Britain, until it was flooded in 1939 to such an extent that even with twentieth-century methods draining was too costly to make further operations worthwhile.

The lead-smelting works of Cox Bros (Derby) Ltd was started in 1781. A shot tower 149 ft high was erected in 1809 near the place where the Council House now stands; this was a well-known landmark until its removal in 1931 (page 47). The other lead works of this company, in Normanton Road, closed as recently as 1965.

The Shot Tower, Derby, 1809–1931

The numbers employed in the mines fell from 1,461 in 1841 to 285 in 1901, of whom 240 were at Mill Close. In 1963 only 93 men were employed partly or wholly below ground. Today, however, the Glebe Mines activity of the Laporte Industries Group is producing over 100,000 tons per annum of fluorspar and baryte, which have acquired important new uses, and lead concentrates. The Ladywash Mine and the Sallet Hole Mine are busier than they have ever been.

IRON AND STEEL

The production of iron from its ores, and the manufacture of articles in iron and steel, have a longer continuous history than that of lead. Although the quest for lead played a bigger part initially in the development of engineering technologies, iron has made by far the greater contribution overall.

Despite the ease with which the local ironstone could be obtained, no traces have yet been found of Iron Age workings in Derbyshire. Owing to the difficulties of transportation, and the eventual exhaustion of the ores, the county has never been a leading producer of iron, still less of steel. Nevertheless, the industry has played an important part in the county's history; from the twelfth century onwards, references to it are frequent. Companies founded in the eighteenth century flourish today, and from the early iron enterprises have developed engineering firms which enjoy a world-wide reputation. There have survived, too, many fine examples of iron products, monuments to the skill of the founders who produced 'Derby castings'.

Early Iron Manufacture

Iron was first obtained by smelting broken ironstone in primitive furnaces, with charcoal as fuel. It was not possible to obtain a temperature of more than about 1150° C, and the result was a semi-molten pasty mass of iron and slag, the 'bloom'. This was then hammered to expel as much slag as possible. The quality of the resulting wrought iron depended upon the composition of the ore and the effectiveness of the working. Originally the bloom of iron averaged only about 7 lb in weight, but by Roman times such things as anvils weighing about 1 cwt could be produced, and until the mid-nineteenth century this was the normal weight of a single piece of iron.

In Derbyshire the ironstone was found as nodules—fairly large smooth flattened balls averaging about 1 ft in length—in the clays of the lower coal measures. These were won by grubbing from the surface, and later by sinking shallow bell pits along the line of bassetting. The overlying coal was discarded. The line of bassetting is well indicated by the places where iron workings were first recorded. From the thirteenth century onwards there are frequent references to forges in the Belper and Duffield areas, at Hulland Ward, Codnor, Horsley, Loscoe and Heanor. Farther north the names of Chesterfield, Brampton, Barlow and Eckington appear. Farey listed twenty-three places where he had seen slag and the remains of old bloomeries. Investigators should note that the Foxbrooke furnace established by Sitwell in 1652 was 'ruinous and in great decay' as long ago as 1749.[22]

When water power was first applied to the driving of bellows for the bloomery furnace is not precisely known, but Sir George Sitwell quoted an early reference. In 1507 John Selyok leased at Norton the 'Syte of a Smethe place to Bylde an Ironsmethe, both blome harth and strynge harth', with 'the Course of the Water called Mossebeck to turne the said Smethes'. The large mounds of slag still to be seen in the now quiet and sylvan valleys of Mossbeck Brook and Barlow Brook, and the ruins of old dams, evoke the atmosphere of these times. The string hearth was the smith's hearth at which were produced scythes, ploughshares, harrow teeth, spades, grates, javelins, cressets for beacon lights, door bands, locks and keys.

Steel was produced in the same way as iron, where the ores were suitable, but more commonly it was converted from iron by heating it, in contact with charcoal or other carburising material, in the absence of air. This produced 'blister steel', the material for the makers of swords and tools. 'XX parvos cultellos de Assheborne' were itemised in Edward III's possessions in the Tower of London in 1334.

Late in the sixteenth century the sixth Earl of Shrewsbury (d 1590), fourth husband of Bess of Hardwick, induced a party of immigrant Flemings to settle in the Norton area. They made scythes and sickles, so establishing an industry which still flourishes. The village of Ridgeway has several workshops surviving, while at nearby Hackenthorpe is the 'Severquick' works of Thos Staniforth & Co Ltd (plate, page 35). This present firm dates back to 1740, but a John Stanyford was granted his cutler's mark to put upon his sickles in 1565.

In 1565 Queen Elizabeth granted Letters Patent allowing the entry into the kingdom of not more than 100 'strangers and alyens', for the 'searchinge, digginge and conveyinge of the mines ewer [ie ore] and stone for the making of steele and iron wyer'.[23] We have already seen how Burchard Cranich brought methods of lead-ore crushing and smelting from Germany, and that a compatriot of his, Christopher Schutz, came to England in 1566 and after some difficulty developed means of drawing iron wire. This was in demand for wool cards, knitting needles, bird cages and, in heavier gauges, for sieves for washing lead ore. William Humphray, Assay Master of the Royal Mint, took care to gain the rights to the processes, and a main centre of wire production was established at Tintern. Of more local interest is the fact that Schutz set up a works at Hathersage for drawing wire for knitting needles and for the new lead-ore washing machines. Sites of old wire and button works are still recognisable here.

In 1740–2 Benjamin Huntsman of Doncaster, needing better steel for the springs of clocks and pendulums, developed the crucible method of casting steel. According to Professor T. S. Ashton,[24] he asked Robert Cocker of Hathersage to draw cast steel wire for him about 1770–80. This establishes a link between the German engineers of Elizabeth's reign and the light precision engineering which was an essential element of the great expansion of the textile industry, for Cockers were still operating as needle-makers in 1857. Samuel Fox lived in Hathersage, and it was here that he first drew his sections for the making of umbrella frames, before moving out of the county to start the present company at Stocksbridge near Sheffield.

In 1581 Sir John Zouch of Codnor set up a wire manufactory at the forge at Makeney, but he was made to cease work by Humphray. He restarted, and was again stopped. This incident makes one wonder if Cranich's lead-ore stamping mill in Duffield Frith (see page 31) was also at Makeney, then in Duffield parish. Two hundred years later Walter Mather of Staveley owned the forge here.

Much of the wrought iron was rolled into sheets. Some of it was hammered into thin sheets of extraordinarily complex shape by armourers. More was cut into strips by water-driven slitting mills, to

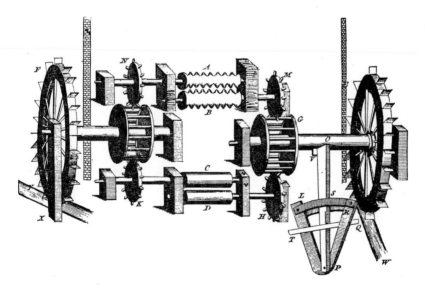

An iron rolling and slitting mill. (W. Emerson, *The Principles of Mechanics*, 1758)

provide rod for nail and horseshoe making. In 1734 Thomas Evans set up an iron rolling and slitting mill on the Derwent at Derby, close to a copper smelting and rolling mill which supplied sheathing for the ships of the Navy. In the 1820s these were operated by Bingham, Humpston & Co; the site of the works was near the lowest great weir, where the Cattle Market now stands.

Belper was an important centre for nailmaking. Indeed this was the town's chief industry until the cotton mills were built. It was essentially a cottage industry. A nailer would be supplied with bar iron by a factor, who would buy back a stipulated weight of nails. The nailer would employ all his family and many nailers' shops still survive in the town. It was a seasonal business, and nails were exported in quantity to North America, for horseshoes and for house building.[25] Derbyshire bar iron was also sent to Dudley, the chief nail-manufacturing centre.

Later, in 1876, Johnson & Nephew set up wire-rod rolling and wire-drawing works on the site of an old forge on the Derwent south of Alderwasley (see Gazetteer). At the 1878 Paris Exhibition the firm attracted great attention by showing a No 3 rod (·261 in diameter), 530 yd long, which it had produced on a Bedson continuous rolling mill.[26]

The Coming of Cast Iron

Temperatures high enough to melt the ore so that it could be run off into moulds were obtained with the development of the blast furnace. This was first mentioned in Germany in 1390, and it was introduced into England from France between 1490 and 1500. The Weald, with its plentiful supply of wood for fuel, became the main area of activity. The first furnaces were pyramidal stone structures, upwards of 20 ft high, with bellows driven by a waterwheel. The height was progressively increased, to raise temperatures and output. About 1600, gross national production was increased by about twenty times, due solely to this new technique of increased blast. (From the

Page 53: (left) George Stephenson's Sighting Tower, Chevin, Duffield; (right) Engine house at Seldom Seen Colliery

Page 54:   (*above*) *Samuel Oldknow's lime kiln at Marple Bridge*; (*below*) *Smalley Pottery*

researches of Dr Joseph Needham, however, we now know that the Chinese were able to produce large castings in iron at the time that Iron Age man in this country was still struggling with his primitive hearth.)[27]

At first the castings produced by pouring direct from the blast furnace into moulds were low-duty non-engineering items such as firebacks, fire dogs and cooking pots, but by 1662 George Sitwell, with a furnace at Foxbrooke and slitting mills at Renishaw, was casting cannon, cannon balls, and sugar-cane-crushing rolls, these last for export to the Barbados. The slitting mill is preserved in the name of a local farm.

The early cast iron was what is known as 'grey', containing between 3 per cent and 4 per cent of carbon, most of it uncombined with the iron, and it was relatively weak and brittle. It was converted into wrought iron, or nearly pure malleable iron, in 'fineries'—furnaces in which the pig was reheated and decarburised and then hammered under a water-driven tilt hammer to expel slag, being reheated as required in a 'chafery'.

In 1581 'two great and auncient heapes of iron slagg or cinders' were seen near the brook in Hulland Ward, and two years later on the Mossbeck Brook.[28] The re-discovery of these sites could be a rewarding exercise. In 1950 the ruin of a charcoal blast furnace on Barlow Brook was reported,[29] but this has disappeared recently, with the removal of material from the slag heaps. The longest-lived charcoal furnace was probably that at Wingerworth, which Farey described as blown by waterwheel, and as having been in use for more than 180 years, until 1784. Farey also mentioned a furnace at Melbourne, which a few years ago was excavated and recorded before being submerged under the new reservoir. This furnace dated from about 1725.[30]

The great consumption of wood by the iron and lead smelters caused a shortage. In 1720 Britain produced 25,000 tons of pig iron and 18,000 tons of bar, but had to import more than 10,000 tons of bar from Sweden, some of which went to Belper for nailmaking. For

D

a long time men tried to overcome the shortage of charcoal fuel by using coked coal, Abraham Darby of Coalbrookdale achieving this in 1709. Even then the process did not expand rapidly, because the difficulties due to variations in the properties of the coke and of the iron ores were not fully understood, and much coke-iron was too brittle. So it was not until 1780 that the first coke furnaces were erected in Derbyshire. The first, by majority opinion, was at Morley Park, 1780 (plate, page 35). According to Meade[31] it was followed rapidly by one at the Griffin Foundry at New Brampton, and another at Stone Gravel just north of Chesterfield. Soon afterwards a furnace was erected at Wingerworth, followed by others at Renishaw in 1782, at Staveley in 1786, Dale Abbey in 1788, and Butterley in 1790–2.

In 1796 Dr MacNab listed the coke furnaces then working in Derbyshire, and Farey listed those of 1806. This information is combined in Table I.

It is interesting to follow the progress of the firms which continued to operate at the original sites until well into the present century. In 1840 G. H. Barrow reopened the works at Staveley, which had been closed down for a time, and in 1861 was 'maintaining the lead in castings from Derbyshire iron used in all parts of Europe for water and gas works'. The works at Dale Abbey was restored in 1846 by Benjamin and Josiah Smith (of Ebenezer Smith of Chesterfield). This firm got into difficulties and was being worked by the bankers Crompton & Co in 1861. The Stanton Iron Works Ltd was formed in 1877. In recent years Stanton & Staveley Ltd has become part of Stewart & Lloyds Ltd, and maintains a big business in iron pipes and cast tunnel-lining segments, eg for the new Victoria underground railway system in London.

Appleby & Co became the Renishaw Iron Co Ltd, and is now a part of Tube Investments Ltd. James Oakes & Co (Riddings) Ltd is now a large brickmaking concern, its ironworks being part of the Stanton Ironworks Co Ltd since 1917. The Clay Cross Co Ltd ceased to make iron in 1958, but retains its pipe foundries, and the Sheepbridge Coal & Iron Co Ltd went out of existence, its works being closed in 1961 when it was taken over by Stanton & Staveley Ltd. The Butterley Company Ltd closed down and dismantled its Codnor Park Works in 1965, but retains its foundries at Ripley. In 1778 the company responded to the increasing use of coal as domestic fuel by making cast-iron cooking ranges, which Farey declared had spread so amazingly that 'there is scarcely a house without these Ovens, even of the Cottages of the first class'.

TABLE I

Works	1796 Furnaces		1806 Furnaces		
	Built	Pig produced (tons)	Built	In blast	Pig produced (tons)
Morley Park, Francis Hurt	1	728	1	1	700
Chesterfield, Griffin, Eb Smith & Co	2	1560	3	2	1700
Chesterfield, Stone Gravel. Top & Co (now Smith & Armitage)	1	940	2	1	700
Wingerworth (1780), Jos Butler	1	1274	2	1	819
Staveley (1786), Ward & Lowe (now Ward & Barrow)	1	761	1	1	596
Dale Abbey (1788), English & Co (now pulled down, 1806)	1	443	1	–	–
Butterley, Outram & Co (now Butterley Co)	1	936	2	2	1766
Renishaw (1782), Appleby & Co	2	705	2	1	975
Alfreton, Saxleby & Co (now Oaks, Edwards Co, 1806)	–	–	1	1	1450
Hasland, John Brocksop	–	–	1	1	723
Duckmanton, or Adelphi (1799), Eb Smith & Co	–	–	2	1	900
Chapel (Alfreton?)	1	1456	–	–	–
Park?	1	853	–	–	–
	12	9656	18	12	10329

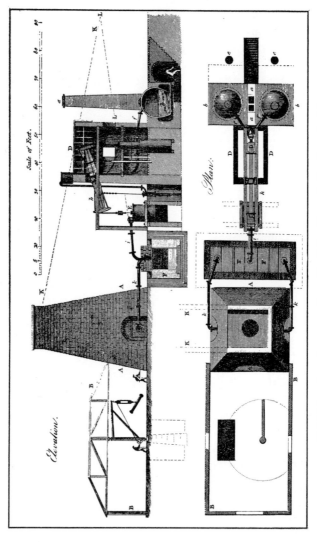

Cold-blast iron furnace, 1810. (By John Farey jr for *Pantologia*)

The methods of iron smelting were thoroughly documented by the sons of John Farey, and by John Jr in particular. Only seventeen or eighteen years old at the time, in 1809–10 he surveyed and described methods of manufacture in many industries, contributing lengthy articles to *Pantologia*, a fourteen-volume encyclopaedia published in 1813, and to Rees' *Cyclopaedia*, the imposing forty-six-volume work of 1819. The lucidity of his descriptions and the high quality of his draughtsmanship are remarkable, and mark a great step forward from the efforts of only a few years previously. Pilkington's drawing of the blast furnace at Staveley, made in 1789, is rudimentary by comparison with the fine drawing reproduced on page 58.

In 1829 the coke smelting process was improved greatly by Neilson's invention of the hot-blast. The Butterley Company was quick to adopt this, as shown by a letter of 18 June 1835 from Mr Joseph Glynn to the editor of the *Mechanics Magazine*. 'The Butterley Company employ in their mines, coal fields, blast-furnaces, rolling mills, forges, boring-mills, and steam engine manufactory, 35 steam-engines of all sizes, from 80 inches of diameter of cylinder, and have six blast-furnaces, of which four are now in work. The whole of these furnaces are blown with heated air. . . .' According to Ure, hot blast increased the output of each furnace from 29 tons per week to 49 tons per week and required less than half as much coal per ton. In 1966 a bank of ruins of these furnaces still stood alongside the recently demolished Codnor Park puddling and rolling mills. They must have been an imposing sight, as the furnaces proper surmounted the present embankment by another 40 ft or so.

An impetus had been given to the production of iron by Henry Cort's invention, in 1783–4, of a method of producing wrought iron direct from cast iron by puddling and rolling. The Codnor Park works of Butterley, established in 1807–11, became an important supplier of wrought iron, and continued in this field until June 1965. Latterly it produced rod for anchor chains for floating harbours, ships, and lightships, the corrosion resistance of high-quality wrought iron having an advantage over steel. Fortunately it was possible in

1964 to take a colour film of the whole process; this is now in the possession of the Industrial Museum, Birmingham.

As the puddling process depends upon manual effort, it is not normally possible to produce a bloom of more than about 100 lb weight. In 1861 Sir John Alleyne of the Butterley Company invented an improved means of handling plate and bar through the rolls, and in 1862 he invented a method of forge-welding together a number of billets. The Derby Red Book of 1863 reported that Butterley was rolling 'the largest masses of iron yet made'. These included the beam for a pumping engine for the Clay Cross Company, comprising two slabs each 34 ft long × 7 ft in the middle, 3 ft 6 in at the ends, 2¼ in thick, and weighing about 7 tons. Alleyne's technique made possible the erection of ambitious structures, the most impressive of which is the roof of St Pancras station. This has a free span of 240 ft, which at the time of its erection, 1867, was the largest in the world. The iron girders were made by riveting sections together; a visual estimate of size of the biggest members suggests that they weigh about 700 lb, and before trimming probably nearly half a ton. On some of them can be seen what may be indications of the weld line. And where the black/brown paint is chipped can be seen traces of the sky-blue paint which must have made the station a striking sight when the roof was first erected. The total weight of ironwork in the St Pancras roof is 6,894 tons, and the roof covers an area of 4½ acres.

In 1827, the Butterley Company was employing nearly 1,500 men. This whole period is characterised by the energy shown in the enterprises. For example, in 1862 Barrow of Staveley produced 400 tons of girders in three months for the London Exhibition Building of that year. Subsequently, with Bessemer's invention of his converter for steel-making, in 1856, cheap steel and large rolled-steel sections became available, and the use of wrought iron declined rapidly.

Derbyshire did not continue to expand as a source of primary iron beyond the 1850s, the cheaper ores from Northamptonshire making local manufacture uneconomical. Nevertheless for a time the products of the leading firms in the county were impressive achievements, many of which can still be seen. Until the advent of cheap steel, cast iron was put to uses which present-day iron founders find difficult to credit. The 'Era of Cast Iron' was inaugurated very largely by such firms as Ebenezer Smith, Butterley, Andrew Handyside of Derby, Staveley, Stanton and James Oakes at Riddings.

In 1777 Ebenezer Smith at Chesterfield was casting cylinders of 70 in bore for Francis Thompson's atmospheric engines. When William Strutt designed his fireproof mills at Milford and Belper, he obtained the cast-iron cruciform-section stanchions and beams from Strutt's local foundry at Milford (now Glow Worm), and from Ebenezer Smith. These pieces, which were required in large numbers, as for the Belper North Mill in 1802, were interchangeable, an early example of prefabricated manufacture. It would be interesting to discover how this uniformity was achieved and controlled.

During the demolition of the Milford Mill in 1964 an unusual coping was noticed on a drystone wall at the outlet of the tail race. This was found to consist of 'skulls'—the dottles from ladles of cast iron. It is reasonable to assume that these date from about the time when the mills were built, and that they came from the local foundry. An analysis is given in Table II, page 67.

The rapid extension of horse-drawn tramroads as spurs to the canals, in which Benjamin Outram of the Butterley Company played a leading part, created a big demand for cast-iron rails. Wagon wheels were also required in large numbers. Another interesting structural application was cast-iron beams. An early one, about 20 ft long, is over the portal of the covered dock of the Peak Forest Canal at Whaley Bridge. Glover mentions in *Peak Guide* the cast-iron beams of the Longcliffe bridge of the Cromford & High Peak Railway, 1825. It was made by Butterley for Josias Jessop. Outram of Butterley was responsible for what is probably the first cast-iron canal aqueduct, carrying the Derby Canal over the old 'cut' of the Derwent, under Cattle Market Road in Derby (see page 149 and plate, page 107). Many cast-iron beams are still to be seen on road bridges over canals and railways. The original railway over-bridges, too, incorporated quite massive examples. The fascia beams still remain in many cases, the permanent way now often being carried on steel girders which have replaced the intermediate castings. Particularly impressive are the skew arches of the two bridges of the London & North Western Railway at Whaley Bridge. In 1868 Andrew Handyside was offering single-casting arched beams of 40 ft span, an 80 ft span being possible with two castings.

More widespread than any other castings are the iron window frames to be seen in large numbers in the neighbourhood of Derby. They vary from the small cottage windows of the Arkwright and Strutt houses at Cromford, Belper and Milford, to the large, light and airy ones of the textile mills and railway workshops, and to pseudo-Gothic church windows as at St John's Church, Bridge Street, Derby, 1827 (plate, page 36), and at St James's Church, Shardlow, 1838. The St John's Church windows were cast in the Britannia Foundry, Duke Street, Derby, by Weatherhead & Glover in 1827. Factory windows especially are an excellent example of the founder's art. Weatherhead & Glover was taken over by Andrew Handyside in 1848, and this firm produced a large variety of sizes and shapes of industrial windows, holding 1,500 different patterns. Many of them are distinctive architectural features, contributing to the good taste of so many of Derbyshire's buildings. The page from Handyside's catalogue of 1873 (reproduced on page 63) shows a few of the designs; the windows cost from 10s to 16s per cwt. Local foundrymen can remember working on these castings, but today only one firm in the country is capable of producing replacements, and then only as two castings, not as a single one. 'Modern' foundrymen find it difficult to believe that a window 10 ft 11½ in high, 5 ft 7 in wide, could possibly be a single iron casting. Production was facilitated by the quality of the high-phosphorus grey iron, as well as by the traditional skill of Derby moulders. Table II (page 67) includes analyses of iron castings of this period.

Another product of Handysides' was post-office pillar boxes. These cost, in 1864, complete with internal canvas bag, door and lock, from £7 10s to £9 12s according to pattern; many are still to be seen in

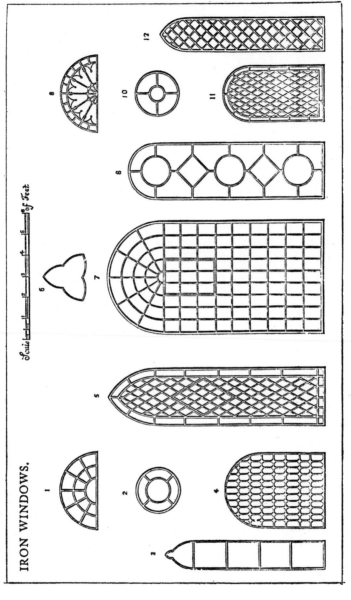

Andrew Handyside & Co., Derby and London.

IRON WINDOWS.

Specimen page from catalogue of Andrew Handyside, Derby, 1873

Derby and in London. Handysides provided water cranes for the railway companies, especially that pattern resembling an elephant's waving trunk, at £28 to £35. Cast-iron vases for gardens, and many excessively ornate ironwork pergolas, lamps, and fountains were also made. And the firm supplied 'one of the most elaborately ornamental iron buildings yet constructed'—a 40 ft high conservatory, for the *steelmaker* Henry Bessemer's house near London.

In 1878 Handysides built two bridges in Derby for the Great Northern Railway. That at Friargate station is probably the 'most elaborately ornamental' railway bridge ever built. Butterley, Handysides, and Haywoods of the Phoenix Foundry, Derby, in fact built iron bridges all over the world. Handysides erected more than 450 on the London, Brighton & South Coast railway,[32] and Haywoods put up in 1861 a many-piered bridge to carry Derby's Cattle Market Road over the Derwent. This bridge is seldom seen at its best, as the roadway aspect is unattractive.

The following advertisement appeared in Freebody's *Directory of the Towns of Derby, Chesterfield*, etc, 1852:

> James Haywood
> Phoenix Foundry, Derby
> Manufacturer of Ornamental Vases and Chairs for Pleasure Grounds. Hot Air and Register Stoves, Kitchen Ranges, with Boilers suitable for heating Baths, Rumford Roasters, Stewing Stoves, Hot Water apparatus for heating Halls, Warehouses and Conservatories, Cast Iron Bridge Girders, up to 20 Tons each, Wrought and Cast Iron Roofs, and every description of Castings for Building purposes.

Haywoods, and another Derby firm, John Harrison, made large numbers of cast-iron mileposts in a range of patterns, to be seen in Derby and on roads radiating for many miles from the town (plate, page 36). John Harrison, whose works was in Bridge Gate straddling what is now Sowter Road, by the Bridge Chapel, built in 1832 a delicately designed and elegant water pump, which was rescued from Elvaston Castle in 1964, to be displayed eventually in the Museum of Technology, Leicester. A four-cylinder table pump, it has a cast-iron table and a thin cast arched framework to support the overhead crosshead bearings. The connecting rods and pump rods are in wrought iron, driven by two wrought-iron cranks from a small iron water-wheel. In 1827–8 John Harrison was building a wrought-iron tank for the Nottingham gas company, 42 ft diameter and 18 ft 6 in deep, which would hold 193,082 gallons of water and weighed 36 tons empty.

Both Butterley and Handyside set an early example of technological thoroughness. The latter especially did much to establish the reputation of 'Derby Castings' for quality and reliability. In trials at Woolwich in 1854, Handysides' irons came best out of fifty samples tested, being 2·6 times stronger than the worst. The firm's guaranteed figures were 450 lb on Fairbairn's test, or 24 cwt on the 3 ft bar. This superiority was ascribed to the excellence of the ores (a mixture of Derbyshire and Scottish), to the good local moulding sands, and to the special skill of the Derby moulders. The Handyside wrought iron had a guaranteed ultimate tensile strength of 20–23 tons per sq in, as compared with the usual 17 tons per sq in. The firm maintained its high reputation until 1911, when due to failure of the management to keep abreast of the times it closed down. Its Britannia Foundry in Duke Street has disappeared entirely to make room for modern housing.

In the days before the introduction of British Standards these pioneer companies established their own levels of quality. Thus the Butterley Company supplied two grades of cast iron: Butterley or 'Special Derbyshire', made from a mixture of oolite and native Derbyshire stone; and Butterley Mine, or 'Derbyshire All Mine', made solely from selected ironstones of the coal measures, obtained on the Butterley Estates.

Five grades of wrought iron were available until quite recently:

Bridge and Girder Quality or	Butterley Crown
Boiler	Butterley B
Best Best	Butterley BB
Treble Best	Butterley BBB
Admiralty Cable	Butterley Special Cable

In 1857 James Eastwood was making engine and carriage wheels, crankshafts, etc for the railway, at the Railway Iron Works at the angle of Cotton Lane, now the southern entrance to the Rolls-Royce foundries. Thomas Swingler was an iron founder, producing railway points and crossings, at the Victoria Foundry, of which the bus depot in Osmaston Road, adjacent to the Rolls-Royce foundries, is a relic. The two companies had merged by 1864, when they were considering opening a railway wagon works. In 1916 they were building railway bridges in steel in many parts of the world, but they went into liquidation in 1925.

Other iron firms which came into existence in Derby during this period were Jobsons, originally of Litchurch Lane and Cotton Lane (1849), now Qualcast Ltd, and Ley's Malleable Castings Co Ltd (1874), now an important supplier of black-heart malleable castings to the motor trade. The long-established companies at Stanton, Staveley, and Riddings (James Oakes) are now merged into one, and an important product is cast-iron pipes. This business had its beginnings in the gas industry. In 1824 the pipes from Strutt's gasholder at Hopping Hill to Mr Ward's warehouse in Belper were of 3 in bore, from thence to Mr Horton's 4 in, and thence to the mills 5 in. In 1835 the 3 in pipes were replaced by 5 in pipes; 500 were ordered from Oakes (Riddings) and 500 from Molds (Morley Park). The Stanton works has some interesting 'jiggers'—hydraulically operated cranes used with the vertical method of casting which has now been replaced by centri-spinning methods of pipe production.

Firms which have specialised in other fields are Smedley Brothers, of the Eagle Iron Works, Belper, and the Radiation Parkray Foundry which began as an offshoot of the Smedley firm. Smedleys now concentrates on foundry equipment. The domestic smokeless stoves of Radiation Parkray are well-known.

This section on iron may end aptly with the story of the failure to preserve the world's first steel railway rail. In 1856 R. F. Mushet, youngest son of the pioneer metallurgist David Mushet, who had worked at Riddings, produced a double-headed rolled rail, from

Bessemer-Mushet steel. It was laid down near the bridge at the north end of Derby station, where wrought-iron rails lasted only six months. Sixteen years later the rail was taken up and lost, despite Mushet's efforts to preserve it.[33]

TABLE II

ANALYSES OF CAST-IRON PRODUCTS*

Composition		'Skull' found as coping on wall at Milford Mill (from Hopping Hill Foundry, now Glow Worm, Milford?)	Cruciform stanchion from Milford Mill, 1782–3	Window from old workhouse, now Royal Crown Derby Co Ltd, Derby, 1838–40
Total carbon	%	3·20	3·64	3·23
Graphite	%	2·80	2·54	2·75
Silicon	%	3·53	1·57	2·48
Sulphur	%	0·80	0·05	0·07
Phosphorus	%	0·20	0·35	1·13
Manganese	%	0·38	0·65	0·33
Chromium	%	0·02	0·07	0·22
Nickel	%	Nil	Nil	Trace
Total iron	%	55·2	91·0 rem.	89·7 rem.

The analysis of the old workhouse window is typical of the high phosphorus iron produced in Derbyshire for the last 140 years or so, but the chromium is unusual. The Milford Mill stanchion is of quite high quality coke blast furnace iron. Its low phosphorus content is unusual for Derbyshire iron. Its high carbon content indicates remelting of the pig without much addition of scrap. The third sample is astonishing for its high sulphur content, and more nearly resembles some furnace 'bears'—tap outs of residual remnants from the bottom of a furnace after a long campaign.†

* With acknowledgments to Mr G. Lee, of Rolls-Royce Ltd.

† Note supplied by Mr M. H. Hallett, Managing Director of Chamberlin & Hill Ltd, Chuckery Foundry, Walsall, and Treasurer of the Historical Metallurgy Group.

COAL

Coal was being mined as early as the thirteenth century, but 500 years were to elapse before it was put to effective industrial use. During the past 200 years, however, the exploitation of the East Derbyshire coalfield has influenced the appearance of the county, and its industrial developments, more strongly than any other single factor. In the eastern coalfields huge spoil heaps dwarf the dead and dying colliery buildings, yet possess a striking beauty, as when the setting sun illuminates the fiery-coloured burnt shales. In the south-eastern corner of the county the wastes of coal and clay workings are still extending, and have not yet been blended into the landscape by time.

Of wider significance to developments in the county as a whole are the improvements in communications, which were developed mainly in response to the demand for easier ways of distributing coal. First came turnpike roads, then canals and tramways—the last very largely a service to local collieries—and the railways, which interacted by imposing at the same time an increased demand for coke, coal and iron.

There is a fundamental difference between mining for iron and coal, and mining for lead, which affects the pattern of economic development. Lead mining was a 'mystery', since the incidence of rich veins of lead was accidental, and their discovery was largely a matter of chance and venture. Coal and iron, occurring in extensive seams, could be 'cropped'. In consequence, when the value of coal came to be appreciated, it was the landowners who played the domi-nant role, in exploiting the resources of their estates. They were quick to appreciate the value of new techniques, encouraging the develop-ment of the methods of the German lead miners, and later of the steam engine, for pumping and for winding.

The clays found with the coal, and the possibility of making use of slack or unsaleable coal, led to a big increase in the manufacture of bricks. This, combined with the need for a large labour force for mining, has given us the nineteenth-century concentrations of brick-built houses in such Derbyshire towns as Swadlincote, Heanor, Clay Cross and Clowne, and around Bolsover. At these places, the original village is almost lost in the rapid urbanisation which has followed the winning of coal.

The coal measures hade, or dip, steeply eastwards. The collieries established a century or more ago at the westward edge of the East Midland coalfield are becoming worked out, and a general move eastwards, to exploit the deeper seams by deeper shafts, is now taking place. Fortunately the National Coal Board is sympathetic towards the preservation of quite important coal-mining machinery which is now reaching its centenary and becoming obsolete.

Early Workings

Derbyshire has three coal-bearing areas. The principal one, in the east, forms part of the largest field in England and at present the most productive; it comes under the jurisdiction of the East Midlands Division of the National Coal Board. The North Derbyshire coalfield is a continuation of the Lancashire & Cheshire field; small in extent, it produces an inferior coal, used locally. The South Derbyshire field forms part of the Leicestershire coalfield and is of relatively recent development.

The most important area, the eastern field, had two zones—the visible and the concealed coalfields. The visible field comprised the west of the region, where the coal seams bassetted along the line running southwards from Dronfield to beyond Belper, and then south-easterly to Stanton (see map, page 20). In this area the earliest references to coal-workings are found. It is a region of fertile farm-lands, interspersed with local concentrations of mining activity which have done little to spoil the countryside. Farther eastwards the con-cealed coalfield is marked by the more modern collieries and by the nineteenth-century urban growths which have accompanied them.

The markedly different properties of the various coal seams were soon recognised by the early coal masters. Thus the Silkstone seam was appreciated as being good for household use, for gas producing and for coking. It was the discovery of good coking coal at Clay Cross which impelled George Stephenson to buy up all the local land he could, and to start a company which later became the Clay Cross Company, in order to have a source of coke fuel for his locomotives. The Top Hard seam makes a hard coke capable of supporting the weight of the charge in tall iron-smelting furnaces. Iron producers were careful in selecting the best coal for their purposes. When nationalisation meant the pooling of coal from different sources, the Butterley Company changed from coal to oil-fuel for its puddling furnaces at Codnor Park, as dependable supplies of the preferred coal could no longer be obtained.

The earliest references to coal working in the area start with the oft-quoted objection of Queen Eleanor to the offensive smoke of the sea-coal (ie coal, as distinct from charcoal), in Nottingham in 1257. This coal was being used mainly by smiths, nailers, brewers, dyers, and limeburners, and for some domestic heating. In 1285 coal was being mined at Morley and Smalley, and at Denby in 1291. In 1290 we hear of an early road death, when William de Naylestone was run over by a three-horse coal cart at Breaston, presumably from the Morley or Stanton pits.

During the next century there are more frequent references. At Hanley (ie Handley—near Stretton and Clay Cross), Godard of Kilburn was killed when the rope he was descending broke. The hazardous nature of coal mining even in those early days is shown by further casualties. In 1313, Emma Culhare was killed by 'le Damp' at Morley, and nine years later Maud Webster was killed by a run-in (the collapse of a shaft) at Wingerworth. Other places mentioned during this period are Duffield, Hulland, Stanton, and Belper. In the fifteenth century lime was burned with coal at Melbourne (1402), and collieries at Codnor are referred to on several occasions. Mention of Tibshelf appears in 1539, and during that century there are many

Page 71 : (*above*) *Waterwheels at Arkwright's Masson Mill, removed c 1927;*
(*below*) *Cat & Fiddle Windmill, Dale Abbey*

Page 72 : (*above*) *Removal of haystack boiler from Park Hall Farm, Denby, to Science Museum South Kensington, 1964;*
(*below*) *Engine house for Francis Thompson's atmospheric engine of 1791, Oakerthorpe Colliery*

references to coal winning in the Middleton Manuscripts, although these are mainly about activities just over the border in Nottinghamshire.

In Derbyshire coal occurs in relatively thick strata of great extent, occurring in soft rock and, until worked out, bassetting over a considerable area. The seams are subject to flooding, and so an early reference (1316) to a 'sowe' or sough (always pronounced 'suf' in Derbyshire) at Cossall, in adjacent Nottinghamshire, is not surprising. It should be remembered, however, that by reason of the soft country rock and the topography, sough drainage was far easier for coal mines than for lead mines.

The earliest workings were by bell pits, originally thought of as shallow, although Godard's fatal accident suggests that they may have been deeper than is generally supposed. As the workings became flooded, new ones would be begun. By the end of the sixteenth century, however, the colliers were just as anxious as the lead miners to avail themselves of the new techniques introduced by the German miners; indeed, the greater involvement of the landowners brought a keener appraisal to bear. A note in the Middleton Papers of 1610[34] on 'An inventor's proposal for improved pumping machine for use in coal pits' will strike a responsive chord with every mechanical engineer. It pointed out that a 'modell allredie made of wood' would show the effectiveness of the device, the key to which must remain the secret of the 'inginere', but 'smale modles often fayle and soune prove defective when they come to worcke upon heavye and continuall weightes in greater proportions'. At this time chain pumps were already at work for drawing water. With a 4 in cylinder bore, they raised water 15 fathoms, or 90 ft, at three pits at Wollaton in Nottinghamshire.

The active agent in this work was Huntingdon Beaumont, who was working at the pits of the Willoughbys, at Cossall, Strelley & Wollaton. Mr R. S. Smith has shown how it was here that the first railway was laid down in this country, in 1603–4, and has dealt sympathetically with the struggles and misfortunes of Beaumont, who went to

E

the north-east coalfield hoping to interest the colliers there in the new devices which he had picked up from the Germans (cf Agricola). Such was their conservatism, however, that he returned unsuccessful, having lost all his money.[35]

A map by Dr J. U. Nef shows the location of those pits which were probably producing more than 10,000 tons of coal per annum about 1610. It includes four pits at Eckington, and others at Totley, Elmton, Shuttlewood, Bolsover, Chesterfield (two), Wingerworth, Tibshelf, Alfreton, Swanwick, Butterley, Ripley, Riddings, Codnor, Belper, Heanor, Shipley, Langley, Denby, Duffield (probably near Hopping Hill), Morley and Stanley, in the eastern field, and at Newhall, Swadlincote, Oakthorpe and Measham in the south-eastern field.[36]

In 1693 Thomas Houghton wrote of Derbyshire coal mining:[37]

> The chiefest coal mines thereabout are at Smaly, four miles, at Heanor, six miles, and at Denby, five miles from Derby; through which abundance in summer are carried as far as Northamptonshire, from whence is brought back barley. These coals at Smaly and Heanor are in the hands of one, Mr Samuel Richardson . . . John Lowe of Denby (has spent) between £900 and £1,000 in perfecting a sough to lay his delf dry . . . and has laid as many coal dry as will be got this forty years. . . . The coals are drawn up by a horse, as in a malt mill, where is a barrel, on which a rope winds. . . . At Smaly my friend went down the pit 20 fathom (120 feet) . . . and presently came to a pit 20 yards deeper than before, out of which they drew water from another pit 20 yards deeper. . . .

This indicates a total depth of working of 240 ft and is exceptionally interesting as an early reference to a horse gin, or whim. These gins continued to be used throughout the nineteenth century. In 1964, with the co-operation of the NCB, the remains of a simple barrel gin and a geared gin were removed from Pinxton Green Colliery to safekeeping at the Colliery Training School at the nearby Bentinck Colliery. The original site has now been obliterated by the M1 motorway.

We have already seen how the reverberatory furnace of Dr Edward Wright was introduced for lead smelting, and how in the second quarter of the eighteenth century its use became general in Derbyshire, where coal was plentiful and peat scarce. The invention of the steam engine by Newcomen in 1710–11, and its introduction into Derbyshire before 1720, created another demand for coal-fuel. Meanwhile increasing amounts of lime were being burnt, using slack coal; and, according to Houghton, Derby saw the introduction of coke for malt-drying about 1643. This is the earliest application of pre-prepared coke so far recorded.[38]

The construction of canals led to a great expansion in the county's coal trade, as it became possible to extend the market southwards. This reduced the long-standing advantage of the coalfields of north-east England, with their coastwise 'collier' traffic, as shown by the following figures (after Nef).

Approximate Annual Output of the whole Midland Coal District*

		Ratio: Midlands/ NE Coast
1551–1600	65,000 tons	1·0
1681–1690	850,000 tons	0·7
1781–1790	4,000,000 tons	1·33
1901–1910	100,000,000 tons	2·0

Little remains of the sites of these early workings, save for areas of disturbed ground to show where bell pits were worked for coal and ironstone. More is to be seen of the coal mines of the late eighteenth and early nineteenth centuries.

Expansion in the Eighteenth and Nineteenth Centuries

Coal and iron were inseparable during this period of rapid expansion, and the first act of a new 'coal and iron' company would usually be to sink a coal pit. The names of the landowners who had exploited the coal previously have been lost in the titles of large industrial enterprises, most of which still survive. They were quick to adopt the Newcomen steam engine, and of seventy-seven early engines in

---

* Including Derbyshire, Yorkshire, Lancashire, Cheshire, Shropshire, Staffordshire, Nottinghamshire, Warwickshire, Leicestershire and Worcestershire.

Derbyshire, twenty-five were installed at coal mines. The earliest was at Measham (then in the county) in 1729, followed by Smalley in 1735, Staveley in 1769, and Alfreton, Stainsby, Barlow and Ilkeston in 1775 and 1776.[39] Further research might uncover many more. For the industrial archaeologist, a pleasing feature of these early applications of steam is that as the seams became exhausted the installations were abandoned, so that there still exist numbers of old beam-engine houses, as at Oakerthorpe 1791, and at the Seldom Seen colliery, which will be dealt with in the next chapter on the steam engine.

When George Stephenson was driving the Clay Cross tunnel of the North Midland Railway he discovered rich seams of coal, admirably suited to coking. Smokeless fuel had become necessary for railways through Acts of 1826 and 1830, and an immediate result was the founding of George Stephenson & Company in 1837. Formerly coal was 'cowkified' by burning it in large heaps on the ground. The beehive coke oven was introduced about 1737 in Durham, to improve the control of speed of burning. This was not so necessary with the coking coals of Derbyshire, and the stack method persisted for a long time. Indeed Farey registered strong disapproval of its survival in Sheffield, where the murky atmosphere, which has only recently improved, was already well-established.

Farey credits David Mushet with the introduction 'a few years ago' (ie before 1807) at Somercotes of the close-way of coking—the provision of a controllable chimney to the heap of coke. According to Dr Mott[40] this method had been used in the north-east since about 1775. After discovering the Black Band iron ore in Scotland, establishing the iron industry there and losing his share through the dishonesty of his partner, Mushet joined James Oakes for a time at Riddings before moving on to South Wales.[41] (It was at the New Deeps pit of the Somercotes works of James Oakes that petroleum was first exploited commercially, by James Young in 1848.)[42]

Beehive ovens were noted by Farey at Dunston (close to the great Sheepbridge Works), Troway, Ponds and various other collieries. Ruined banks of ovens, many hardly distinguishable under dense growth, are to be seen at Unstone, Barlow Brook, along Mossbeck Brook, and east of Eckington.

Other great coalmasters of the nineteenth century are to be identified with the iron companies. John and Charles Mold sold much coal at the site of their furnaces in Morley Park, at prices ranging from 2s 6d to 4s 6d per ton. In this area, too, the researches of Mr A. Guest show that there were formerly great banks of coke ovens to feed the furnaces. Perhaps the greatest coal producer of his time was G. H. Barrow, who reopened the site at Staveley, 'opposite the former buildings', thus establishing the Staveley Ironworks in 1840. In 1858 Smith's Stanton Ironworks was taken over by George Crompton the banker, and later the Stanton Ironworks Co Ltd became the largest colliery owner in the Midlands.

The 1860s saw further considerable expansion in the trade. The Clay Cross Company (formerly George Stephenson & Co) sank a number of new shafts. Three of these, at Parkhouse, Morton, and Shirland, were stopped in 1965 after being worked continuously for 100 years. Their winding engines are exceptionally interesting and are described later (page 118). These collieries show that there was little change in the appearance of coal mining until the advent of the covered-in winding gear of the new collieries which are replacing them to the east. It is greatly to be hoped that one of these old sites will be preserved complete with its classic old winding engines, gear, and buildings. But at least the engine of the Morton Colliery is safe (see page 118).

Some of the largest industrial installations to be seen in the Derbyshire coalfield today are concerned with the production of coke and producer gas. Although there is little resemblance to the 'crozling' or cowking heaps of 150 years ago, the coke-ovens of the Stanton, Staveley and Sheepbridge companies, and the low-temperature carbonisation plant of the NCB at Wingerworth, are in direct line of succession.

The small coalfield in the north-west shows little activity today, but interesting ruins remain of a beam-engine house and a ventilation stack at the Dolly Pit, near Whaley Bridge. The other area, in the south-east around Swadlincote, has developed during the past century, along with an important earthenware industry, which is described elsewhere. At Bretby is the Engineering Development Establishment of the National Coal Board.

STONE, FOR USE AND ORNAMENT

It would have been atypical of Derbyshire men not to put to profitable use the stone which is so prominent a feature of the landscape. The range of uses and applications matches the geological variety. From early times limestone was burnt to produce lime for agriculture and for cement. Its use as building stone is still evident. Its employment as a flux for smelting iron ores has continued to increase, and today large quantities are quarried for road metal, and for firedamping dust for coal mines.

'Derbyshire marble' enjoyed a wide reputation until a century ago, and it inspired the development of complicated sawing and polishing machinery. Chert, a siliceous rock allied to flint, which occurs in limestone, was for a time quarried for the pottery and china industry. Fluorspar, in its 'Blue John' form, enjoyed a vogue for ornaments from Roman times and was one of the tourist attractions to the county in the early nineteenth century. The production of Blue John vases with ormolu mounts was one of Matthew Boulton's ventures. Later, fluorspar was valued as a flux in steel-making, a use which is now being exploited on a large scale.

In the south of the county gypsum, the sulphate of calcium, achieved an even wider reputation. During the Middle Ages the alabaster (large blocks of gypsum) of Chellaston was much used in England and France, being exported as far as Fécamp in 1414, for ecclesiastical effigies and church decoration. Gypsum was put to practical use as 'plaster of Paris' and employed extensively for floors and walls.

Gritstone has been used for centuries for field walls, buildings, and grindstones. Its use as a building material endows many of Derbyshire's towns and villages with their characteristic appearance.

In deep pockets of the limestone there occur 'accidental' deposits of siliceous clays, which support an important industry producing refractory bricks for furnace lining. Loams have long provided material for brick-making, and the clays of the coal measures have been the basis of an important earthenware industry. Finer clays support potteries which are closely identified with the county.

Limestone

Burning limestone to produce lime has been practised since the time of the Greeks and Romans. A Roman bath excavated at Buxton was found to have been constructed of limestone blocks, with a lime mortar, and faced with a lime cement.[43] Cameron thinks that the field name of Oldeofne, in Alsop-en-le-Dale, refers to a lime kiln. It is not known when the value of lime for improving the soil was first appreciated, but at the end of the fifteenth century it was being burnt for that purpose, using wood, peat or coal as fuel.

According to Farey, the agricultural value of lime seems to have been better realised in Derbyshire than farther south, and he mentions the eagerness with which the local farmers would seek out limestone for burning. Farmers from Lancashire and Cheshire would bring their carts 20 miles to collect lime, and by the new canals it was being distributed from Crich and Peak Forest for 40 or more miles around—to the astonishment of Farey himself. In his second volume he lists about seventy-six places where limestone was burnt for 'land sale', ie buying on the spot and carting away. In addition, most large farms had their own usually primitive kilns. In 1964 one of these old kilns, at Monyash, was excavated and a model of it commissioned by ICI Ltd is exhibited in the Derby Borough Museum.

Several interesting points emerge from Farey's list. The first industrial kilns were at Ashover, and he describes them as 20–25 ft deep. To canal wharves at Aston-on-Trent, Breaston & Draycott, Bull Bridge, Borrowash & Spondon, Codnor, Derby, Horninglow, Ilkeston Common, Langley Mill, Pinxton, Pye Bridge, Sandiacre, Sawley, Shardlow, Shipley, Stanton-by-Dale, Swarkeston, Twyford, Weston-on-Trent, and Willington, the firm of Edward Banks & Co brought limestone from its Hilts Quarry at Crich and burnt it on the spot. It was sold at prices ranging between 2s 9d and 3s 7d per quarter of eight bushels.

Enthusiasm for land improvement led also to the manufacture of bone-meal. Farey reported that 'several Ship Loads of the Bones, collected in London (some from the Churchyards, as I have heard) find their way into the interior of Derbyshire, and are there ground by Mills, erected on purpose, into a most potent and valuable Manure.' He listed nine mills where this was done, and apparently bone-crushing was a mill sideline ancillary to lead and iron making. Although Farey felt sure that Middlesex farmers (evidently a backward lot) would be surprised at this use of bone-meal, not everyone appreciated the importance of crushing the bones. At the Duke of Portland's Park at Welbeck Farey saw large bones, the skulls of horses for instance, broken into only two or three pieces, and strewn over the lawns, which must have been a grisly sight.

A few years after Farey's report, Banks' kilns at Bull Bridge appear to have been taken over by the Butterley Company, which continued to use them until thirty years ago. They are now extremely ruinous, but something can be seen of the extent of the enterprise. It was mechanised, with a horse tramroad to bring the stone from the quarries, and a 'tipple' to tip the stone from the wagons. Some was tipped directly into barges, some to a level space from which barges could be loaded, five at a time being accommodated in a covered dock. Much of this stone was used as a flux in the Butterley iron furnaces, upwards of 1 ton being needed for each ton of iron smelted. At Bugsworth was another extensive establishment, shortly to be reported on by Mr Brian Lamb, who has made a thorough study of the workings and of the railway and canal complex which distributed the lime.

At Marple Bridge, by what was then the county boundary, Samuel Oldknow, who was as interested in agricultural improvement as he was in his textile mills, erected a large lime works, which Farey claimed to be the most complete he had ever seen. These kilns still stand, with their façade in imitation of 'an ancient Castle' (plate, page 54). Oldknow had close ties with Derbyshire, being financed by Richard Arkwright II and hiring Derbyshire lead miners for his building work.

The enclosure of land increased the demand for lime, and the transportation of limestone and lime was a main reason for the building of the Cromford & High Peak Railway in 1825. This line, and the later railway from Ashbourne to Buxton, preserve for us some excellent limestone work in their bridges. The tunnel under the A6 road at Parsley Hay, built from dressed limestone, is as clean and sharply cut as the day it was erected 140 years ago, even to the masons' marks.

When George Stephenson was building the North Midland Railway, he perceived that railway transport would greatly benefit the export of lime to other parts of England. At the same time that he was buying land for the railway company at Ambergate he bought adjacent land for his own Clay Cross Company, already mentioned. In 1840 he began to build eight large lime kilns on the Cromford Canal at Ambergate, adding twelve more before the first were finished. The joint where the extension was made could still be seen until the kilns were demolished in 1966 to make way for the East Midlands Gas Board's £7,000,000 petroleum-gas plant. The curved bank of kilns was an imposing sight and was in use until October 1965. The kilns were 30–40 ft deep and of 11 ft diameter, with cones 20 ft high; the cones illustrated by Smiles were later replaced by steel structures. Supplied with limestone from Crich Cliff quarries by a tramroad which ended in a long, steep gravity incline (see Gazetteer), the works produced 50–60,000 tons of lime a year and in the 1850s employed 120 men. Lime was being sent to most of the principal towns in the country. Coal came from Clay Cross by the North Midland Railway.

Lime-burning has continued, especially in the neighbourhood of

Dove Holes, Burbage and Stoney Middleton. These areas had been worked for a long time, Dove Holes being mentioned in 1650, and Pilkington (*A View of the Present State of Derbyshire*) referring in 1789 to the people living in caves hollowed out in the huge spoil heaps of lime ash at Grin Low. Under the action of rain this ash became cement-like and must have offered adequate shelter, although tourists visiting the caves thought poorly of them. Old kilns can still be seen amongst the quarries in Middleton Dale, which today produce much of the limestone dust used by the National Coal Board for fire-damping. Some lime kilns of impressive size remain, as those near Peak Forest station. A particularly fine example can be seen by the footpath from Spend Lane to Bostern Grange, still in sufficiently sound condition to warrant preservation.

The lime-quarry workings in the Buxton and Wirksworth areas are vast in extent. At Middleton-by-Wirksworth is a rare example of a modern limestone mine. Lorries drive for ¼ mile underground to the working face. Excavation is carried out by bord-and-pillar working on a noble scale, with 'roads' about 20 ft high and 35 ft wide, and pillars 40 ft square. A large stone-crushing plant has been installed underground. Where the terrain is suitable, this method reduces disfiguration of the countryside. The topography in the immediate vicinity of Wirksworth town is, however, changing visibly, as whole hills are being removed by the more usual method of open quarrying. At the huge cement works at Hope an effort has been made to reduce the unsightliness of the quarries by making them of horseshoe shape in plan to conceal the scars. The tall chimney, with its plume of white smoke, is, however, a prominent feature for miles around.

The properties of the lime vary considerably. That at Hope occurs adjacent to clays which make the production of Earle's cement a profitable venture. Crich lime is particularly pure, as William Jessop found to his cost: shortly after he had built the imposing aqueduct to carry the Cromford Canal over the Derwent, at Wigwell, it collapsed. He admitted that the fault was his, and offered to repair the damage at his own expense. The Crich lime is lacking in the argillaceous matter necessary to provide the 'bind' needed for good mortar.[44]

Gritstone

The gritstones, which vary greatly in hardness, fineness of grain and durability according to their provenance, have for many centuries been important both as building material and for grindstones. A grindstone quarry at Alderwasley (where half-finished stones can still be seen) was earning high rents in 1257.

A flourishing business in grindstones was maintained for a long period, until the invention of the French burr stones—which are fabricated by cementing small pieces of stone together with plaster of Paris. Before this, 'Peak Stones' from Derbyshire were regarded as the best for flour milling, and they were in great demand both in Britain and on the continent. A pair of 5 ft diameter stones cost ten guineas in Farey's time. Smaller stones were used for paint-grinding, and very large ones were exported to Finland for grinding wood-pulp for paper. Examples of these can be seen at the Poor Lots Quarry at Tansley.

The quarrying and shaping of gritstone blocks for building is a more expensive business than brick-making, so that stone is no longer the principal building material in the county, although artificial stone is providing a not unsatisfactory substitute. At the time of the building of the North Midland Railway, however, stone was put to uses which are perhaps the finest monument to the railway pioneers. The long cutting through Belper, and the embankment retaining wall at Ambergate, created a great impression when they were built and attracted many visitors. The skill of the stonemasons persisted, and it is particularly evident in that stretch of wall alongside the A6 road at Ambergate which was built of random-sized blocks of stone, some of considerable size, carefully fitted together, when the tracks were doubled in 1931 (see page 221). Even these efforts are dwarfed, however, by the huge stone blocks which were used at lead mines as engine foundations, many of which are still lying as evidence of their former purpose.

An interesting example of how knowledge was accumulated from experience is given by Farey. Some stones repelled paint, and so made poor milestones, but White Watson found that stone from quarries at Woodseats, in Norton, held paint on its surface excellently.

A notable feature of the uplands of Derbyshire is the drystone walling, in limestone or gritstone according to the locality. In Farey's time a wall from 5 ft to 6 ft high cost from 6s to 12s per rood of 7 yd, for getting the stone, carting it and building the wall. Farey was impressed by the walls around Ashover, consisting of large upright slabs, which are still to be seen.

Gypsum

The gypsum pits of Chellaston had been known for their alabaster for church monuments at least since the fourteenth century. In 1367 Edward III had ten carts and eighty horses to draw blocks of the stone to Windsor, for the Chapel of the Garter. Altar pieces and images were carved in Nottingham, many going overseas to France, Spain, Italy, Holland and Iceland, from 1382 until the Reformation. The exports to France went via Nottingham and Hull, to Harfleur, those to Spain via Dartmouth. When plaster of Paris was first made by burning gypsum is not known, but it was made in Paris in the thirteenth century. Pilkington stated in 1789 that 800 tons of gypsum were raised yearly at Chellaston, 500 tons being sent to the Potteries where it was used for moulds.

A common use of gypsum plaster in Derbyshire was for flooring— for cottages, and later by William Strutt for his fireproof cotton mills. Cottages would often use a mixture of crushed lead slag and plaster, sometimes bound with ox-blood. The plaster was also used to make a wash for walls. In 1782 Francis Thompson wrote to James Watt that he had whitewashed the inside walls of the engine house at

Gregory Mine to make it lighter—a reminder that engine-tenders in those days must have worked their long hours in dark and gloomy surroundings, with only a few candles to illuminate their reciprocating charge.

Derbyshire Marble

Occurring locally in mines at Ashford, the 'black marble' of Derbyshire was used for church furnishings in medieval times, and for chimney pieces at Hardwick Hall in 1580. Later it was to have a great vogue, along with the grey 'marbles', or limestone containing crinoids ('Derbyshire screws') of Sheldon, Monyash, and Hopton, for table tops and chimney pieces in smaller houses.

The oldest marble works was that being run at Ashford by Henry Watson in 1748, and it continued in use until 1905. Part of it was demolished when the A6 road bypassed Ashford, and since the site was taken over by the North Derbyshire Water Board a few years ago the original buildings, identified by Dr T. D. Ford, are disappearing.[45] The sawing, grinding and polishing shops were all worked by water. This works produced, in addition to plain polished slabs, a variety of ornaments, vases, pillars and brooches of inlay work. Mr Robert Thornhill of Great Longstone has made an important collection of these items, which although commonly on sale as souvenirs at Matlock Bath in the heyday of Victorian tourism are now rare. Mr Thornhill has also gathered together the tools and materials used.[46]

The sawing and polishing of these large blocks of hard limestone posed mechanical problems, the solution of which, at two works in Derby and one at Ashford, attracted many sightseers. Brown, later Brown & Mawes, set up a manufactory in the old Silk Mill at Derby, and a detailed description of the complex machine was given in Rees' *Cyclopaedia*, 1819–20 (drawing reproduced on page 86). It could saw two blocks into five plates and polish two plates at the same time. The drive was by waterwheel to the crank located under the polishing tables at the left-hand side of the machine, as shown in the drawing.

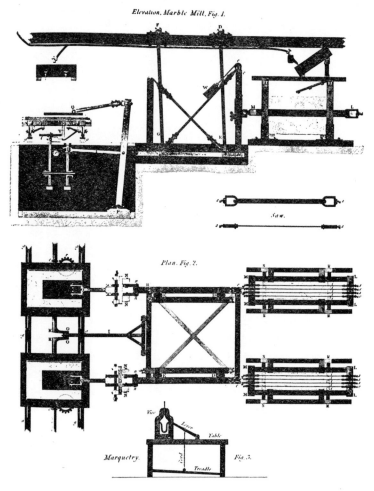

Brown's marble-sawing machine, Derby, 1802. (Rees' *Cyclopaedia*, 1819)

In 1802, Brown's lease of the Silk Mill having lapsed, he erected a large works in King Street, Derby. He had a steam engine, and he also made quantities of vases in Blue John. Later the enterprise was taken over by Joseph Hall, and in 1916 R. G. Lomas & Son was continuing to work in alabaster here. The buildings are hidden behind the showrooms and works of Batterby & Hefford.

Blue John, another mineral greatly sought after by collectors from Roman times onwards, is now extremely scarce, and the industry is carried on only by a few families in Castleton.

POTTERY, EARTHENWARE AND CHINA

Pottery-making is one of man's earliest activities, and it is fitting that some of the oldest industrial sites yet discovered in Derbyshire should be the Romano-British potteries of Hazlewood and Holbrook. Painstakingly excavated from 1958 onwards (see the *Journal* of the Derbyshire Archaeological Society), these potteries revealed a high degree of standardisation of cooking pots, some of which have been identified at army garrisons on Hadrian's Wall. This would imply a measure of organisation for the ordering, collecting and distributing of the utensils, probably to some army staging-post on the route to the north which has not yet been identified.

An early medieval pottery existed at Burley Hill, Quarndon, and in the fourteenth century there was one at Dale Abbey and another at Repton. Chesterfield had a brown-pottery manufactory before the end of the fifteenth century, and there is today at Whittington the 157-year-old stoneware works of Pearson & Co (Chesterfield) Ltd. The brownware pottery at Brampton no longer exists. Crich had an old pottery, about which little is known, and Ticknall had one in the sixteenth century. Little remains of this but a well-wooded pool which was once a clay pit, a picturesque open drying shed, and the ruins of a rectangular kiln, which has more probably been used for bricks. Ticknall pottery was listed in the inventory of one of the Melland family of Alport-by-Youlgreave, in 1635, and slightly earlier in the inventories of the Wirksworth branch of the Wigley family. Wirksworth, too, had a pottery, and a brick works, in 1787.

Many local potteries have disappeared, but an interesting relic is that at Smalley, with its single bottle kiln still standing. Here were made the earthenware pots for the fireproof buildings of William Strutt in the 1790s. This works was operating until twenty to thirty years ago, making teapots (plate, page 54).

William Bourne (1747–89) of Eastwood set up a pottery at Belper. In 1809 or slightly earlier his son Joseph Bourne established kilns by the claypits at Little Ryefield in Denby. He sent clay to the pottery at Belper until 1816–19, when this was closed down and the Denby pottery was continued, to establish its present world-wide reputation for oven and tableware, which is made in part from clay still quarried on the works site. Also at Denby is the works of W. H. & J. Slater Ltd, established by William Drury-Lowe, who died in 1827, and worked by Slaters from 1874. Bricks, sanitary pipes, sinks, gullies and chimney pots are made. The thirteen beehive kilns are in process of conversion from coal to oil firing, as requiring much less labour. Clay was at one time mined in an adjacent pit, and coal comes from the colliery at Moor Green.

The big expansion of the coal industry stimulated in two ways the growth of brick and earthenware manufacture. Coal mining unearthed quantities of clays, of varying properties, and there was much 'slack' or unsaleable coal which could be used in the kilns. The turn of the eighteenth century saw the establishment of brick works at Loscoe, at Ambergate, and at Church Gresley and Swadlincote. This last-named area has become an important refractory- and stoneware-producing region, with three large firms dating from 1810. One of these, T. G. Green & Co Ltd, still has twenty bottle kilns, two over a century old. John Knowles & Co (Wooden Box) Ltd started as a result of John Knowles recognising fire clay as he was driving a tunnel for Robert Stephenson's Leicester & Swannington Railway, in 1849. Other clays subsequently discovered by this firm have led to an extension of the business into the manufacture of salt-glazed drain-pipes.

A brick works near the centre of Derby has just ceased to operate. It had a Hoffmann kiln, of the type invented in the 1850s for sequen-

Page 89: (above) *Clock-gear cutting machine, bought from Whitehursts 1855, still in use by Wm Haycock, Ashbourne, in 1966;*
(below) *Planing machine from Strutt's Mill, Milford; probably by James Fox, c 1820*

Page 90: (*above*) *Warehouse and dock, Trent & Mersey Canal, Shardlow*;
(*below*) *Horse swing-bridge, Cromford Canal, Bull Bridge*

tial heating and cooling. This kiln, which was started up in 1866, was reputedly the second in Britain, and it was not shut down until it needed repairing in 1945. The Derby Brick Company Ltd has used the local loams, which have been quarried right up to the edge of the Derby Ring Road. The firm, which was established in 1835, will continue at its works at Aston-on-Trent, where gypsum too has been exploited. Another large Hoffmann kiln was in use until recently at the Oakwell Brick Works, on the coal measures at Ilkeston.

At Longcliffe, near Brassington, and at Friden there are important producers of refractory bricks, using the highly coloured siliceous clays which occur locally.

To many people, Derby is better known for its fine china than for any other of its products. 'Crown Derby' probably owes its success as much as anything to the abilities of the artists it employed. The enterprise began in 1750 in Derby, at a site in Nottingham Road just across from the Exeter Bridge. It was George III who in 1773 gave to the company the right to mark William Duesbury's wares 'Crown' Derby, Queen Victoria adding the 'Royal' in 1890. The original company declined and went out of formal existence in 1848, but a small number of its employees under W. G. Larcombe moved into a house in King Street and continued as the Old Crown Derby China Factory. This building, with its small kiln house behind, is now an antique shop. Until about 1963 the door of the house had a somewhat chipped Crown Derby letter-box frame.

In 1878 a new firm was established as the Crown Derby Porcelain Co Ltd. It took over the old workhouse in Osmaston Road, which was built in 1832. In subsequent years the front of the central bay of this building has been changed, though the cast-iron windows of the two flanking bays are original (see Table II, page 67). The workhouse rooms are exceptionally lofty, light and airy, with cast-iron columns, brick roofs of arches of 6 ft span, and stone staircases with iron banisters. Eventually, in 1925, the King Street works was closed and merged with the main establishment. The Derby Borough Museum has an exceptionally fine collection of Crown Derby china.

F

In 1795 John Coke started a china factory at Pinxton. He persuaded William Billingsley, who had been apprenticed to Duesbury in 1774, to leave the Crown Derby works and join him, but Billingsley left Pinxton in 1800 or 1802, to take up work in turn at china works at Torksey, Worcester, Nantgarw, Swansea, and Coalport. The Pinxton works closed down in 1818, but not before the company had sued Francis Thompson, the steam-engine builder of Ashover, for failure to fulfil his contract for the supply of a steam engine of specified horse power.

CHAPTER THREE

The Evolution of Engineering

THE word 'engineer' has evolved from the Latin 'ingenium', implying one with an aptitude for invention or construction. An 'engine' is not, in the true sense of the word, a prime-mover, but rather a mechanical contrivance, a machine, an implement, a tool. 'Engineering' has been defined as 'the art of directing the great sources of power in nature for the use and convenience of man'.

Within these meanings, Britain lagged a long way behind the continent in the development of 'engineering'. It was in fact in the efforts to increase the efficiency of winning metallic ores from the earth that the art was first developed in the civil sense as distinct from the earlier application to engines of war. The story of these developments, as illustrated by contemporary writers of the sixteenth century and later, has been retold by Keller.[1] It is significant to the subsequent developments in Derbyshire that a number of the German mining engineers who came to this country in the late sixteenth century did important work in the county.

A century later George Sorocold, a Lancastrian who had settled in Derby, was probably the first to be awarded the title 'Engineer' for his work in a predominantly civil/mechanical field. It is difficult to identify a definite starting point in any story of evolution, but there can be no doubting the important part played by this man in laying the foundations for the Industrial Revolution. Sorocold's contribution in developing water power and applying it to the driving of complicated machinery has not yet been fully recognised.

The industrial enterprises which came into being in the latter half of the eighteenth century are not easy to classify. 'Ironmasters' and 'coalmasters' also built iron bridges and canals, steam engines and tramroads. They were acutely conscious of the importance of good engineering design, and they employed architects who helped to establish the lasting good taste of Derbyshire's old industrial buildings. Many of the products of these engineers still stand, as impressive and as serviceable as when they were built a century or more ago. Equally noteworthy is the longevity of these local firms.

Engineering cannot be separated from each of the broad areas of activity which are discussed in this book. In this chapter an attempt has been made to trace the growth of engineering skill, experience and knowledge, as a basis for the later industrial developments.

THE DEVELOPMENT OF WATER POWER

Water power was applied to the grinding of corn in Roman times. At the Domesday survey there were seventy-two mills in Derbyshire, and this number increased considerably during the following centuries when many were put to other uses, such as papermaking and the fulling of cloth.

Today many of these watermills have disappeared, their sites indicated only by a pond on a small stream. Others have survived, sometimes with fine wooden machinery intact, as in the mill on the Lathkill at Over Haddon. Mill buildings which have had their machinery removed often do service as barns, the wheel pit, the axle-bearing supports, and the worn circular grooves being the only evidence of their former use.

A particularly fine mill stands on a site which has had a watermill for 800 years, at Alport-by-Youlgreave. Its present machinery is of nineteenth-century date, and is in excellent condition. Another mill of attractive design, which until recently was grinding chicory for an 'instant drink', is at Longford. A much older one, desperately in need of rescue, is the Tideswell Mill in Millers Dale.

We have seen how water power was applied to the tilt hammer for forging, and to blast for smelting. The German engineers Cranich and Schutz applied it to ore-crushing in Duffield Frith, and to wire-drawing, which was carried out at Hathersage, where mill buildings still stand, and at Makeney, by the lower weir. In 1581 a commission of three gentlemen was appointed to survey the resources of Duffield Frith. They recommended that small overshot wheels might be erected on Black Brook near Chevin, and on Hulland Brook, for lead smelting. They recognised at these places signs of earlier iron smelting.[2] Another site is indicated in the name Slitting Mill Farm, near Eckington, and one at Smelting Mill Brook, Little Rowsley.

It was George Sorocold, however, who at the end of the seventeenth century really developed the application of water power to the driving of intricate machinery, and who in so doing initiated the activities which culminated in the pioneering growth of the textile industry in Derbyshire half a century later.

Born into a family with academic traditions, about 1668, probably in Ashton-in-Makerfield in Lancashire, Sorocold's early years were lived in an area noted for its fine smithing—lock making and clock and watch making. He was a student at Emmanuel College, Cambridge, where he would probably have had access to the works of Agricola, Besson, Ramelli and Zonca. He settled in Derby in 1684, marrying Mary, one of the daughters of Henry Francis the apothecary, in December of that year. In 1687 he was concerned with the rehanging of the bells of All Saints Church, an act recorded on a brass plate fixed to a wall of the vestry. He went on to install a public water supply in the town. In 1692 he erected a waterwheel on the site of an old gunpowder mill on the Derwent below St Mary's Bridge. This drove pumps which lifted river water to a cistern in the yard of St Michael's Church (*not* on top of the church, as stated by Hutton and often quoted), whence it was distributed through pipes made of bored-out elm trunks to a number of private houses and to a stone conduit in the Market Place. There were about 4 miles of these pipes, some of which were dug up a few years ago and one of which is preserved in the Derby Borough Museum. The waterworks remained in use until after 1829.

During the next few years Sorocold erected similar installations at

Bridgnorth (which remained in use until 1857), Bristol, Deal, Exeter, King's Lynn, Leeds, Marchant's Water Works in London, New-castle-on-Tyne, Norwich, Nottingham, Portsmouth, Sheffield and Great Yarmouth. All this was done between 1692 and 1700, and it is by no means certain that the list is complete.[3]

In 1701 he reconstructed the waterworks at London Bridge, which had been built by Peter Morice, a Dutchman, in 1582 (see opposite). This was his finest installation, and it received much notice. Henry Beighton's description of 1731, in the *Philosophical Transactions*, is one of the best. The wheel was 20 ft diameter, with floats, or paddles, 14 ft wide and 1½ ft deep. It drove four four-throw crankshafts through 2·2 to 1 gearing. The crankshafts worked connecting rods to overhead beams to which were fixed pump rods. The pumps had bores of 7 in and a stroke of 30 in. At 6 rpm of the wheel the displacement was 880 gpm against a head of 120 ft, equivalent to 32 hp. The machine was noteworthy for its early use of cast iron for cranks, rods, and cylinders, the stiffness of cast iron, which would break rather than bend, being adduced as an advantage. This is possibly the earliest instance of designing to reduce consequential damage in the event of failure of a component.

These works earned for Sorocold a great reputation. Savery, his contemporary and the pioneer of the steam pump, said of him: 'In the composing of such sort of engines, I think no person hath excelled the ingenious Mr George Sorocold.' To Ralph Thoresby he was 'the great English engineer'. In 1703 'Mr Sorocold the Engineer' gave evidence before the House of Lords in support of a scheme for making the Derwent navigable from Derby to the Trent. Rhys Jenkins considered that he was probably the first man concerned with non-military projects to be given the title Engineer, and the first expert engineering witness to be examined in Parliament.[4] He worked on many other important projects before undertaking the work on the silk mills of Derby which gives him his due, but as yet unrecognised, claim to the title of one of the world's first mechanical engineers (page 120). The part played by Cotchett and the Lombes, largely

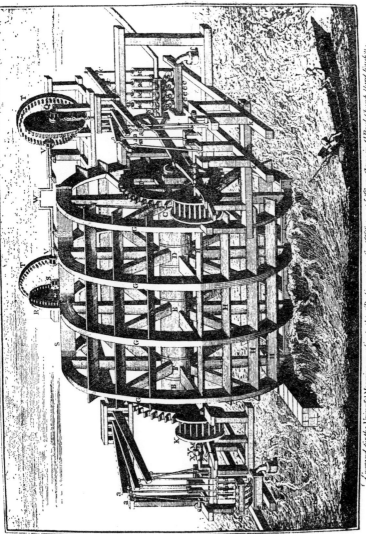

The WATER WORKS at LONDON-BRIDGE for the supply of the CITY of LONDON with THAMES Water.

Engraved for the Universal Magazine according to they Parliament's after K. Hinton at S. Kingaltine in S. Paul's Church Yard, London.

Sorocold's London Bridge Waterworks, 1701. (*The Universal Magazine*, 1749) that of entrepreneurs or initiators, will be described in dealing with the textile industry. In 1702 Sorocold carried out the mill-wrighting and probably the whole installation for Thomas Cotchett's silk mill, which was built adjacent to the waterworks and contiguous with the flour mills, of which at a later date there were three, operated by one Sowter whose name is commemorated in the relatively new Sowter Road. The underground water passages of these corn mills, still working about sixty years ago, could be seen in 1964 when the new offices of the East Midlands Electricity Board were being erected.

Cotchett's venture was not successful, and in 1717 Sir Thomas Lombe, of London, decided to build a mill with machinery on the Italian principle. We have it on the authority of Daniel Defoe that it was Sorocold who constructed the machinery and the mill. Mechanically the project was successful, and it was for a long time a main venue of visitors to the town, including Defoe in the 1720s. 'When Lewis Paul and Richard Arkwright came forward with their spinning machines, the one in 1738 and the other in 1768, the ground had been prepared for them.'[4]

By 1734 important works had been set up at the great weir at Derby, about 600 yd downstream from the silk mill. These, belonging to the Evans family and later to Bingham and Humpston, rolled and slit iron sheet for nailmaking, and rolled copper sheet for sheathing naval vessels. All that remains apart from the imposing weir is an underground sluice and its control which may have been connected with the works. The whole of the area now covered by the Cattle Market, the Bus Station, the New Market, and the Municipal Buildings in Derby must have been a busy place in the succeeding years, with water-powered lead-smelting and rolling mills, gypsum and plaster works, and colour works, while across the river were several foundries.

Despite the sound construction of Sorocold's works, his water-wheels, in common with the others of his time, must have been extremely inefficient. There had indeed been little development since the earliest times, many of the wheels being undershot, with simple flat radial paddles, open at the sides. There was, however, an appreciation of the value of dams, to maintain water supply in times of drought, and these were used with overshot wheels having rudimentary buckets. Great boldness was shown in the building of weirs across even such turbulent rivers as the Derwent. There were weirs at Makeney in the sixteenth century, and at Masson, Hopping Hill and Derby in the early eighteenth century.

In 1759 John Smeaton presented before the Royal Society the results of his experiments to improve the efficiency of waterwheels.[5] He showed that the overshot wheel was far more efficient than the undershot, 63 per cent as against 22 per cent, and the optimum circumferential speed of the buckets was established at about $3\frac{1}{2}$ ft per second, although 6 ft per second was often used. This latter figure gives a rotational speed of nearly 6 revolutions per minute for a 20 ft diameter wheel. With the increasing use of iron instead of wood, this new knowledge led to a big increase in the amount of power developed. Pegg & Ellam Jones, colour manufacturers with works established in 1820 on the site of the present Derby Bus Station, still showed a waterwheel of 300 hp in their advertisement of 1916 (see figure, page 100). The paper mills at Peckwash, below Duffield Bridge, had the right to take 800 hp from the Derwent, and the imposing flow still to be seen in the fine wheel house at Calver Mill provided 140 hp.

A great extension of water power came in response to the demands of the textile industry. Arkwright seems to have been cautious in his first attempt at Cromford, being content with the modest flows of water from Bonsall Brook and Cromford Sough. His subsequent works at Masson Mill, and those of Jedediah Strutt at Belper and Milford, were much more ambitious, and the weirs built by these men, usually as improvements to older weirs, remain as imposing monuments to their efforts.

The Derwent, which has been referred to as the cradle of the Industrial Revolution, is stepped by great weirs along its whole length from Bamford Mill just below the huge reservoirs near its source to Wilne, near its junction with the Trent. These weirs would form a worthy subject for study, from Bamford's straight weir, the unusual downward-curved one at Masson, Strutt's fine and more usual up-stream-curved ones at Belper and at Milford, the latter with its double weir, to the skew weirs of Peckwash and Dale Abbey, and Derby's great weirs. At Borrowash there can still be seen traces of the weirs set up by the monks of Dale in 1278 for their corn mills, which cut off Derby from access to the Trent and the sea until Sorocold's navigation was built in 1720.

Advertisement in Derby Chamber of Commerce *Year Book*, 1916

Lead mining had created the demand for new applications of water power, mainly for pumping. It provided scope for another form of prime mover, the water-pressure or 'hydraulic' engine, which enjoyed a limited vogue for roughly a century, until it was supplanted by the steam engine. It is important as pioneering the use of high pressures and so giving a lead to the eventual further development of the steam engine, once the restrictive patents of Watt had expired.

These engines worked by the pressure of a head of water upon a piston, and they could be single- or double-acting. Their definitive history remains to be written, and they are interesting as making early use of quite high working pressures. Ure thought that they were first used in Germany about 1748, and in 1765 one was erected in Northumberland. From the fact that Francis Thompson was consulted about a hydraulic engine working under a head of 120 ft of water at lead mines near Aberystwyth in 1788, it may be that such an engine had been used in Derbyshire before that date.

In 1803 Richard Trevithick, the great Cornish engineer, installed a hydraulic engine at the Crash Purse Shaft, near Youlgreave, and it ran until 1850. The working piston operated under a pressure of 150 psi, developing 174 hp.[6] In 1841 a much larger engine was installed at Guy Shaft, nearby, and a few years later another one at Pynet Nest mine. John Darlington, chief engineer of the Alport Company, is generally credited with the design of these engines, although they were built by the Butterley Company and by Graham & Co of the Milton Ironworks.[7]

On the tributaries of the Derwent, with their smaller flow, it was necessary to impound the water in dams. The hunger for power is shown by the extent to which quite small streams were harnessed. The Ecclesbourne had from early times nine mills along its 8 mile course, and the tiny streams which unite to form Bonsall Brook still carry many dams and mill ruins. Some of these were used for lead smelting, others for colour grinding and bone grinding. The brook, together with the outfall from Cromford Sough, was used by Arkwright for the first powered cotton mills in the world. Page 71 shows a rare photograph of the waterwheels at his later mill at Masson.

Where the topography was difficult, as in the steep narrow valley of Sydnope Brook, great ingenuity was employed. The quiet and beautiful dams filling this valley, the uppermost 96 ft above the mill, would repay study of the means employed for their control. To cope with the head of water, the flax spinners Edward and James Dakeyne patented a 'disc' engine in 1830 (Patent No 5882). The most striking characteristic of this ingenious machine is perhaps the difficulty which is experienced by those trying to describe it; the patentees, and Stephen Glover, succeeded only in producing descriptions of monumental incomprehensibility. The engine did, however, have the advantage that it could work under high heads of water. The casing of the first machine was cast at the Morley Park Foundry. It was 10 ft outside diameter, weighed 7 tons, and the motor developed 35 hp.

Another beautiful dam is that at Bakewell, which until 7 January 1955 provided the water for two fine wheels used by the DP (Dujardin-Planté) Battery Co Ltd, on the site of Arkwright's mill. Fortunately the wheels and the machinery were recorded in minute detail by Mr Robert Thornhill, the engineer of the company, at the time when a gear segment of the older wheel broke, jammed, and caused much consequential damage, to which the replacement of the old flat-belt drive by V-belts, with their reduced tendency to slip, may have contributed.[8]

These wheels were examples of the increasing skill in making the best use of available materials. The older wheel, built in 1827 by Hewes & Wren of Manchester, was 25 ft in diameter, 18 ft wide. It had a cast-iron axle of cruciform section and a segmental cast-iron rim, to which the gearing was fixed, also in segments, to reduce the stresses due to the $\frac{1}{2}$ ton of water held by each bucket, $10\frac{1}{2}$ tons in all. The rim was fixed to the hub by forty wrought-iron spokes, $2\frac{3}{16}$ in diameter. The smaller wheel, built in 1852 by Kirkland & Son, Mansfield, was 21 ft in diameter, 7 ft wide, and had cast-iron spokes, reinforced by ties. Together they drove a 66 kV generator.

Wheels of more unusual size were one of 52 ft diameter shown on Sanderson's map of 1834 at the Mandale lead mine on the Lathkill, and the 40 ft wide wheel installed by Jedediah Strutt in the North Mill at Belper in 1804. This latter was so wide that its axle had to be constructed from staves, like a barrel.

Waterwheels in the larger installations were gradually replaced by steam engines or, where the water flow was dependable, by the more efficient water turbines. Often steam would be used as a standby. Turbines were installed at the Bamford Mill to generate electricity, a Musgrave steam engine (1907) driving the spinning and doubling machinery. Evans' Mill at Darley Abbey still uses water turbines, and the waterwheels of the DP Battery Works, just mentioned, have been replaced by a horizontal Francis turbine, by Gilbert Gilkes & Gordon Ltd, which will generate 150 hp.

Other applications of water power were to the 'jigger' or hydraulic crane, invented about 1850 and still in use on a noble scale at the Stanton Ironworks, and to hydraulic lifts. In 1832 John Harrison, of Derby, made an elegant four-cylinder table-pump, driven by water from the lake, to raise water to Elvaston Castle. Later it provided water for the elevator in the Castle. An interesting and unusual application of a small waterwheel was by Herbert Frood, in 1897 or earlier, to develop friction materials for brakes. This wheel was erected on a tiny stream in the garden of his house, Rye Flatt, in Combs. Frood's work led to the present great enterprise of Ferodo, not far away in Chapel-en-le-Frith. The immediate outcome of Frood's efforts was described in the advertisement shown (see page 104).

WIND POWER

Windmills were a much later development than watermills, the first English reference being in the twelfth century; no windmills were recorded in the Domesday survey. They saw their widest application in East Anglia, where there was little fall of water available and much low-lift pumping was needed. Windmills suffered from severe limitations, however, as they were at the mercy of the weather, being useless in calm and liable to be destroyed in storm. Moreover, they were incapable of developing more than a few horse-power.

In 1808 Farey listed forty-five windmills in Derbyshire. Today, although many stumps remain, only three are recognisable. The

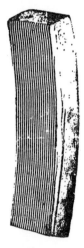

oldest is the finest—the Cat & Fiddle mill at Dale Abbey which has, fortunately, been preserved by the Stanton Ironworks Company Ltd, and is open for inspection. Dating from 1788, this post mill (the earliest type of windmill) is in excellent condition (plate, page 71). The skeleton of another post mill, perhaps of date 1699, still stands at South Normanton. It is not now easy to see, as it is entirely surrounded by new houses. At Heage, in a striking position on top of a hill, what has been a fine example of a tower mill still stands. It has, unusually, six sails, and on a stone by the side of the door is 'WM. 1850', which may date it. At the time of writing Derbyshire County Council is at work on preserving its structure, but urgent action is needed if it is to be restored in entirety.

In Farey's time some of the forty-five mills were 'of considerable dimensions, by which a good deal of the Flour of the District is ground'. Today even the one capable survivor is idle.

THE STEAM ENGINE

For nearly 2,000 years man has known that power could be derived from heat by 'the expansive force of steam'. It was not until 1643, however, that Torricelli made the vital discovery of the pressure of the atmosphere, and so prepared the way for the development of the reciprocating piston engine.

During the reigns of Elizabeth I, James I and Charles I, one-seventh of all the patents granted referred to pumping, so great was the need to unwater lead and coal mines. Thomas Savery, who in 1698 invented the steam pump, hopefully entitled his descriptive book, published in 1702, *The Miner's Friend*, although the pump's limited lift (it was a vacuum pump), diminished its value in this field. Savery's engine was not successful in its time, although it was revived in 1876 as the Pulsometer pump, which is still made.

It was Thomas Newcomen of Dartmouth who invented the first really practical steam engine for pumping, in 1711–12. At one great imaginative bound he combined boiler, cylinder, piston and automatic valve gear into the progenitor of the modern steam engine, indeed of the modern automobile engine. By his use of the rocking beam and a long rod, or spear, to operate a pump at shaft bottom, he was able to force water up from great depths. His invention preceded the improvements of James Watt by fifty-seven years; and throughout this period, and for long afterwards, Newcomen engines were used successfully to unwater mines, and later to drive textile machinery.

The rocking-beam arrangement gave the engines their characteristic appearance, and determined too the style of the lofty buildings which housed them. Newcomen's beam itself was not novel, as it had been used by Sorocold and his predecessors for their water-driven pumps. It was retained by Watt, and indeed by the builders of the great Cornish engines of the nineteenth century, although the original wooden beams were replaced by massive iron castings.

To distinguish the early Newcomen engines from the horse- and water-driven winding, pumping and crushing 'engines' of the miners, they became known as 'fire-engines'. More properly they were 'atmospheric engines', since power was derived from the weight of the atmosphere acting upon the upper surface of a piston in a cylinder in which a partial vacuum had been created by the condensation of the steam filling it.

Although it was Newcomen who evolved a practical engine, Savery had worded his patent of 1698 so cleverly that Newcomen was compelled to take him into partnership. In the words of his patent, Savery's engine did work by the 'Impellent Force of Fire'. With such a broad claim it is fortunate for today's builders of engines of all types that the patent has lapsed.

The first Newcomen engine may have been erected in 1711 in Cornwall, but the first of which we have any record was erected in 1712, either at Willenhall, within sight of Dudley Castle, or at the Griff Colliery, near Nuneaton.

The lead miners of Derbyshire were quick to take up the new prime-mover, as it did not suffer from the waterwheel's disadvantage

Page 107: (*above*) *Cast-iron aqueduct, Derby Canal, Derby;*
(*below*) *The foot of Sheep Pasture Incline, Cromford & High Peak Railway*

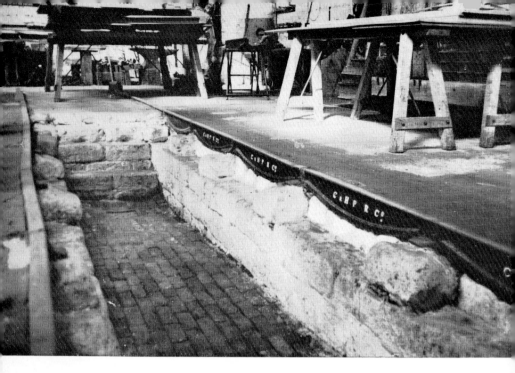

Page 108: (*above*) *Engine inspection-pit, High Peak Junction, Cromford & High Peak Railway*
(*below*) *George Stephenson's penetration of the Cromford Canal, Bull Bridge*

of being dependent upon an adequate supply of water. By the end of the eighteenth century a large number of 'fire engines' had been installed at lead and coal mines in the county. It is not surprising that engines came to be built locally, work which provided impetus for the expanding iron and engineering industries. One local man, John Barber, actually patented the gas turbine in 1791, thereby showing a prescience of the leading part which the county would come to play in the production of the sophisticated and advanced gas turbines, for the aircraft and industrial applications of today.

By 1720, and possibly as early as 1717, there was an engine at the Yatestoop lead mine, near Birchover, mentioned in a contemporary Barmaster's book which is at Chatsworth House.[9] In 1730 the Rev James Clegg, of Chapel-en-le-Frith, reported seeing near Winster (ie at Yatestoop) '3 curious Engines in which by ye force of fire heating water to vapour a prodigious weight of water was raised from a very great depth, and a vast quantity of lead ore laid dry'.

These early engines had brass cylinders, but very soon brass was replaced by the much cheaper cast iron, and Abraham Darby at Coalbrookdale became a major supplier. Darby was a Quaker, and at this time another Quaker enterprise, the London Lead Company, was actively mining lead in the Winster/Wensley area. In 1748 this company bought an engine from Coalbrookdale for use at the Mill Close Mine.

The history of early steam engines has inspired many industrial historians to enthusiastic effort. Newcomen, of course, is commemorated in the title of the Newcomen Society for the Study of the History of Engineering & Technology, founded in 1920 and the pioneer and senior body in this field. Despite the great amount of research work already done, discoveries are still being made. The present author was able to compile in 1957 a list[9] of seventy-seven early steam engines in Derbyshire, a list which has recently been augmented by Miss Nellie Kirkham.[10] There is considerable scope for further work, and to do justice even to existing knowledge a whole volume could be written.

G

By 1777 at least twenty atmospheric engines were at work in Derbyshire, thirteen of them at lead mines, the rest at coal mines. In 1777
Francis Thompson, of Ashover, erected an engine at the Norbriggs
Colliery, Staveley. In the same year he built an engine with a 70 in-
bore cylinder, for the Yatestoop Mine. For its time this was a big
cylinder, especially since it was most likely cast and machined by
Ebenezer Smith & Company, of the Griffin Foundry, New Brampton,
a firm then only two years old. The engine was of the Newcomen
type, but it probably embodied the improvements of John Smeaton.
In the 1760s Smeaton had greatly improved the efficiency of the
Newcomen engine, mainly by boring the cylinder more accurately so
as to get a better vacuum. He more than doubled the efficiency,
raising the 'duty' from 4·3 to 5·6 million ft lb of work done per bushel
(84 lb) of coal burnt, to 9·4 to 12·5 million.

James Watt's improvements of 1769 doubled and eventually
trebled even Smeaton's performance, by keeping the cylinder hot
throughout the cycle, by jacketing it and condensing the steam in a
separate vessel. None the less, engine-users in Derbyshire, where
coal was plentiful and cheap, persisted in using the Newcomen or
internal-condensing type of engine, not wishing to pay the high
royalty, one-third of the estimated saving in coal consumption, which
was demanded by Boulton & Watt. (In the third quarter of 1782 the
Gregory Mine partners paid to Boulton & Watt the sum of £67 8s 9d,
which was compounded of 1,348,750 strokes of the engine at 10s per
10,000 strokes.) (An extract from the accounts is shown opposite.)
There were, too, long delivery delays caused by the growing demand
for B & W engines. There is much poignant correspondence to indicate that two or three years might elapse from the first inquiry to the
first drawing of water at potentially rich lead mines in Derbyshire.

These factors presented an opportunity to Francis Thompson, who
achieved a fairly wide reputation as a builder of atmospheric engines
of his own (Newcomen) design, and as an erector of engines according
to the Boulton & Watt plan. In 1774 he made a drawing of the old
Mill Close engine of 1748, which had been sold to the Gregory Mine

			£	s	d
James Plant	as by	Bill		13	
George Allen	Pick Sharpener	d°.		14	8
Thomas Burton	Blacksmith	d°.	5	2	6
William Forest	Plumber	d°.		5	
Mr. Manley	Attorney	d°.	49	14	
Mess.rs Boulton & Watt		d°.	2	17	8
D°. Composition for ye Engine having made 1348750 Strokes at 10/. for every 10,000 {First Payment}			67	8	9
Sweeds Iron ... 3. 1. 24			3	14	6
Candles 5 Doz a 6/9 & 5 Doz" 6/6			3	6	3
Oil 7 Gallons at 3/. ... 2 Gal d°. 4/.			1	11	4
Linseed d°. 2 Gallons 4/. 8 Flax 10/11				18	11
Cloth 7/. Whiting 4 Soft Sope 7/4				14	8
Nails 400 & 4 500 at 6 and 900 at 8				9	10
Hemp 2/4 Files 3/6 Brushes 7 Gimblets 3				6	8
Bask 1/ Duck 2/8 Besoms 3 paper 4				3	3
Renderd Tallow 1. 2. n ... 46/6			3	9	9
Paid for a Bell				1	10
Widow Wood Meal 26 wks 2 Pks P. week a 8			1	14	8
Abram Burks for Lime 3 Load				2	3
Mr. Hodgkinson for 665 Square yards of Land for Hillock Room			8	6	3
Assistance at ye Mine and keeping Accts 13 wks a 10/.			6	10	

Carried forward £ 764 | 17 | 6

Extract from Account Book of Gregory Mine Partners, 1782

An early sales brochure: a drawing by Francis Thompson of the old
Mill Close engine of 1748

partners in 1768. This drawing, probably an early example of a sales brochure, has been preserved in the school at Ashover (see page 112). In 1782 Thompson erected an engine of $64\frac{1}{2}$ in bore at the Yatestoop Mine, about 510 ft below the surface. This and the 70 in engine were sufficiently remarkable to attract the notice of John Smeaton, whose drawings and notes are preserved by the Royal Society. The underground engine had a single haystack boiler of 20 ft diameter, possibly the biggest boiler of this type ever made, since the largest quoted by John Curr in his list of recommended sizes is 17 ft (see below).

In 1775 Boulton & Watt obtained an extension of their patent for twenty-five years. This caused bitter frustration, not least to the

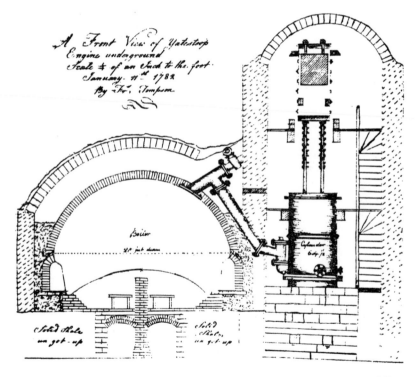

John Smeaton's sketch of Thompson's engine underground at Yatestoop Mine

Cornish engineer Richard Trevithick, who was anxious to use much higher steam pressures than the $2\frac{1}{2}$ psi or so deemed right by the cautious Watt. (As we have seen, hydraulic pressures of 56 psi and upwards were already common.) Many engineers tried to circumvent the patent, which without doubt stultified progress for at least a quarter of a century. In 1792 Thompson took out a patent (No 1884) for a double-acting engine; John Barber of Smalley, who was almost certainly known to Thompson, had taken out his patent for the gas turbine the year before (see drawing below).[11]

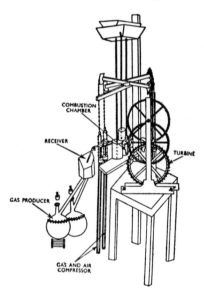

John Barber's gas turbine, 1791

Thompson continued to expand his business, building small whimseys or winding engines, and installing two-cylinder engines in cotton mills. From the extent of his activities locally, as reported by John Farey Jr,[12] it is likely that the haystack boiler which for many years stood in a hedgerow at Park Hall Farm, Denby, had been installed by him at a coal mine nearby. Happily it was made available to the

Science Museum in 1964, and the plate on page 72 shows the tricky removal operation.

The first cotton mill to have a steam engine appears to have been Arkwright's Cromford Mill, which in 1780 had a Boulton & Watt engine of 8 hp to raise water to the wheel.[13] In 1792 a Boulton & Watt engine of 16 hp was installed at the Woodeaves Cotton Mill, near Ashbourne. Francis Thompson installed engines of up to 40 in bore in 1793–4 at a worsted mill at Arnold, at a cotton mill in Macclesfield, and at four cotton mills in Manchester. Thompson's business was carried on by his son Joseph, and the last mention of engines built by this family of engineers is probably that appearing in the bill of sale of the equipment at the Morley Park Ironworks, in 1856, reproduced in part on page 116. In 1965, the effort to surmount the high brick safety wall around the engine shaft at Morley Park was rewarded by the sight of a broken-off spear and a rising main. Local tradition has it that the engine continued to pump water from this shaft until well into this century.

With one happy exception, nothing remains of the engines of this period save the ruins of the buildings. In 1791 Francis Thompson erected an engine of $57\frac{1}{2}$ in bore at Oakerthorpe Colliery. It was moved to the Pentrich Colliery in 1841, where in 1917 it came to the notice of the late W. T. Anderson, when he was installing electrical machinery there. Anderson, who had worked with Henry Royce in Manchester, and who when a service engineer maintaining arc lamps had actually used the second two-cylinder car of 10 hp built by Royce, wrote a fascinating paper on the old colliery engine.[14] To the great credit of the authorities (this was in 1917, let it be remembered), the engine was removed to the Science Museum at South Kensington, where today it occupies a proud place side by side with the engines of Watt and Trevithick. The site of the Pentrich colliery engine has disappeared, but in 1965, investigating some small indications of buildings on the $2\frac{1}{2}$ in Ordnance Survey map, the present writer came across a truly magnificent ruin of an old engine house (plate, page 72). By local tradition, and on the authority of the East Midlands Division

THE WORKS AND MACHINERY

Comprise the following Particulars, *viz.*:—

Two Cold Blast Furnaces, with one Condensing Blowing Engine (60-horse power), with four good Boilers attached; and one High-pressure Blowing Engine (46-horse power), with three new Boilers attached, together with receivers and blast pipes;—Refinery, with water boxes, pillars, blast box, two-irons and race plates complete, with blast pipes;—Air Furnace cupola, covered-in pig beds;—large and small Foundrys, with cranes and moulding boxes;—Drying Stove, with iron carriage and railway models and patterns;—Blacksmiths' Tools with bellows, anvils, vices, tongs, bores, drifts, wedges;—Boiler-makers' Tools;—Furnace for heating Plates, with powerful shears and punching machine;—Machine for bending and shaping Boiler Plates;—Valuable Collection of Tools for turning and shaping Wood and Iron, consisting of rounds, levels and squares, models and patterns, and all other tools and 3,074 yards of tramways, and moveables requisite at Blast Furnaces;—One 3-valve Pumping Engine, by *Thompson* (136-horse power), at work, with cast-iron beam and 3 boilers and 170 yards of 16-inch pump trees, and excellent powerful capstans, shear legs, pulleys and gearing;—One Winding or Drawing Engine (35-horse power), with flat and round rope drums, and pit ropes, chains and gearing with indicator and signal bells complete, with head gearing and slides to pit, together with 2,455 yards of underground Edge Railways, with 6 trolleys at work, and 1,469 yards of jig chain, iron sleepers, iron props, and all other underground tools, appertaining to a modern-worked Colliery;—One Atmospheric Winding and Pumping Engine (10-horse power), with bell crank and slide rods and plates;—Two running Lime Kilns, and one stand Lime Kiln;—Four Weighing Machines, winds, planks, poles, ropes and boxes;—One Balance Waggon;—   common stand Weighing Machines hand pumps and gins, at the Ironstone Pits; together with the planks, wheelbarrows, poles and pins at the Ironstone Open Works, saw pit, shed, cranes, turn tables stages for loading and unloading, &c;—Chills for making Castings, cast iron patterns and models, turned pipes models —One valuable Boring Rod, of large size turned and fitted complete, new flat wire pit rope 250 yards in length;—Stocks of Coal, Coke, Limestone, Ironstone, (raw and calcined) Lime Timber, Fire Bricks, Fire-stone, Sand-stone, Common Bricks, Stock of Pig and Refined Iron about 50 Tons of old anvils, hammers, broken rolls, &c.

Extract from bill of sale of Morley Park Ironworks, 1856

of the National Coal Board, it is likely that this building is the original engine house of 1791.

Most of the engine houses still to be seen at derelict lead and coal mines were built for engines of relatively high pressure, and date in the main from the mid-nineteenth century. Exceptionally picturesque are those at the Magpie Mine, Sheldon, at the Old End Mine, at

Crich, and at the Watts Shaft at Mill Close, this last now merely a solitary arch of massive proportions. The Warren Carr engine house at Mill Close housed an exceptionally large Cornish engine of 80 in bore built by Harvey of Hale, Cornwall, installed in 1875 and working until 1932. It was known as 'Jumbo'. Visible for many miles are the two chimneys of the Ladywash Mine (still being worked, now for fluorspar) and of the New Engine Mine, which stand like sentinels overlooking Eyam Edge.

Beam-engine houses, becoming increasingly rare, are a worthy subject of study in themselves. They were built of local material, and so in general limestone was used at lead mines, gritstone, and later brick, at coal mines. An exceptionally large engine house, in brick, still stands at the aptly named Seldom Seen coal mine on Moss Beck Brook near Eckington (see plate, page 53).

With the lapse of the Boulton & Watt patent in 1800, Richard Trevithick was at last able to realise his ambition to use high-pressure steam. The Cornish engine, so-called because it was first used in the tin mines of Cornwall, gradually supplanted the less powerful and less efficient low-pressure engines.

A set of four fine Cornish engines, built in the 1870s, still operates just over the Staffordshire border at Clay Mills, near Burton-on-Trent. These engines were built by the Gimson Company, of Leicester, which also built the great engines destined to form the nucleus of the Museum of Technology at Leicester. They are compound engines, low-pressure cylinder 38 in diameter by 6 ft stroke, high-pressure cylinder 22 in diameter. Steam is supplied at 80 psi by five Lancashire boilers. Two old engines which have only recently gone out of use and which may yet be preserved are that built by Butterley, at Middleton-by-Wirksworth, and the Graham engine at Whatstandwell. The former, installed in 1825 to haul trains of wagons up the Middleton incline of the Cromford & High Peak Railway, operated at 5 psi. The latter was built in 1849 at the Milton Iron Works to raise water from the Derwent to the Cromford Canal.

In 1803 Trevithick broke with tradition by building an engine with its cylinder horizontal. In 1965 three twin horizontal-cylinder winding engines ceased work after 100 years' use at collieries originally sunk by the Clay Cross Company. Two of these engines, at the Parkhouse Colliery (Clay Cross No 7 shaft) and at the Morton Colliery (Clay Cross No 5 pit) are identical, although they bear the names of two different builders, the Butterley Company and Andrew Handyside of Derby respectively. They were designed by William Howe of the Clay Cross Company, and they incorporate the Howe link motion. They provide an early example of the sub-contracting of a design of some complexity to more than one manufacturer. The engine at the Morton Pit has been excellently documented.[15] It shows also the way in which engine-men come to identify themselves with their charge: the cylinder covering carries the names of the winding teams which have served the engine, much as we see in churches a list of incumbents; a member of the Wheeler family has been included in the team from 1865 until the present day, through three generations. This engine has been removed by the NCB to Leicester, for re-erection in the Museum of Technology. The engine house at Morton Pit was interesting for its cast-iron roof trusses. A contemporary engine of like age, at the Shirland Pit, was built by Thornewill & Warham, the engine builders of Burton-on-Trent.

A tandem compound engine which although of twentieth-century vintage is worthy of preservation is that built by the Musgrave Company of Bolton in 1907 and used until 1965 at the Bamford Mill. It has a magnificent flywheel lined with mahogany, and transmitted its power by multiple ropes to line shafting on each floor. The cast ironwork supporting the pulleys and the spiral staircase is unusually elegant. The mill was closed down by Courtaulds in July 1965. The whole installation, including the millwright's shop, is exceptionally well equipped for its period and will be preserved by the new owners (see Gazetteer, Bamford).

These surviving engines are of considerable potential value in the teaching of engineering design. A necessary part of any curriculum is the study of the evolution of the art, and examples of early mechanical engineering products are all too rare. The steam engines of the eighteenth and early nineteenth centuries were built by men who had only cast iron and wrought iron as the principal materials of construction. The way in which they minimised the deficiencies of these materials are object lessons in themselves. For example, these early engines made extensive use of cottered fastenings, which derived from the wedges of timbered building construction. At the time screwed fastenings were not properly understood, nor were the materials or the manufacturing techniques available to produce such fastenings of the necessary quality and reliability for connecting rod big-end bolts, for instance. The study of the design of early cotters, their evolution through the more sophisticated screw-drawn and locked wedges, and their eventual replacement by bolts and studs, could provide an interesting exercise.

So, too, could the study of the development of steam pressures, from 'atmospheric', to James Watt's conservative 5 psi, and on to Trevithick's 100 psi, with all the problems that this presented. There is the long persistence of the vertical cylinder/beam arrangement, and its replacement by the horizontal cylinder with crosshead and crankshaft. Then, too, there are the increases in speed from the 5–13 strokes per minutes of the early engines, to rotational speeds a hundred times as high, as kinematics came to be better understood; and there are the fascinating subjects of valve and boiler design. It is greatly to be hoped that educational establishments will appreciate the opportunities and support action for the preservation of these surviving engines.

MACHINERY AND MACHINE TOOLS

That great engineer Leonardo da Vinci, writing in about the year 1480, said: 'A tool is but the extension of a man's hand, and a machine is but a complex tool. And he that invents a machine augments the power of a man, and the well-being of mankind.'

In this area of activity, as in so many other cases, the continent of Europe was at first ahead of Britain. Here, too, the ingenuity of man had been applied to the design and development of machines for far longer than is popularly supposed. Biringuccio illustrated a water-wheel-driven boring-mill for cannon in 1540,[16] and in 1703 Sorocold took out a patent for a similar machine to bore elm-tree trunks for water pipes and used this machine at the original silk mill at Derby. The lead-ore stamping mill of Burchard Cranich, erected in Duffield Frith in 1552, used the cam, and we have seen how the crank was used by Sorocold at the London Bridge waterworks in 1701 and, presumably, at all the other waterworks which he built up and down the country, after the designs illustrated by Agricola in 1556.

It was in constructing the complicated machinery for the Silk Mill at Derby in 1717, however, that Sorocold established his reputation as a mechanical engineer. The machines, 'filatoes' or spinning mills, 'tortoes' or twist mills, and winding mills, required more than 10,000 spindles, more than 25,000 spinning reel bobbins and 2,923 star wheels, 9,050 twist bobbins, and 1,870 star wheels, and 45,363 winding bobbins. As Rhys Jenkins said,

> The erection of John Lombe's Silk Mill in the years 1718 to 1722 is an outstanding event in the history of machine building . . . it involved the making and fitting of, what was for that time, an enormous number of small parts—toothed wheels, spindles and bearings . . . to ensure that all the spindles, bearings and wheels in a machine were even moderately exact in shape and size, with the skill and appliances then available, must have been a great task.[4]

Sorocold's great contribution was to construct intricate machinery, requiring the production of large numbers of more or less interchangeable parts, to install it in a single five-storey building, and to drive it from a single large waterwheel. This first factory in a modern sense provided work for 300 employees.

This was a very different type of problem from those which Sorocold had faced in the construction of waterwheels, pumps and navigations. Already well established, however, was a tradition of fine engineering in the making of clocks. The late seventeenth century was a period of intense activity in this field, Thomas Tompion, the master, being at the zenith of his powers from about 1675 onwards. Moreover, as mentioned earlier, Sorocold himself came from an area in Lancashire, around Prescott and Ashton-in-Makerfield, which was renowned for its fine smithing of clock and lock components.

According to Houghton, there were only two watchmakers in Derby in 1693. There would, however, be knitting-frame-smiths, and it is not impossible that Sorocold brought in other people from outside the town. Some of these may have come from his native Lancashire, but he would have had no difficulty in recruiting talent from other places, as his work on water supply for towns had given him many contacts throughout the country.

This light engineering was continued in Derbyshire through the clockmakers of such places as Derby and Ashbourne. In 1736 John Whitehurst set up as a clockmaker in Derby, in the old gabled building in Irongate which is now occupied by Haslams. His business prospered until 1856, and he found time to indulge in such other activities as geology, the advocacy of clean air, and of standardised weights and measures. In Ashbourne the Harlow family started up as clockmakers around 1740. Thus there was an established technology and industry on which Arkwright and Strutt could draw, as shown by their advertisement in 1771, for 'two journeyman Clock-Makers, or others that understands Tooth and Pinion well'.[13] Arkwright's own patent of 1769 was in the name of Richard Arkwright of Nottingham, clockmaker.

The clockmaking industry in Derby has been continued by John Smith Co Ltd, which builds important clocks throughout the country. This firm was founded in 1856 by an apprentice of the Whitehursts, a year after the death of John Whitehurst III, when the old firm was sold.[17] There is also the firm of John Davis & Son (Derby) Ltd, established towards the end of the eighteenth century to make surveying instruments, and now producing safety equipment for the mining industries.

Two Ashbourne firms, William Haycock and Samuel Barton & Sons, still retain the skills and some of the methods of their founders, although today they make more components for computers and meters than for clocks. The bow drill is still used occasionally, and

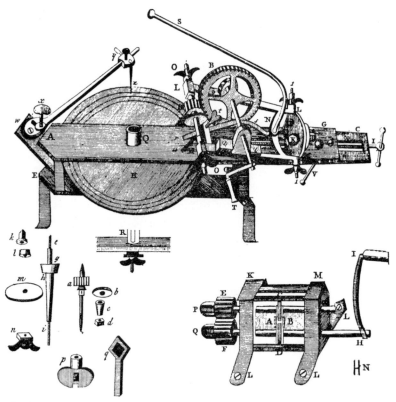

Clock-gear cutting machine. (Emerson's *The Principles of Mechanics*, 1758)

Haycocks employ a gear-cutting machine which was bought from Whitehursts (ie before 1855). This machine (plate, page 89) closely resembles that illustrated in Emerson's *Mechanics*, 1758 (see above). It differs little in basic design from the oldest gear-cutting machine known, that of Robert Hooke of 1672.[18] The cutter is advanced towards the work on an arcual path, not parallel to the axis of the wheel to be cut, the discrepancy being unimportant in gears of very small width. The fly cutter has only one cutting tooth. These cutters are still shaped by hand-filing to cycloidal form. The cutters for gears of 150–264 diametral pitch, which are typical sizes still being produced, are little thicker than a safety razor blade. Yet such is the traditional

Hand-made cutter, and gear made on a machine
of the type shown on page 89
Pitch circle dia 0·33 in (150 DP)

skill of the Ashbourne clockmakers that they are found to be correct to profile when examined subsequently by the customer at a magnification of 30 x. The figure on this page shows a projection of such a cutter and the gear it produced, prepared by Mr L. J. Stead from components made available by Bartons. It has been pointed out, however, that a high degree of accuracy of clock gears is not a strict requirement, as they are lightly loaded in only one direction.

Roughly contemporary were the marble-sawing and polishing works at Ashford and Derby, already described.

In 1760 Job and William Wyatt of Tatenhill, just over the border in Staffordshire, took out a patent for a method of cutting wood-screws on a lathe. Their business was taken over soon after 1776 by Shorthouse Wood & Co, who set up a factory at Hartshorne. The ivy-covered derelict building, known as the Screw Factory, still stands. It was operated by a wheel on Repton Brook, and it must have been one of the first establishments to be concerned with the con-tinuous mass-production of small components. By 1796 it was em-ploying fifty-nine pairs of hands, and by report turning out 1,200 gross of screws per week on thirty-six lathes worked by the one waterwheel. Stebbing Shaw, the onetime rector of Hartshorne, des-cribed the lathes as producing eight or nine screws per minute, the operations requiring the stopping and starting of each lathe eighteen times per minute. Children were employed, and they could earn from 1s 6d to 19s (sic? 1s 9d?) per week. It is difficult, however, to reconcile the rate of production with the total output, which would be expected to be about three times as great as quoted. In 1846 the works was shut down, apparently because it could not compete with the Birmingham firm of Nettlefold & Chamberlain, which had adopted new American machinery.[19]

With woodscrews there was no need for strict interchangeability, as was so desirable with bolts and nuts. It is generally assumed that (Sir) Joseph Whitworth, who came to live at Stancliffe Hall, Darley Dale, introduced interchangeability, but this is not so. He was antici-pated by Eli Whitney, with his mass-produced rifle, by the makers of cheap wooden clocks in the United States and, who knows, possibly by George Sorocold. Whitworth's great contributions were the pro-duction of a flat plane, and the evolution of a standard range of screw threads. He announced his proposed screw-thread standards at a meeting of the Institution of Civil Engineers in 1841, when he pro-

Page 125: (above) Northern portal of Clay Cross Tunnel, North Midland Railway, 1840; (below) Original station at Rowsley, by Paxton

Page 126: (*above*) *From small beginnings—Rolls-Royce Ltd, Nightingale Road, Derby, 1908*; (*below*) *Mr George Holdworth, hand-frame knitter, Longdons, Derby, 1967*

posed a range of diameters and pitches, and a thread angle of 55°. He had found this angle to be the average of a large number of screws which he had measured, but unfortunately he failed to report the details of his measurements, and so we have no record of the thread angles commonly used up to the time of his investigations.

When the old buildings (1780–1806) of Strutts at Milford were demolished in 1964 a large amount of structural ironwork was available for examination. Many nuts were tried on many bolts, and in no case was any difficulty experienced in fitting a nut to its size of bolt. A number of the bolts were taken for measurement, with the following results:

Sizes of Sample Wrought-iron Bolts from
Strutt's Old Mill (1780), Milford

Diameter	Threads per inch	Thread angle
$\frac{1}{2}''$	11	65°
$\frac{3}{4}''$	11	53°
$\frac{3}{4}''$	10	64°
1″	10	54°

Although obviously there was need for standardisation, there was nothing lacking in interchangeability within a given size. It is not known where these bolts were made, but Strutts had, at a later date, some fine machine tools for making their own textile machines, which will be mentioned later. They evidently appreciated the value of interchangeability, as already seen with the cast-iron stanchions and beams, obtained from two different sources.

It was the practically simultaneous inventions of James Watt and Richard Arkwright which created the need for more accurate machining of forgings and castings. The atmospheric engines of Newcomen type had been improved as a result of Smeaton's development of the boring mill, but Watt's engine required a steam-tight piston, and it was John Wilkinson of Bersham who in 1775 was able to bore a large cylinder at first to a tolerance equivalent to the thickness of an old shilling, and then, in the same year, to the thickness of a thin sixpence.

H

Derbyshire was not far behind, and in 1775 Ebenezer Smith, a Sheffield man, set up a company with ironworks at New Brampton, Chesterfield, and later at Duckmanton, which was to enjoy a long period of prosperity. Mr Philip Robinson of Robinson & Sons Ltd, the firm occupying the site of the Griffin Foundry, suggests that the company was established to meet the demand for steam engines.[20] Certainly by 1777 it had supplied a 70-in bore cylinder for Francis Thompson's engine at Yatestoop. The firm's name is cast on the cylinder of Thompson's Oakerthorpe/Pentrich engine in the Science Museum. From correspondence in the Boulton & Watt Collection at Birmingham it also supplied castings for Boulton & Watt engines erected in the district, probably by Thompson.

In 1779 the Griffin Foundry had produced the cannon which were fired in the streets of Chesterfield to celebrate the acquittal of Admiral Keppel at his courtmartial following the battle with the French at Ushant. The continuance of cannon manufacture is indicated by a cast-iron plaque showing a cannon and a pyramid of balls and the date 1816, which is inserted in the wall of the Cannon Mill, restored by Robinson & Sons Ltd. This manufacture of engine cylinders and cannon implies skill in accurate boring.

Little is known of the manufacture of early textile machinery. The hand-frame knitting machines had a massive timber framework, and needles were made locally from wire produced at Hathersage. The machines were constructed by framesmiths also working locally, usually in a small way of business. When they established their large spinning mills, the Arkwrights and the Strutts probably made their own machines, as we have already seen that they were recruiting clockmakers. At an early date cast iron was being used for machine frames, and the locally available expertise in ironfounding may have been a factor in the rapid advance of industry in Britain. In the United States even machine tools continued to be constructed on timber frames for many years—although this did not prevent the eventual American supremacy in this field.

Meanwhile, demand and supply interacted and in 1785 James Fox, who had been butler to the Rev Thomas Gisborne of Foxhall Lodge in Staffordshire, set up an engineering works, with the help of his master, in City Road, Derby, on the left bank of the Derwent. He had started at a good time, and soon established a successful business making lathes, and machinery for the lace and hosiery industries. In 1806 Simon Goodrich, Mechanist in the office of the Inspector General of Naval Works, reported that Baron de Bode had bought from Fox for export to Russia a 10 hp condensing steam engine for £480, with a boiler costing £96; a large boring, turning and screw-cutting lathe for £296; a machine for cutting and dividing wheels from 6 in to 9 or 10 ft diameter, for £208; and a slide lathe for cutting screws, £106. 'All, I have no doubt, very good machines, particularly the large lathe, and very cheap . . .—an excellent choice and a good bargain.'[21]

Commemorative plaque at Ebenezer Smith's
Griffin Foundry, Chesterfield

Pantalogia, 1813, mentions a very good lathe by Fox of Derby, and in 1816–17 John George Bodmer, a Swiss inventor of spinning machinery, visited Derby where Fox took great pains to provide him with information about his lathes and about a steam engine which he was building for use in a boat on the Trent at Nottingham. According to Smiles, Fox has some claim to being regarded as one of the first to build a successful planing machine, in 1814. Before 1833 he had produced what was possibly the prototype of the first effective production gear-cutting machine.[18] In 1859 he was credited with building the largest planing machine in England. He was busy, too, in the foundry industry, producing kitchen ranges, tomb railings and garden rollers.

When the Old Mill at Milford was demolished in 1964, several old machine tools were transferred to museums. From a room with structure bearing the date 1817 a small slotting machine went to the Science Museum; a fine planing machine and a lathe are preserved in the Museum of Science & Industry at Birmingham (plate, page 89). There is little doubt that these were the work of Fox. Mr K. R. Gilbert of the Science Museum ascribes the date 1817 to the slotting machine, the planing machine being possibly a little later. His recent researches indicate that in the early 1820s Fox was building large machines of advanced design. These deserve to be studied in detail. The story of machine tools is one of great breadth and diversity, and it has been brought together in a valuable account by Mr L. T. C. Rolt.[22]

The late eighteenth century saw the birth of a number of iron companies in Derbyshire, whose exploitation of their raw material led them to become engineering firms of world-wide repute. William Jessop, the brilliant civil engineer so much concerned with canals, and Benjamin Outram, whose speciality was tramroads, joined forces in 1790 with John Wright and Francis Beresford to form Benjamin Outram & Co: two years later this became the Butterley Company. Amongst its early projects were the supply of cast-iron rails and wagon wheels for the early tramroads, cast-iron troughing for the Derby Canal, steam engines, ships for dredging, and lock mechanisms for Telford's Caledonian Canal, steam engines, winding gear and cast-iron bridges for the Cromford & High Peak Railway, and steam engines for draining the Fens, as at Stretham where an engine of 1831 has been preserved. Farey noted that there were four builders of steam engines in Derbyshire—the Butterley Company, James Fox, William Mosedale of Derby, and Joseph Thompson of Ashover. Later, Mosedale had circular-saw mills.

In 1839 Joseph Glynn reported to the Institution of Civil Engineers that the Butterley Company was sawing the ends of railway rails square, in twelve seconds for the 78 lb rail. The rails were sawn while still hot, with circular saws 3 ft diameter, ⅛ in thick, revolving at 1,000 rpm, cooled by the lower edge dipping in water. The coming of the railways created an enormous demand for rails, wheels and bridges, for which the company became a major supplier. The improvements in the rolling of wrought iron introduced by Sir John Alleyne (see page 60) and the construction of the roof of St Pancras station required engineering of a high order, which was developed as a further response to the new demands.

In 1818 Weatherhead, Glover & Co established the Britannia Foundry in Duke Street, Derby. At first this firm was concerned mainly with decorative iron work. The sudden and rapidly increasing demands imposed by the railways changed all this, and in 1848 the foundry was taken over by Andrew Handyside (page 65). Besides establishing the reputation of 'Derby castings', this company built steam engines and very many bridges for roads and railways all over the world. The composite cast- and wrought-iron bridge to carry the Great Northern Railway over the Derwent at Derby was built in 1878, being first erected in the works yard, and tested by having six locomotives run on to it.[23] Other notable structures built by Handyside were Central station, Manchester (a cruder St Pancras, on a reduced scale), and that wonderful period piece of cast and wrought iron, the Albert Suspension Bridge over the Thames at Chelsea.

In 1844 (Sir) John Smith established the brass foundry which is today situated in Cotton Lane, Derby. Eastwood & Frost was also established as engineers in Cotton Lane and in the Morledge in 1852, at the same time that Frost & Swingler was making axles, cranks and wheels of wrought iron, also at Morledge. James Eastwood was soon to establish himself at the Railway Iron Works at Litchurch, as a millwright, engineer, and manufacturer of wheels for the railways; his works was on the site now occupied by the foundry of Rolls-Royce Ltd. Thomas Swingler meanwhile had moved to the Victoria Foundry, Litchurch, as an ironfounder and manufacturer of railway points and crossings. His works, too, was close by the railway, and the fine buildings, with noble cast-iron windows and iron lintels over the large doors, form today the Osmaston Road depot for the Corporation trolley buses. The works of the two firms were adjacent, and soon the firms combined into Eastwood Swingler & Co, to survive until after the first world war, mainly as railway-bridge builders and constructional engineers.

In 1840 the Midland Railway built an important engineering works opposite to the Midland Railway station at Derby. In 1873 it decided to make the building of carriages and wagons a separate activity, and this led to the erection of the large complex of buildings between Osmaston Road (opposite Eastwood Swingler & Co) and London Road, Derby[24] (see page 167). So big was this works that on its completion the Midland Railway Company occupied an area in the town as big as Derby had been before the arrival of George Stephenson. Even before this, in 1851, it had been determined that 43 per cent of the adult population of Derby had been born outside the county, so rapid had been its industrial growth.

Derby's pattern as an engineering town with a strong railway bias was thus established. Its central situation and good railway and canal communications increased the attractiveness of the town to industrialists. In 1849 John Jobson came to Derby from Sheffield and set up his iron foundry for the manufacture of stove grates in Cotton Lane, before taking over the Derwent Foundry, moving to Victory Road in 1929, and then expanding to the Sunny Hill Works. The company is best known today for its Qualcast lawn mowers, but it is in addition an important supplier of iron castings to the automobile industry. George Fletcher, who had been an apprentice of George Stephenson, moved to Derby in 1860 the works which he had established at Southwark, to construct sugar-processing machinery and steam engines. This company, still in its original premises at the Masson Works by the railway in Litchurch Lane, has an extensive overseas trade. Only recently it has been asked to supply spare parts for an engine delivered nearly a hundred years ago.

Five years later Sir Searle Haslam founded the Haslam Foundry & Engineering Company, in City Road, Derby. This company specialised in hydraulic machinery, and worked for some years to develop dry-air refrigerating machinery as used in the SS *Orient*, which in 1881 arrived in the Thames with the first consignment of frozen meat from Australia. In 1928 the electrical engineering firm of Newton Brothers Ltd, founded in 1899, took over Haslams, changing the name to Newton Brothers (Derby) Ltd in 1935.

In 1874 Francis Ley, who in his teens forsook the study of agriculture to become a draughtsman at Handysides, left the company at the age of twenty-eight to set up in business on his own as a manufacturer of malleable-iron castings. He paid frequent visits to the United States to study production methods there, and soon obtained the British rights for the manufacture of Ewart Chain Belt. This company has expanded into a major supplier to the automobile industry. It too is located by the railway in Litchurch, in what has become a traditional founding area, from the time of Eastwoods and Jobsons to Rolls-Royce.

Derby Chamber of Commerce (established 1864) set up in 1906 the Borough Development Committee which succeeded in attracting to Derby two companies which have continued to expand and which are now completely identified with the town. In 1907 came Aiton & Co Ltd, a company which had been founded in 1900 in London to make prefabricated steel pipes and, later, sea-water distillation plant. At about the same time Rolls-Royce Ltd of Manchester chose Derby as the site for future expansion (see Chapter Four).

Chesterfield too has an industrial history of note, but of later date. In 1855 the Sheepbridge Coal & Iron Company was founded near the town, by the brothers William and John Fowler. Today, its blast furnaces have gone, and the site is occupied by Sheepbridge Engineering Ltd and its subsidiary Sheepbridge Stokes Ltd. In Chesterfield itself, in 1860, Oliver & Co was formed, moving to Broad Oaks in 1870. This firm built steam engines, including one for the Magpie Mine. C. P. Markham, managing director of Staveley, bought the company for himself in 1889, and today, a part of John Brown & Co Ltd since 1937, it makes colliery winding engines, water turbines of up to 300,000 hp, and wind tunnels for research. The Bryan Donkin Co Ltd, founded in 1803 in Bermondsey, moved to Chesterfield in 1903, and its near neighbour the Chesterfield Tube Company Ltd was established in 1906. The latter produces pressure-cylinders by hot extrusion, in vast numbers and in a wide variety of sizes, from small ones for emergency oxygen kits for airliners to large ones 24 in bore by 27 ft long.

Although much of the work of these engineering firms is exported, their products are often to be seen. Since so many of them owe their existence to the development of means of communication—canals, tramroads, railways, motor-cars and aircraft—these will best be discussed in the next chapter.

CHAPTER FOUR

Communications

TRADE and industry are dependent for their survival and growth upon adequate means of communication and transport. Cut off from the sea, yet so rich in minerals, it is not surprising that Derbyshire should be well-favoured in examples of all types of communication, from pre-Roman trackways, through Roman roads, pack-horse roads, turnpikes, canals, tramroads and railways. Typical too of the initiative and enterprise which characterised pioneer efforts in each of these fields is the most recent development—the restoration and preservation of electric tramways (street-cars) by the Tramway Museum Society in the quarry at Crich.

Canals and railways hold a special fascination, as shown by the number of societies which exist for their study and protection, and by the extensive literature. Their story is so full of incident that it can only be indicated here. Remains on the ground are so plentiful that their study and survey could occupy a lifetime, and an added attraction of such a pursuit is the rare quietness and solitude of many of the routes.

Local developments in every type of communication—road, canal, tramway and railway—fully confirm Miss Phyllis Deane's comment that in Britain it was 'almost entirely native private enterprise that found both the initiative and the capital to lay down the system of communications which was essential to the British industrial revolution.'

TRACKWAYS AND ROADS

The need to transport smelted lead to the sea in Roman times may well have provided the first instance of truly industrial transport in the area. The number of Roman pigs of lead already found (see page 24) indicates the large scale of the industry, and there can be little doubt that the weight of the pig was determined by the carrying capacity of the pack pony.

It is known that many of the turnpike roads of the eighteenth century followed the earlier pack-horse roads, and the routes to the Humber may well have followed pre-Roman trackways. The main Roman roads are well authenticated, but these were for the most part made up and paved for military purposes. The network of minor roads would be unpaved, dirt roads being kinder to unshod hooves. Some indication of the early routes may be provided by the locations of pack-horse bridges, of which at least eleven remain; one, formerly at Derwent village, was removed and re-erected to the north when the village was submerged under the Derwent reservoir. These bridges, of unknown date, vary in width from 2 ft 3 in (at Upper Booth, Edale) to 4 ft 10 in at Coalpit Lane, Youlgreave. Others can be seen near Bradford, on the Youlgreave–Harthill road, at Alport, at Hollinsclough, Washgate, Bakewell, Goyts Bridge, Hayfield and Randall Carr.[1]

The trains of pack-horses were often of considerable length. The men who tended them were called 'jaggers', each of whom looked after five horses, and whose name is preserved in Jaggers Clough and in the Jaggers Lanes at Outseats and at Ashover.

During the Middle Ages and into the eighteenth century the roads, which must have been in fair condition in Saxon and Norman times, became neglected. Effective communication was possible only in dry seasons, as shown by the letter of George Sitwell of Renishaw in November 1664: 'I purpose to send your wife a chimney back as soon as our Derbyshire ways are passable.' In 1749 the main Chesterfield to Derby road was blocked by several hundred tons of colliery spoil at Clay Cross, and in 1758 the coal roads around Swanwick had become impassable as early as October. There are many reports of the hazards of travel in the seventeenth and eighteenth centuries. Thus Viator, of the *Compleat Angler* (1676), described the Derby to

Ashbourne road as 'large measures of foul way'. In 1784 Barthelemy Faujas de St Fond wrote that the turnpike road from Buxton to Manchester via Chapel-en-le-Frith was 'neither agreeable nor commodious' and that the journey took seven hours.[2] A vivid impression of overland transport in the eighteenth century, with its dangers from footpads, has been given by H. S. Twells,[3] who has dealt particularly with the carriage of goods by stage-wagon.

Attempts to improve the roads throughout the county by transferring the responsibility for them from the manor to the parish had been made as early as 1555—a date which, as a matter of passing interest, coincides with the increasing activity in lead and coal mining. But because of the inability of many of the local authorities to meet the requirements of the Highway Act, it could not be properly enforced, and not until the setting up of the turnpike trusts in the eighteenth century was the problem tackled with energy. The Trusts, composed of private individuals, were allowed to recoup the costs of road maintenance by exacting tolls at 'turnpike' gates. Derbyshire's first Turnpike Act, 1725, was for the improvement of the road from Buxton via Chapel-en-le-Frith to Manchester.

In general the turnpikes followed the earlier roads, being 'improved' merely by throwing down stones (sometimes of large size) on to the existing mud. They are often extremely hilly, since the earlier travellers had kept to the high ground, avoiding the muddy 'bottoms'. Indeed, when modern roads have been impassable during floods, the now minor routes of the old turnpikes have again come into their own. Many of them are still usable, 'those steep precipices' and 'almost perpendicular descents' reported by Edward Browne in 1662 and by Celia Fiennes in 1697 necessitating in these days a sharp change of gear.

A now discarded stretch of the Ashbourne–Buxton turnpike of 1738 turns off the present main A575 road at Sandybrook, to go by the Dog & Partridge Inn, via Spend Lane and Gag Lane, to rejoin the main road where what has been a toll house stands just south of the New Inns at Alsop-en-le-Dale. The Sheffield–Manchester turnpike of 1725, via Castleton, formerly ascended the Winnats Pass. Other notable inclines are on the Derby to Chesterfield road of 1756, via the Hazlewood Road, Duffield, at Blackbrook, Bole Hill and Cromford, the hill at Conksbury Bridge and the disused road over Sir William Hill (1757).

In 1802 the Ripley to Derby road was made to allow easier transportation of the products of the Butterley Company. Strutts built the Milford Bridge in 1795, and with Hurt and Arkwright made the valley road to Cromford available to the public in 1818.

The eighteenth century brought a spate of bridge building, Glover listing in 1829 thirty-nine bridges which had been built (or rebuilt) since 1729. This period too saw the great developments in road-building techniques. First came 'Blind Jack' Metcalfe of Knaresborough, who built roads 'in the vicinity of Buxton' in the 1770s, followed by Telford with his soundly-based construction in the early 1800s, which was superseded by McAdam's cheaper waterproof topping. However, well into this century many roads in the limestone areas remained on the Telford pattern, surfaced with small stone. Farey commented on the 'stratum of Dust almost as fine as Hairpowder, and almost as easily moved as a fluid'—a limestone powder which is today ground by machine to be used for fire prevention in coal mines. Within living memory travellers on these roads had to wear the smoked or blue-tinted spectacles which preceded today's more scientific sunglasses to reduce the glare from the white roads.

In 1709 an Act was passed making it obligatory to set up signposts on the highways. An early one, clearly incised 1705, is near Sycamore Farm on the Wirksworth–Hopton road, and that at Alport-Height is dated 1710. One, marked 'Derby Coach Road, 1739' is by the Holly Bush Inn at Makeney. There are also many interesting old stone mileposts, as at Hazlewood and above Wirksworth on the old Derby to Chesterfield turnpike. The hundreds of cast-iron mileposts erected in the early nineteenth century, made mostly by Harrisons and by Haywoods, both of Derby, have been mentioned in Chapter Two. A survey of types and patterns would be worthwhile (plate, page 36).

By 1832 the road system had so improved that Guiseppe, Count Pecchio, was writing 'England has more roads and canals than all the rest of Europe put together—and more civilization. . . . this is an unfailing effect of an infallible cause. From the want of easy communication, men remain disjoined and isolated; their minds grow cold, their spirit slumbers, they feel no emulation, they experience not the spur of the necessity for satisfying new desires, have little moral development, energy, or activity'.[4]

The turnpikes were abolished by Acts of Parliament in 1888 and 1894, but many tollhouses can still be recognised. The map of Derbyshire prepared by Burdett in 1762–7, and revised in 1797, is useful as showing the turnpiked roads and the probable location of tollhouses, the position of the mileposts, and the location of coal pits, lead mines, smelting cupolas, and watermills.

CANALS AND NAVIGATIONS

Man has always made use of rivers to transport heavy goods. Derbyshire was unfortunate in having only the Derwent below Derby, and the short stretch of the Trent along its southern boundary, capable of being made navigable.

The Derwent was obstructed by the monks of Dale Abbey when they built weirs for their corn mills at Borrowash in 1278. In consequence much of Derby's market in lead was lost to Chesterfield, which used Bawtry on the river Idle as its port for shipping to London and overseas. Charles I made an effort to open the Derwent to the Trent in 1638, when he commended to the burgesses of Derby that great engineer Sir Cornelius Vermuyden, whose work unwatering the Wirksworth lead mines has already been described. More research is needed to discover if anything was done at this time, but at the beginning of the next century repeated efforts were made to obtain the permission of Parliament to carry out the works proposed by George Sorocold in 1702. Owing to opposition, mainly from the road hauliers, this was not completed until 1721.

Meantime difficulties were experienced in keeping the Trent open as far as Burton. Shallows, rapids and drought were the difficulties. Boats were winched up the river at Redhill, and a 'flash' was used at Kings Mills, which place has an interesting history of competing factions.[5] The shoaling caused by the Dove led to Willington becoming Derby's main port, until the Trent & Mersey Canal brought about the transfer of this business to Shardlow.

Even after this canal was built shallows in stretches of the Trent still caused difficulty. Farey reported having seen a 'Gravel Plough' at work near Trent Lock, which must have been a truly noble machine 'consisting of a large iron Shovel, suspended between 4 large Wheels; which machine is drawn by 4 horses, in dry seasons, a man riding on an elevated seat behind, to drive the horses over the shallow places in the River, until 18 or 20 cwt of Gravel is collected in the Shovel, which is then drawn on to the sloping bank of the River, where its contents are shot out, by means of a Winch-handle, roll and ropes, that tilt up the hinder part of the shovel'.

The first canal in England since the days of the Romans was cut at Exeter in 1563. England lagged far behind the continent in canal building, however, and not until the last quarter of the eighteenth century, under the stimulus of vastly increased industrial production and ever-inadequate roads, did the building of inland waterways begin in earnest. The first canal of this phase was opened over most of its length at Sankey Brook, St Helens, in 1757. By this time James Brindley, who was born at Wormhill, near Buxton, in 1716, had been engaged by the Duke of Bridgewater to engineer the Bridgewater Canal, opened in 1761. Brindley was the pioneer of what became during the next forty years the canal boom, of which the climax was the 'canal mania' starting about 1793, when people sought frenziedly to buy shares in the projected canal companies. He was followed by two other local men, William Jessop and Benjamin Outram, who played a great but not yet fully recognised part in the later developments.

Although most of Derbyshire's eighteenth-century canals are now derelict, there is much to be seen of the work of the pioneers. Dealing with these chronologically, first came that stretch of Brindley's great Trent & Mersey Canal (the 'Grand Trunk') which passes through Derbyshire. It is still open, kept in order by the British Waterways Board and used increasingly by pleasure craft. Along its quieter lengths the skill of the engineers of 190 years ago can perhaps be better appreciated than anywhere else, lest it be in old lead-mine workings. The Act for this canal was passed in 1766, and it runs from Preston Brook on the Bridgewater Canal near Runcorn, to the Trent at Derwent Mouth, a distance of just over 93 miles. It was initiated by Erasmus Darwin and Josiah Wedgwood to serve the needs of the Potteries and the Midlands, James Brindley being appointed engineer. The canal was open from Derwent Mouth to near Stafford by June 1770, and completed throughout in 1777, five years after Brindley's death, when the work was taken over by his brother-in-law Hugh Henshall. It was the first canal to be made available for public use, ie to be opened to people other than its proprietors on payment of dues.

Many items of interest can be seen along its Derbyshire stretch although, in common with the other canals of the county, it did not make use of engineering devices such as lifts and inclined planes. Where it enters the county at Clay Mills it crosses the Dove at Monks Bridge by a typical Brindley aqueduct—twelve low brick arches over the river, and eleven more in the total length of the raised channel. At Stenson Lock, only 4 miles from the centre of Derby, there are features which excited the interest of Farey, a lock, a lock-keeper's cottage and a road bridge, all together. The now derelict Derby Canal joins the Trent & Mersey at Swarkestone, and at Weston Cliff is an interesting juxtaposition of the Trent & Mersey with the Trent. There used to be a transfer wharf here, busy over a century ago when one of the mills across the river at Kings Mills ground gypsum from the pits between Aston and Chellaston. The stone was taken by tramroad to the canal, through Aston and Weston Locks, to Weston Cliff, then down river to the mills for grinding, and back again by the same route, finally using the Derby Canal to the plaster works of Pegg & Co, at Morledge in Derby.

Shardlow, near the old Wilden Ferry across the Trent, became an inland port of great importance. It has retained much of its original appearance, with wharves, warehouses, docks and inns of contemporary date, but busy now as a marina (plate, page 90). A ropewalk can still be recognised, where the boatmen left their short canal ropes in exchange for long river ropes as they travelled towards the Trent. The scenes of confusion, with goods arriving from all over the country, can well be imagined. Clerking of a high order must have been necessary, and it is not really surprising that a large steam-engine cylinder, despatched by Boulton & Watt for the attention of Francis Thompson, should go astray and turn up in North Wales instead of Ashover. Iron mileposts along the canal, indicating the distances from Shardlow to Preston Brook, are in good condition still.

Throughout its Derbyshire length and just beyond to Horninglow, the canal was capable of taking boats of 40 tons burden, 13 ft 6 in beam. The principal trade was in the export of coal, limestone, freestone, gypsum, bar iron, lead, pottery, ale, cheese, etc, and in the import of deal and pig iron from Scandinavia, flint, chert, malt and barley.

Brindley's next venture in the county was the Chesterfield Canal. Mr Charles Hadfield, in his detailed account of the canals of the Midlands,[6] believes that this was promoted by the London Lead Company, which had lead to export from Kelstedge, by the Cavendishes, who owned the ironworks at Staveley, and by other landowners wishing to exploit their coal resources. The canal was surveyed and planned by Brindley in 1769, to run from Chesterfield via Worksop and Retford to the Trent at Stockwith. It was completed in 1777, so that it was being driven contemporaneously with the Trent & Mersey. On Brindley's death in 1772 the work was taken

Page 143 : (*above*) *The Old Silk Mill, Derby*; (*below*) *Calver Mill, 1804*

To SAM.ᵗ OLDKNOW ESQ.ᴿ THE PROPRIETOR.
This West View of MELLOR MILL in Derbyshire

Page 144: (*above*) *Samuel Oldknow's Mill, Mellor, 1790*
(*below*) *Long Row, Belper, a fine example of Strutt's Housing*;

over by John Varley, with the help of Hugh Henshall, who later succeeded Varley. The work of both Varley and Henshall deserves further study. Today the canal is in a sorry state. The Norbriggs Tunnel, originally 2,850 yd long, just outside the county boundary, collapsed and was closed in 1908, which ended the usefulness of the Derbyshire stretch. There are now only the remains of locks, bridges (eg at Killamarsh), embankments and the aqueducts over the Doe Lea stream.

Brindley is rightly looked upon as the father of canals in Britain, and the site of his birthplace has been marked by a bronze plaque on a stone plinth, bearing the inscription:

James Brindley
1716–1772
Millwright and Civil Engineer

Here stood the cottage in which James Brindley was born.
Of humble birth, he became famous as the pioneer builder of the great canals of England.
This plaque was erected by the Local History Section of the Derbyshire Archaeological Society and unveiled by J. L. Longland Esq., M.A., on November 1, 1958, when Miss Y. H. B. Hartford planted the adjacent ash tree.

The next canal to be made was the Erewash from the Trent at Sawley to Langley Mill. This was proposed by colliery owners in Nottinghamshire and Derbyshire, to link up with the Loughborough Navigation along the Soar. The Act was passed in 1777, the engineer being John Varley, and the $11\frac{3}{4}$ mile length was opened in July 1779. The canal can still be navigated, though with difficulty; despite its proximity to towns and collieries it has some beautiful quiet stretches. Where it crosses the Erewash at Shipley Gate an interesting small arched aqueduct clearly shows the influence of Brindley. At Trent Lock something can still be recaptured of the original atmosphere of the eighteenth century.

Brindley's successors were Telford, Rennie, Outram and Jessop. The first two were famous. The names of Benjamin Outram and William Jessop are far less known, save by local people and canal

I

enthusiasts. Yet it is undoubtedly to Jessop that the credit for the greatest achievements should be given, while his partner Outram played a great part in the early development of engineering in Derbyshire, and especially of tramways as feeders to canals. Both men had Derbyshire connections, and Outram and Francis Beresford, by buying the Butterley Estate from the ironmaster Horne, laid the foundations of the great Butterley Company, in which Jessop and John Wright were founder partners. Outram was born in Alfreton in 1764, son of James Outram, surveyor, engineer and ironmaster (1732–1810), and Elizabeth his second wife, who was a daughter of Edmund Hodgkinson of Overton Hall. One of Benjamin's sons became General Sir James Outram, of Indian Mutiny fame. In the Butterley Company, it appears that Jessop was, most of the time, the civil engineer, the surveyor and builder of canals; Outram was the mechanical engineer and the builder of early railways. This formed an admirable partnership. When the Caledonian Canal was being driven by Telford, from 1802 to 1822, Jessop visited it frequently to give advice, and the Butterley Company provided the locks and structural ironwork, the temporary tramways used on the eastern half of the canal, and two steam dredgers designed by Jessop. Outram will be noticed again when considering the use of tramways as extensions of the canal system.

Jessop was born at Davenport in 1745. His father Josias, who is thought to have been of Derbyshire stock, worked for Smeaton, and on his death when William was sixteen years old, he left his family in Smeaton's care. Jessop became Smeaton's pupil, and later his assistant on the Aire & Calder Canal, working for him until about 1771. His great ability is now being recognised despite the screen of his innate modesty. Mr L. T. C. Rolt has been the first to draw attention to this,[7] but a detailed biography remains to be written. From scattered sources it is obvious that Jessop had stupendous energy and ability. In 1772 he became principal engineer to the Grand Canal in Ireland and from 1782 until about 1805 he was employed as surveyor or as chief engineer on at least twenty-five navigational and canal projects. These were as far scattered as the Surrey Iron Railway, the Thames navigation from Dorchester to Lechlade, the West India Dock, the Sussex Ouse, and the Caledonian Canal. In addition he had considerable influence upon the thinking of Telford, who held him in high regard and who consulted him on many of his projects, for example the Ellesmere, Shrewsbury and Caledonian Canals. Telford, however, owing to habitual forgetfulness, failed to give credit to Jessop at the time, and contemporary and much-repeated sources, such as the writings of Farey in his Derbyshire survey and in his section on canals in Rees' *Cyclopaedia*, are misleading.

Jessop's first venture in Derbyshire was the Cromford Canal. It had been proposed in order to extend the Erewash Canal towards Pinxton, but nothing came of this, and in 1788 Sir Richard Arkwright, who was anxious to develop the area around his mills, took more forceful action, along with the Gells and Beresfords, Benjamin Outram, the Jessops and the Hodgkinsons, who were Outram's in-laws. These men represented interests in iron, coal, limestone, lead and cotton, and when William Jessop submitted his plan and an estimate of £42,697 in December 1788, half of this sum was raised immediately, and the rest within two weeks.[6]

The Cromford Canal is derelict, cut by the collapsed Butterley Tunnel and the new East Midlands Gas Board plant blocks the north entrance to the tunnel at Bull Bridge. The Pinxton branch, via Pye Bridge, made as a broad canal, is in the same condition. Nevertheless the Cromford is still an exciting canal to survey. Its close juxtaposition with railway, road and river in the narrow Derwent valley affords interesting views, which are augmented by the warehouses and wharves at Cromford, the pumping station at Whatstandwell (see page 117), and the aqueducts. At the time of its building, according to Hadfield, Jessop was not fortunate in his construction of aqueducts. That at Bull Bridge gave trouble early in 1792, and later in the same year the noble bridge of 80 ft span over the Derwent at Wigwell failed. Jessop accepted the blame, attributing it

to the use of Crich limestone (see page 82); he re-made it so good
that it is still sound. Farey, evidently depending upon hearsay, is not
quite accurate about this incident.

The long aqueduct at Bull Bridge, crossing roads, river and railway, is extremely interesting, with its old lime kilns and wharves, the
horse swing bridge (plate, page 90) and the iron trough inserted by
George Stephenson when he drove his railway underneath the canal
(plate, page 108). Here history repeats itself. At the time of Stephenson's achievement, in 1839–40, the use of this iron trough was looked
upon as something extraordinary. Yet in 1794–5 Jessop's partner
Outram had used an iron trough, probably for the first time ever, at
Derby. At about the same time Jessop had recommended the use of
iron troughs to Telford for his aqueducts at Longdon-on-Tern on
the Shrewsbury Canal, and at Pontcysyllte on the Ellesmere Canal.
The trough at Derby had almost certainly been made by the Butterley
Company, as was that for Stephenson. What is more likely than that
someone remembered what had been done forty-five years before?
The Bull Bridge aqueduct is soon to disappear to permit road
widening.

The tunnel at Bull Bridge, 93 yd long, can still be traversed, but
the much more important one at Butterley, originally 2,966 yd, is
closed, since it subsided when coal was mined beneath. The reservoir
in Golden Valley still exists and provides recreation for fishermen.
Possibly it was the rich deposits of iron and coal found here which
inspired the formation of the Butterley Company.

Following the Cromford Canal, in date order, came the Nottingham Canal, which linked Nottingham with the Cromford Canal.
Jessop was the engineer-in-charge, the Act was passed in 1792 and
the canal was finished in 1796. As it runs from Nottingham along the
eastern side of the Erewash up to the junction with the Cromford
Canal at Langley Mill, it is wholly outside Derbyshire.

On 7 May 1793, an Act was passed approving Outram's survey for
the Derby Canal, to connect the town with the Trent & Mersey Canal
at Swarkestone, and with the Erewash Canal at Sandiacre. Outram

was appointed engineer, and at Jessop's suggestion the northward spur was continued to Little Eaton, whence a tramway (the 'Gang road') went on to Denby (page 153). The Gang road was opened in 1795, the canal throughout its length in 1796 (not in 1794 as Farey wrongly reported and Lyson and Priestley later repeated). The Derby Canal is now utterly neglected and derelict, but it still retains features of interest. It crossed the Derwent just above the lowest of the great Derby weirs, which was repaired and raised. A narrow wooden bridge, the Long Bridge, crossed the river here, for men and horses, and this stood until 1959. Where the canal crossed over Sorocold's 'cut', which formed the island of the Holmes, it was carried in an aqueduct (1795), a trough made up of cast-iron sections, bolted together (plate, page 107). There are five sections 6 ft deep, 8 ft along the upper edge, 9 ft along the lower, to produce a scarfed effect, with flanges 3 in deep and an average thickness overall of 2 in (see page 148).

In the heyday of the canal, Derby was an important inland port, bigger in extent even than Shardlow. There were four large basins and a number of bays, with extensive coal wharves both at the Morledge and Nottingham Road branches of the canal. Few traces remain, save for an interesting warehouse dated 1820. The spur to Little Eaton was filled in some years ago, and the terminal basin is now occupied by a garage, although the Clock House still stands. A small stone building, by tradition a warehouse for whetstones from the local quarries, was demolished in 1965 to make car-parking space for the local inn.

Contemporary with this venture was the Nutbrook Canal, only $4\frac{1}{2}$ miles long, to connect the collieries of Edward Miller Mundy and Sir Henry Hunloke at Shipley and West Hallam with the Erewash Canal at Trowell. Although the canal has mostly disappeared, the large reservoirs at Shipley and Mapperley still exist, the latter becoming widely known in 1930 for the $26\frac{1}{2}$ lb carp caught there, which for some years held the British record.

In 1794 the first Act was passed enabling the construction of the

Peak Forest Canal. It was intended to join the Manchester, Ashton & Oldham Canal with Chapel Milton and Whaley Bridge. Samuel Oldknow was one of the moving spirits behind this project, his interest in agriculture and his appreciation of the value of lime probably being motivating factors. Benjamin Outram was the engineer, and the canal was finished in 1800. Some of its most impressive features lie just outside the county, at Mellor and Marple—the 90 ft high aqueduct over the river Goyt and the stair of locks. The Bugsworth terminus was once an important place for the collecting and burning of limestone, and the quarrying of building stone from Crist Quarry, for the growing towns of Lancashire. Today the large complex of canal basins and wharves, lime kilns and quarries is silent and decayed.

Indicative of Outram's predilection for railways is the extension to Chapel Milton and Townsend, by an inclined plane 600 yd long, with a slope of 1 in 9. This, now surfaced, is used by Ferodo & Co Ltd as a testing track for brake materials. The Whaley Bridge branch, which still contains water, led to the point of transfer with the Cromford & High Peak Railway of the 1830s. A large basin and a covered dock still stand. The latter has an imposing cast-iron lintel beam of 20 ft span, and date 1832.

The last and smallest canal in the county is not, strictly speaking, a canal at all. It was built as a dam for the Woodeaves Mill, by the Bentley Brook, near Tissington, in 1802, the narrow valley determining its form. It was 1¼ miles long, and was used by small boats to bring limestone downstream from its upper end.

Ancillary to the canals are the sources of water for locking. Particularly picturesque, and now used for sailing, is the Combs Reservoir of the Peak Forest Canal and its Todd Brook reservoir in Whaley Bridge. Another one, outside the county, is Rudyard Lake, while others have already been mentioned.

Despite the voluminous literature on the canals of Britain, much work remains to be done. More needs to be known about the difficulties of surveying, and about the marshalling and deploying of large bodies of men—the 'navigators', whose work is better known in connection with railway constructions.

The interest of walking along old canal towpaths can be increased by taking note of the width of the canal, of bays and passing places; of the type of locks, lock gates and lock-keepers' cottages, and of the paddle machinery and sluice controls; the style of the accommodation bridges, which sometimes varies on different stretches of the same canal; the iron lamp brackets still remaining on some bridges, eg on the Trent & Mersey and the Cromford. Roving bridges, enabling the horses to pass from one side of the canal to the other, horse tunnels as at Marple and horse bridges such as the swinging one at Bull Bridge, and the modern replacement in concrete over the Trent at Derwent Mouth, are worth noting. Mileposts, wharves and warehouses, cranes, docks and boat-building yards may be found; there is still the occasional tavern, often with employees' cottages nearby; and the number of references in Farey suggests that there should be traces of lime kilns at many of the wharves, from which can sometimes be traced the track of an old tramroad.

An additional cost imposed upon the canal builders was the fencing off of their property from the local farms. In Derbyshire stone walls were often used, but there are many miles of quickthorn hedges, used again when the railways came; a main source of these was Melbourne, from whence men travelled long distances to plant the trees.

TRAMROADS

The German mining engineers who came to England in the sixteenth century already had a knowledge of the use of rails for underground transport stretching back for at least a century. Roughly fifty more years were to elapse before there was any recorded use of rails in England, to increase the efficiency of coal transportation. This has been established by Mr Richard S. Smith[8] as the work of Huntingdon Beaumont, who in 1604 laid rails from coal pits at Strelley to the usual collecting point for the road hauliers at the end of Wollaton Lane, 2 miles outside Derbyshire's eastern boundary.

Beaumont went to the Newcastle area in 1605 to try to exploit ideas for increasing the efficiency of coal mining which he appears to have gained from Agricolas' *De Re Metallica* of 1556, but such was the conservatism of the coal-masters in that area that he returned to Wollaton practically penniless. Nevertheless, the use of rails extended, and in 1734 Desaguliers illustrated a wagon with flanged wheels and edge rails used to carry limestone at Prior Park, near Bath. In 1756 Smeaton was using flanged (ie 'plate') rails and a turntable to move stone from the works to the quayside at Mill Bay, Plymouth, for shipping to the Eddystone Lighthouse. His chief assistant was Josias Jessop, and his pupil a few years later was Josias's son William Jessop. It is not surprising therefore that railways came to be used extensively in Derbyshire, although it was Benjamin Outram, Jessop's partner, who were their chief exponent.

Much inaccurate information has been disseminated about these early railways. The story has been repeated that it was Outram who invented the flanged wheel, and that the railways were called 'tram'-ways in recognition of his work. In fact, the earliest railways had rails of squared timber. Agricola shows a wagon being kept on the rails by an iron pin running in a groove between them. Flanged wooden wheels were in use in Germany in the sixteenth century and Mr C. E. Lee[9] quotes Dr Edward Browne as describing flanged wheels which he had seen in Germany in 1669. The illustration by Desaguliers is also of flanged wheels.

Smeaton's flanged rails had the advantage of allowing the wagons to pass from railway to road, and with wheel tyres wide enough to be acceptable to the turnpike trustees. They had the drawback, however, of requiring deep, wide channels where they crossed the roads, a disadvantage combated by indenting the edges of the channels so that ordinary road vehicles would not skid into them and be compelled to travel to the terminus.

Information is still incomplete and contradictory about the first use of iron for rails, about the use of wood and of stone for sleepers, and about flanged rails, and flanged wheels, wooden wheels, and iron wheels. According to Farey, the first use of flanged rails above ground was by Joseph Butler, to take coke to his iron furnaces at Wingerworth, in 1788. Although this claim cannot be substantiated, the probable route followed by the railway can be traced; while the line of the Lings–Ankerbold railway, also built by Butler, can be more easily followed along the route of the 'zig-zag' railway, described by Mr S. L. Garlic.[10] Along this route stone sleepers can still be found, sometimes incorporated in old buildings of now disused coal mines.

With the coming of the canals, it was quickly realised that railway spurs and extensions provided a cheap means of increasing their scope. Many of the canal Acts included proposals for railways, sometimes without restriction. Others contained clauses permitting local mine owners to run their own railways to the nearest canal wharves; as the coal mines were widely spread, there were many of these tramroads in Derbyshire. They have been thoroughly documented by the late Bertram Baxter,[11] who has listed fifty of them, all but five being connected with the canals of the county. Their total length was 77 miles and the tracks of many of them can still be traced, usually as grassgrown ways between parallel walls or hedges, with occasionally a bridge, under or over, or a short tunnel, to indicate their former purpose.

At Jessop's suggestion, the northward spur of Outram's Derby Canal was terminated at Little Eaton, and continued on to Smithy Houses, Denby, by railway. Its track can be followed from the now filled-in terminal basin along a footpath, 'The Gang road'. A small tunnel still exists in Jack o'Darley's bridge over the steam railway to Ripley, and at least six branches ran from the main line to stone quarries and coal mines. Stone sleepers and cast-iron rails are still found occasionally. This railway, probably Outram's first, had flanged rails and plain wheels. A typical stone sleeper is roughly triangular in plan form, 27 in × 17 in and 12 in thick, and a weight of 150 lb was stipulated.[12] Two holes of $2\frac{1}{2}$ in diameter were drilled to take oaken plugs, and the rails were affixed with iron spikes very probably made by the nailers of Belper. Somewhat surprisingly, since Outram's foundries would then be operating, the first of these cast-iron rails were bought from Joseph Butler, in 1793 and in 1794, at £10 10s per ton.[13] The railway was in operation from 1795 until 1908, when fortunately many photographs were taken of the last run, and it was described in detail by a local historian, Mark Fryar. Two of the original wagons have been preserved. The box, bound with iron, could be lifted from the bogie to be loaded into the barge at Little Eaton.

Another railway, the Crich (or Fritchley), can be traced from the Cromford Canal wharf at Bull Bridge to Hilts Quarry at Crich. Jessop was concerned with this canal, so that Outram may have built the railway. Edward Banks had a battery of lime kilns at Bull Bridge, and Farey described in detail how a tippling device emptied stone from two wagons directly into iron barges, and from four others on to the ground. The site is now in a ruinous state, but the barge bay and the site of the tipples could be identified in 1967. A cast-iron bridge can be seen near Lime Grange, and what has been a large blacksmith's shop. There are tunnels, a long stone-walled embankment, cuttings, and many stone sleepers. At the Old Factory is a wagon-repair shop.

On this Crich railway Brunton's Walking Locomotive was run for several years. This extraordinary machine, patent number 3700, 1813, which propelled itself by a pair of 'ski-sticks', was built at the Butterley works at Ripley in 1813. Its inventor said that it performed very well, at 2½ mph. Another engine was built for the Newcastle Colliery Railway in Durham, but the explosion of its boiler in 1815, killing eleven people, brought this project to an end.[14]

Farey described the wagons of this line as having wheels of cast iron, with round holes instead of spokes. This was to enable the wheels to be locked by passing a pole through them, when the wagons were being slid down 'hurries' at the quarry. The poles were moved occasionally so that excessive flats would not be worn on the wheels.

Wheels of this kind were used much later on the wagons of George Stephenson's railway from Crich Cliff Quarry to his great battery of lime kilns at Ambergate. The line, which was in use from 1842 until 1957, had an impressive gravity-incline, a slope of 1 in 7 and a large cable drum. A number of wagons still exist, which may be preserved.

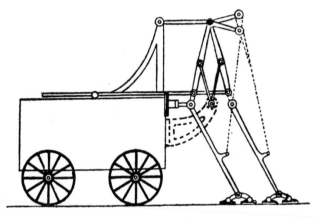

Brunton's Walking Locomotive, 1813

Another interesting tramroad was projected in 1794 and completed in 1802 to carry limestone from Ticknall to the Ashby-de-le-Zouch Canal at Willesley Basin, 12½ miles. Many stone sleepers are buried in the ground, and there is a tunnel of such small cross-section that it seems surprising that men and ponies could traverse it. The handsome single-arched bridge over the road from Derby and Melbourne to Ticknall has long been a landmark for motorists and a hazard for double-decker buses. Outram was the surveyor, but drainage problems caused trouble and a lawsuit arose.

At the end of a spur of the Peak Forest Canal at Bugsworth was an extensive complex of horse-drawn railways to bring limestone and gritstone to the canal basins, and to carry limestone to the kilns. Here was a tipple, mentioned by Farey, which survived long enough to be photographed. Mr Brian Lamb has already succeeded in mapping many of these railways, and recording details of them. Surprisingly, more than one gauge was in use at this site.

Of later date than the horse-drawn tramroads was the Cromford & High Peak Railway. There had been proposals for a canal to join the Cromford and the Peak Forest Canals. Fortunately for the promoters, the much more practicable alternative scheme for the railway, first put forward in 1814, received parliamentary consent in 1825. The engineer was Josias Jessop, son of William, named after his grandfather. By any standards the line was a remarkable achievement, which still commands the affection and respect of railway enthusiasts. Starting at Cromford, at canal level, it rose 990 ft by a series of inclines, to a summit altitude of 1,264 ft. It then fell 747 ft to its junction with the Peak Forest Canal at Whaley Bridge.

As confidence in the capabilities of locomotives was still slender, horses were used on the levels until 1833-4, when locomotives began to be introduced, completely by 1841. The inclines, with gradients as steep as 1 in 7, were negotiated by steam winding engines, with the exception of the final slope at Whaley Bridge, where a horse chain-gin was used. One winding engine has survived, at the Middleton Incline: it was built by the Butterley Company in 1825, and remained in use until June 1963. This entire site may be preserved by British Rail. Near the foot of the Sheep Pasture Incline (plate, page 107) is a catch pit, installed after runaway trucks had been shot right over the main (A6) road and the canal beyond, to land where the filter beds now are. Passengers were carried from 1833 to 1877.

In the workshops at the foot of the incline at High Peak Junction is a shop where locomotives were overhauled, and where some of them were assembled, certainly in 1859, and possibly earlier. The rails here are the original fish-bellied castings. All bear the letters C & HPR and some, in addition, S.W.C., probably for Samuel Wharton, iron founder of Tapton, Chesterfield. Of the shop's former bank of smiths' forges only one remains, with an elegant horn handle on the bellows lever, and a fairly complete set of smith's tools. In an outhouse is a hand-driven overhead drill, capable of drilling $1\frac{1}{2}$ in diameter in steel. High Peak Junction has a simple rotating plate signal, and a signal system for communication between the winder at the top of the incline and the despatcher at the foot.

Although the line is now closed, to walk its whole length (with permission) is a worthwhile pilgrimage, bringing appreciation of the work of the railway pioneers—steep inclines, sharp small-radius curves, tunnels, and deep cuttings through hard cherty limestone, as at Hopton, wharves, as at Parsley Hay, and striking bridges. The portals of Newhaven Tunnel, under the Ashbourne–Buxton road, carry two elegant medallions, bearing the names of Josias Jessop and of W. Brittlebank Esq, Clerk to the Railway Company, of Wirksworth. The masonry of this tunnel is remarkable for its quality and durability, the white limestone blocks being as clean-cut and well-fitting as when they were made: the masons' marks can be seen as clearly incised as if they had been applied yesterday. The railway has been described by Mr A. Rimmer.[15]

RAILWAYS

Since the early days of Watt men had conceived the idea of using steam power for locomotion over the ground. It was not until Watt's patent lapsed, however, and Trevithick was able to apply higher steam pressures, that steam locomotion became feasible. Stephenson's breakthrough, with the Stockton & Darlington Railway in 1825 and the Liverpool & Manchester Railway in 1830, marks the beginning of the great industrial expansion of the nineteenth century. Derbyshire benefited particularly, owing to demands for large quantities of ironwork for rails, locomotives, rolling stock, bridges and machinery; for coke (obligatory for the next thirty years as smokeless fuel for locomotives); and for bricks for stations and tunnels.

Full-scale passenger-carrying railways did not come to Derbyshire until 1839, by which time experience had been gained in other parts of the country. At the same time, the spirit of competition and emulation was keen, while the topography of the county offered especial challenges; these attracted the master, George Stephenson, and a consequence is that the works of the earlier Derbyshire railways are on a scale and of a style which have remained largely unaltered. There are many relics which merit preservation, and there is, too, scope for research into the influence of these railway works upon local industry. At Chesterfield Public Library is a collection of Stephensoniana, recalling the long period in which Stephenson lived in Derbyshire; a railway exhibition was held in Chesterfield in 1948, on the centenary of his death.

Public interest in railway-building ventures was extreme at the time, and the flow of literature abundant; indeed, Professor Jack Simmons gives a whole chapter of his delightful 'introduction' to railway history to available literature and maps.[16] The columns of the *Derby Mercury* show the great contemporary excitement about the progress of local railway ventures, whose pace would put today's motorway works to shame. The building of the North Midland Railway is an example. George Stephenson and his 'ardent and indefatigable pupil Frederick Swanwick', the resident engineer, made a preliminary survey of the Derby–Leeds route (72¾ miles) on 5 and 6 August 1835. Swanwick, aged twenty-five, surveyed the route in detail, mostly on foot, made drawings, and detailed estimates, attended committees in London, and helped prepare the proposals for submission to Parliament for the Act which was passed in 1836; the first ground was broken in February 1837. But during 1835 he had done work on 119 miles of other projected railways and in 1836–7 worked on the Whitby & Pickering Railway, besides surveying the 22 miles of the Doncaster, Midland & Goole Railway.[17] Meanwhile, George Stephenson was working not only on the North Midland, but also on the Birmingham & Derby Junction and other railways.

Actual construction of the North Midland took place between 1837 and 1840. Right through the winter months continuous day and night work proceeded, and the inhabitants of Belper were grieved that work did not stop on Sundays. Mr Terry Coleman has corrected many misconceptions of the way in which the railway navvies worked.[18] When their contracts were ended for work on the Derby–Belper stretch of line, 1,509 of them sat down to dinner in a field by Duffield station on 10 June 1840; cooked victuals were brought by train from Derby. The size of this gathering may help to solve the puzzle of Stephenson's Sighting Tower, on the top of Chevin Hill (plate, page 53). It does not command a view of a sufficient length of line to justify such a substantial structure, and one wonders if it could have been built to keep the men busy during a slack time, or to help in the surveillance of a regiment of workers.

The Midland Railway has had, from its formation by amalgamations in 1844 to the present time, a great influence upon the pattern and growth of the county's industry. For five years, until George Hudson effected their amalgamation, three independent and competing railway companies existed, the Midland Counties, the Birmingham & Derby Junction and the North Midland. The Midland Counties Railway was conceived at the Sun Inn, Eastwood, on 16 August 1832, to enable the local coal owners to meet the threat of Robert Stephenson's newly opened Leicester to Swannington Railway, which had been built to compete with the Erewash Canal coal trade up the Soar to Leicester. The Midland Counties was intended to link Leicester, Nottingham and Derby, with an extension up the Erewash to Pinxton. It would provide access to London by joining the Birmingham to London line near Rugby. Its engineer was C. B. Vignoles, a past President of the Institution of Civil Engineers. The first sod on the Derby–Nottingham stretch was cut in May 1837 and the first train entered Derby on 30 May 1839, the line being opened to the public on 4 June 1839.

The Midland Counties and the Birmingham & Derby Junction Railway competed keenly for the traffic to London. George Stephenson surveyed the route of the latter from Hampton to Derby, and his son Robert pressed on with the work with all speed. The first train entered Derby on 5 August 1839, and the line was opened to public passengers one week later.

Meanwhile the North Midland was being built to join Derby and Leeds. The line from Derby to Masborough, the junction for a spur to Sheffield, was opened on 11 May 1840 and throughout to Leeds on 1 July 1840. The North Midland had undertaken to build a joint station for the three companies at Derby. Francis Thompson was the architect for what was and can still be recognised as a very fine station indeed. The handling of hundreds of passengers from a single train posed problems which had not been met before. It was felt that they should be required to walk the minimum distance to and from the train, and one platform, 1,050 ft long, with a bay for each company, was constructed, with waiting rooms and offices having a fine frontage, some of which is still visible, and a glass-covered 'market place' for locomotives.[19] Unfortunately, the keen competition between the three lines led to their obstructing each others' trains, and the idea of a single platform was not developed. The glazed roof inside the station was damaged by bombing in world war II and was replaced by the present structure.

Despite his failings, Hudson inculcated a spirit in the Midland Railway which for a long time kept it aggressively ahead of others. Pride in the Derby station is shown by the fact that, within living memory, engine-drivers made it a point of honour not to blow off steam inside it.

The whole area around Derby Midland station provides excellent material for sociological study. The elegant headquarters offices, neighbouring warehouses, the houses in Railway Terrace—formerly occupied by the élite engine drivers—and the old Midland gas lamps give an excellent impression of the times. The solid Midland Hotel (1841), although originally a private venture was in keeping with the rest of the area; it was purchased by the Midland in November 1860. Across the tracks are the extensive locomotive works. Not visible from the passenger platforms is the round house, described in 1840 as having sixteen sides, 134 ft across, with a conical roof, the lantern of which was 54 ft above the floor from the top of 18 ft columns. It was approached by two wings 48 ft long. There were shops 160 ft × 70 ft, three storeys high, for the repair of engines and carriages. These workshops took *only nine months* to build, and some are still in use.

The next twenty years saw the Pennines crossed from Ambergate to Buxton and Manchester, and from Sheffield to Manchester via Woodhead and Glossop. In addition, a dense network of lines was established in the eastern coalfield (see map page 162). The ambitiously-named Manchester, Buxton, Matlock & Midland Junction Railway reached Rowsley from Ambergate on 4 June 1849. The Midland Railway had rights on this line, but in 1852 the London & North Western secured a joint lease with the Midland, for nineteen years. The Midland opened the line from Rowsley to Buxton in 1863, reaching Manchester in 1867. Worried lest it should lose the right to use the Ambergate to Rowsley stretch, a line was opened from Duffield to Wirksworth in 1867, with the intention, should need arise, of penetrating the hills northward to Rowsley.

Only a few of the main features of local railway engineering can be mentioned. Vignoles's Midland Counties line has little of note in the area save the bridges over the Derwent at Derby and over the Trent at Red Hill, both much altered, and the Red Hill Tunnel. The Birmingham & Derby Junction had an easy level route, in marked contrast with that of the North Midland. Where the latter passed over the Nottingham Road in Derby the road was lowered to provide headroom; the dip so formed still floods after heavy rain.

Stephenson planned the NMR to pass through Milford on the left bank of the Derwent, but the Strutts objected, fearing that the water supply to power their mills would be disturbed, and the present route through Chevin Tunnel was adopted, the tunnel being started in 1838. The narrow Derwent valley posed other problems, and it was necessary to make the 1 mile long deep cutting, with its eleven bridges, right through the town of Belper. This fine cutting, lined

K

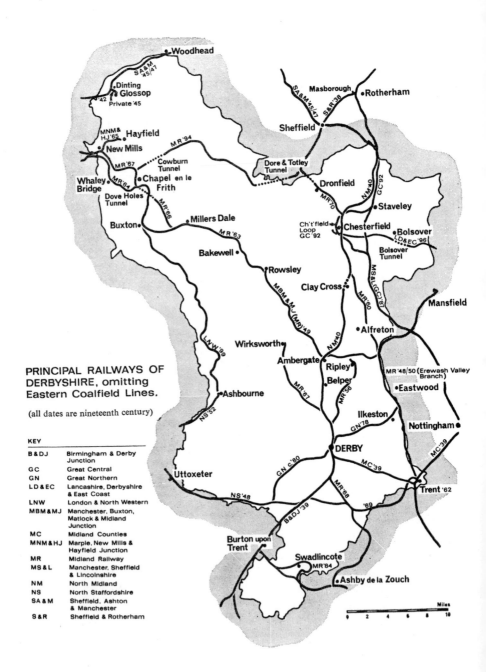

PRINCIPAL RAILWAYS OF
DERBYSHIRE, omitting
Eastern Coalfield Lines.

(all dates are nineteenth century)

KEY

B & DJ	Birmingham & Derby Junction
GC	Great Central
GN	Great Northern
LD & EC	Lancashire, Derbyshire & East Coast
LNW	London & North Western
MBM & MJ	Manchester, Buxton, Matlock & Midland Junction
MC	Midland Counties
MNM & HJ	Marple, New Mills & Hayfield Junction
MR	Midland Railway
MS & L	Manchester, Sheffield & Lincolnshire
NM	North Midland
NS	North Staffordshire
SA & M	Sheffield, Ashton & Manchester
S & R	Sheffield & Rotherham

with gritstone masonry, was one of the sights of the time. At Bull
Bridge, Stephenson's route was blocked by the Cromford Canal. The
story of his tunnelling through the embankment is well known,
although most accounts are inaccurate, being based probably on
Smiles's story that three 50 ft long sections of iron trough were
welded together to seal the canal. The contemporary account in the
Derby Mercury, 13 March 1839, is altogether more credible:

> A very interesting process took place late on Saturday night, the 2nd inst.,
> on the portion of line which is to pass under the Cromford Canal at Bull
> Bridge. In consequence of the railway having to be carried under the bed of
> the canal an iron tank, 150 feet long, nine feet wide, and 6 feet deep, was
> made at the Butterley iron works, for the purpose of preventing the water
> escaping from the canal. The tank, having previously been conveyed in five
> different parts near to the place where it was intended to be fixed, was
> rivetted together about midnight, and floated to the spot and there sunk and
> embedded. The whole of the proceedings were finished in 24 hours, without
> having interrupted the traffic on the canal. The execution of the work
> reflects the greatest credit on the engineer, as well as upon the contractor. A
> large concourse of persons were present to witness the proceedings, with
> which they appeared highly interested.

The dried-up bed of the canal is lined here with engineering blue
brick. A magnetic compass shows signs of confusion at points 150 ft
apart, over the railway, and it may well be that the trough is still
in situ (plate, page 108).

The hilly nature of the county has necessitated many long tunnels
and high viaducts. The Toadmoor Tunnel at Ambergate gave trouble
through slipping shale and today the flat-arched tunnel described by
Smiles is reinforced by steel hoops. Making the Clay Cross Tunnel
(plate, page 125) through wet shale and coal measures, 1,784 yd long,
was another difficult task. Tunnelling through rock of a different kind
was required at Dove Holes, 2,984 yd long. The Dore & Totley
Tunnel, of 1893, 6,230 yd, ending at Grindleford station, is mostly
in Derbyshire, and the Cowburn Tunnel, driven in 1892–5, is unusual in having only one air shaft. This was because of the great
depth of the tunnel, 800 ft below the surface. The square stone
structure of the shaft is a landmark on the skyline north of the

Castleton–Chapel-en-le-Frith road, A625. The viaducts, at Buxton (1863) and especially at Dinting (1842), are also impressive structures which, as expressed succinctly by Coleman, deserve to rank with the cathedrals of the Middle Ages.

The North Midland Railway has a number of exceptionally well-designed stations which aroused admiration when they were opened. The architect was Francis Thompson, of whom little is known save that he was thought to be a Derby man. He received a salary of £1,000 pa until the shareholders complained that too much money was being spent on stations and the chairman, George Carr Glyn, said that he would prefer to see 'smaller stations in the cottage style'. Thompson went on to design the station at Chester, another with a long single platform, after the style of Derby, and he 'architected' the Britannia Tubular Bridge for Robert Stephenson.

The best-known example of Thompson's works in the county is Wingfield station, surely worthy of preservation. A less-known station is at Ambergate. In response to a request by a deputation from Matlock, it was agreed to build a First-Class Station here. According to an engraving in Adams' *Gem of the Peak*, 1845 edition, this was a single rectangular building, in dressed stone, with Elizabethan gabled ends and mullioned windows. It was originally located north of Toadmoor Tunnel, just north of the goods shed which still stands. When the line was driven from the junction south of the tunnel to the Rowsley line in 1863, the station was dismantled and rebuilt in the fork of the new junction. This building still stands, and strongly resembles the original Thompson externally, but is much altered, in having two blocks, on a V plan, the northern ends being joined by a curved wall. It is less decorated than was the earlier building. It is visible from the bridge on the steep minor road from the main A6 road to Heage, which is a good viewpoint too for the Toadmoor Tunnel. It went out of use as a station when the present triangular station was built in 1876. This last station has interesting cast-iron 'furniture' such as platform number-plates, seats and a drinking fountain. The embankment walls by the main A6 road are particularly impressive; they are of two dates, one stretch having been replaced when the two bridges were reconstructed in the 1930s.

Despite Glyn's plea, the stations on the Rowsley line were equally well 'architectured'. That at Cromford is thought to have been designed by G. H. Stokes, son-in-law of Paxton. The original terminal station at Rowsley stands on the north side of the road to Bakewell (plate, page 125). This was probably designed by Paxton himself, a director and major shareholder of the Midland Railway Company. The station at Matlock Bridge, also probably designed by Paxton, had an interesting beginning, being completed on a Saturday, and found on the Sunday morning to have had all the lead stolen from its roof. Just north of this station one of the old cross-bar signals remains.

When the line was continued by the Midland Railway to Buxton in 1862–3, the Dukes of Rutland and Devonshire both wanted the local station near to their own home. As a compromise an elegant stone station was built at Bakewell, and another one only a mile away at Hassop (1862). The latter is now used by an agricultural engineering company as a depot. Buxton had twin stations, both with end façades like that remaining on the London & North Western station. The balanced appearance was lost when the Midland Railway's end wall was demolished.

It was not unusual to replace an original station when its site was found inconvenient. Traces of original stations exist at Belper, at Ambergate (just north of Toadmoor Tunnel) and at Whatstandwell (north of the tunnel). This last shows how primitive were some of the local stations until traffic justified something bigger. Ashbourne has an elegant small brick and stone building, now neglected, which was the terminal station for the 1852 North Staffordshire Railway until the line was extended to Buxton in 1899. Here too is a particularly fine engine shed, in stone, its elegant windows having contemporary glass. Representative of the 'cottage style' mentioned by Glyn was a small brick station which stood at Kilburn, on the Ripley line of 1856, until it disappeared almost overnight in 1965.

There is much of interest still to be recorded of the developing layout and construction of railway stations. The juxtaposition of buildings of 1850 and 1862–3 at Rowsley offers a good opportunity for comparison, and the later building can be related to Trent station, built in 1862, with its continuous length of glass canopy, demolished January 1968. The influence of local conditions on architectural style and materials is interesting (cf Glossop station of 1845–6, with its decorative lion, and elegant frontage), as too is the state of the company's finances at the time. The wooden stations of the Ashbourne–Buxton line of 1899 are of the L & NW system's contemporary standard for wayside stations. The 'Knotty's' (North Staffordshire) station at Hatton (ie Tutbury) is typical of a desire to economise. Warehouses, goods yards, cranes, and sometimes elegant iron footbridges can be observed, along with cast-iron 'furniture', old lamps, and an intriguing variety of shapes of water cranes, and their sources of water. The stationmaster's house and the hotel are often contemporary and designed by the same architect. When in 1878 the Great Northern Railway connected the Potteries to the East Midlands coalfield, it built two fine bridges in Derby, the handsome one in Friargate and that over the Derwent (see page 131).

The work of the great companies did not entirely exclude the enterprise of smaller ones. In 1863 'Mr Fell', who was a partner of Thomas Brassey, the great railway contractor whose navvies had put fear into the hearts of soldiers of both camps in the Crimea in 1855, constructed an experimental stretch of mountain railway near to the Cromford & High Peak Railway north-east of Buxton. It has been described by Mr W. H. Hoult,[20] and it can be traced. The coal-mining companies built many spur lines of 'steam railway' in the late nineteenth and early twentieth centuries, and quite elegant tunnels and bridges remain, for instance the composite double-tiered line near the western entrance to the Butterley Tunnel of the Cromford Canal. In 1925 the Ashover Light Railway was built by the Clay Cross Company to transport lime from the quarries at Ashover. It had a short life, ending in 1950, but it enjoyed a wide popularity throughout the county, passengers being carried until 1940. Traces of it are still visible.[21]

The tremendous activity involved in building hundreds of miles of railway, with bridges, cuttings, tunnels and embankments, and with a huge demand for rolling stock, required the support of a greatly expanded engineering industry. At first the railways depended upon such firms as Butterley and Handyside, but later they began to build locomotives, carriages and wagons on their own account. Other firms started up to meet the demands of railway builders both at home and overseas and Derby in particular became an important engineering centre. When the North Midland, the Birmingham & Derby Junction and the Midland Counties Railways were amalgamated as the Midland Railway in 1844, Matthew Kirtley was appointed locomotive superintendent to the new company. He had a great influence upon its technical policy, and in 1851 it began to produce its own locomotives at the Derby works. On his death in 1873 it was decided to have one superintendent for the Locomotive Department and another one for the new Carriage & Wagon Department.

This marked the beginning of the huge establishment lying between London Road and Osmaston Road, Derby. The works, which have been described in detail,[22] cover an area of 128 acres in total, the vast shops accounting for 38 acres. The shops, which were built from 1876 onwards, remain in use, as does some of the carriage-handling gear. The works may be significant in the story of industrial development as pioneering the use of large single buildings, the biggest covering 120,000 sq ft. Structural engineers will find an interesting variety of mixed cast and wrought iron roof trusses, and some of the cast-iron windows, almost certainly from Handysides, are of noble size.

Across the Osmaston Road are the onetime shops of Eastwood Swingler & Co, who were builders of iron bridges and railway rolling stock. The long cast-iron lintels should be noted, and the architectural windows, again almost certainly from Handysides. The building is now an omnibus depot.

With the expansion of the railway workshops the area of housing stretched across London Road. The company continued to buy land, and Derby Corporation took Litchurch into the borough in 1877, by which time the Midland Railway occupied an area as great as that occupied by Derby town before the advent of the railways. Today the wheel has turned full circle, and the main centre of research for British Rail has been established at Derby. The background atmosphere of the town, and the ubiquitous signs of railway activity dating back to 1839, and indeed to the early horse railways of 1793, must inevitably help the planners in preserving a due sense of balance and perspective as they look ahead.

STREET TRAMWAYS

Electric streetcars are still remembered by many people, as they have been abandoned only during the past thirty years. They had a brief reign compared with other means of transport, and it is greatly to the credit of the Tramway Museum Society that a living museum has been set up in George Stephenson's quarry at Crich.

Derby possesses relics of the even earlier horse-drawn streetcars. Rails are still in the ground in what was an overnight parking place for the cars, in an enclosure, formerly gated, by the side of the Great Northern Railway viaduct near Friargate station. The horses were stabled under the arches of the viaduct. This tramway was opened in 1880, and in 1899 Derby Corporation bought it from the Derby Tramway Company for £32,000. Electrification was put in hand in 1903, and in the next year electric tram number 1, made at Loughborough, went into operation. It ran until 1933, covering 660,390¼ miles, and is to be preserved at Crich. The electric tramway depot was situated on Osmaston Road, where it still stands, near Abingdon Street.

Horse trams persisted until 1915, although the routes were completely electrified by 1909. The first trolley buses were introduced in 1932, and conversion to this form of transport was completed by 1935. The last trolley bus ran on 9 September 1967, since when motor buses have been used exclusively.

The electric tramway in Glossop, operated by the Urban Electric Supply Co Ltd, was closed down in December 1927. Chesterfield went over to trolley buses in the same year, and Ilkeston closed down its tramway in 1931, having started it in 1903.

What must have been one of the world's most exciting rides was provided in Matlock from 1893 until 1927. One year after Travis's London tramway had begun to operate, and in the year that the San Francisco cable tramway was inaugurated, John Smith of Matlock, who was working in the United States, wrote to John Smedley suggesting that a cable tramway should be established in the town. A route up Matlock Bank, by Rutland Street, was actually surveyed in 1885, but the street was then too narrow. It was widened in 1890, and by this time Smith had returned home and was on the Matlock Local Board. His suggestion was noted by Marks, the engineer of the Lynton Cliff Railway, and by George Newnes, MP, a native of Matlock. A company was formed, Newnes subscribing most of the capital. Work was begun in 1891 on the depot and engine house which still stands at the corner of Rutland Street and Wellington Street.

The tramway was opened on 28 March 1893. A mere $\frac{5}{8}$ mile long, it was claimed to be the only single-line cable railway in Europe, and the steepest, with an average gradient of 1 in $5\frac{1}{2}$, a gauge of 42 in and a 3 in diameter cable. The lower terminus was in Crown Square, and the ornate cast-iron shelter, donated by Robert Wildgoose, has been moved to the riverside gardens close by. A passing place was provided at Smedley Street. There were 252,633 passengers in the first nine months, and they paid 2d for the ascent, 1d for the descent. The three cars were made by G. F. Milnes & Co of Birkenhead, and seated thirteen inside and eighteen outside. Dick Kerr & Co Ltd provided the power plant, which consisted of two high-pressure horizontal steam engines of 14 in bore × 28 in stroke, 400 hp.

In 1898 Sir George Newnes gave the tramway to the Urban District Council, which then became the first municipal authority to own and operate a cable railway. Heavy cable wear contributed to high operating costs and by 1910 the venture was losing money. Major alterations were made in 1920, the steam engines being replaced by suction gas engines, but by the mid-1920s motor buses were able to surmount the hill. On 23 September 1927 it was decided to shut down the line; on 30 September the cable broke. The tram shed is now a milk depot.[23]

THE MOTOR CAR

No work on Derbyshire can ignore the motor car, since it was in Derby that the young Rolls-Royce Company established in the early years of the present century the most widely known reputation for quality of design and workmanship and for reliability of performance. The world-wide acceptance of 'Rolls-Royce' as the synonym for all that is best in quality and reliability is a fitting culmination to the efforts of those local engineers, starting perhaps with Sorocold and progressing by way of Handyside's 'Derby Castings', who 'never failed in what they undertook, because they considered the perfections and success of their work first, and their profit afterwards'.

By 1907 the Rolls-Royce Company was requiring for the production of the new 40/50 hp six-cylinder motor car, later to become known as the Silver Ghost, more space than was available at Cook Street, Manchester. The reasons for the choosing of Derby are well expressed in the following letter:

To the Directors   *11th February, 1907*

Mr Royce and Mr Johnson are of opinion that Derby is a good centre for works on account of

    (a) Cheapness of land.
    (b) Cheapness of labour.
    (c) The large variety of trades connected with automobile manufacture which are carried on at Derby, e.g.

foundry, malleable iron works, wheel making, and the various
trades included in the works of the Midland railway (1500 hands).
  (d) Its close proximity to sources of raw material (Birmingham 25 trains
each way daily—Sheffield 36 miles).

The wages current in Derby were 3s per week lower than those
in Manchester, and it was decided to maintain the higher rate, thereby
ensuring that many of the Manchester personnel moved to Derby
and that the flow of skilled workers was in the right direction.[24]
  Henry Royce made himself responsible for the layout of the new
factory to be capable of turning out 200 cars a year. Eight firms were
invited to tender and on 9 February 1907 Royce wrote to the Derby
solicitor C. R. B. Eddowes: 'Mr Royce and Mr Johnson are of
opinion that if the work of erecting the buildings is entrusted to such
a firm as Messrs Handyside, of Derby, it would be quite unnecessary
to employ an architect to prepare drawings, or to supervise the erection of the buildings, as Messrs Handyside are engaged, and have
for some years been engaged, in erecting buildings of a similar nature,
and are a thoroughly competent and trustworthy firm. . . . when
architects are employed to prepare drawings . . . they are in the habit
of asking Messrs Handyside to give them drawings and specifica-
tion. . . .' By September 1907 the buildings, of 1½ acres (65,340 sq ft)
were ready, and the removal of plant and personnel from the Cook
Street works began. The Derby works was opened officially on 9 July
1908 (plate, page 126).
  This phase of the Company's progress began with a total capital
of £63,500, which allowed £23,500 to be spent on new works, buildings and machinery. That first works, erected by Handyside & Company, is still in use at the main site in Nightingale Road, Derby.
It provides a direct link between the company of Weatherhead &
Glover, the predecessors of Handysides, founded in 1827, and the
great firm which is today predominantly concerned with aircraft
engines. There can be little doubt that the innate ability of those
employed in railway engineering, whose roots ran back through canal
construction, iron manufacture, textiles, and coal and lead mining,

has contributed greatly to the 'Magic of a Name'. Motor cars are
no longer made in the county (the motor-car activity of Rolls-Royce
was transferred to Crewe in 1945), but the skills and abilities which
they called for have continued to maintain pre-eminence in the still
more demanding fields of aviation, space, and marine nuclear pro-
pulsion.

At the same time the advent of the motor car has had a permanent
effect upon the pattern of the county's industry. The large Ferodo
works in Chapel-en-le-Frith is an important supplier of brake linings
for the trade. A major part of the output of Leys, Qualcast and
Sheepbridge consists of iron castings of many kinds for the large
automobile manufacturers. In Belper the firm of Daltons, formed
through the prescience of a veterinary surgeon who saw that the
horse would be replaced by the motor car, produces refined oils and
lubrication additives in what was one of the warehouses of the hosiery
firm of Ward, Sturt & Sharp. More recently, the research laboratories
of Lubrizol (Great Britain) Ltd have been established at Hazlewood,
for work on problems of lubrication.

CHAPTER FIVE

Textiles

THE mid-eighteenth century developments in the mechanisation of the knitting, spinning and weaving of textile fibres have had a profound influence upon industrial life—an influence extending far beyond the confines of this one particular industry.

In response to a need for national self-sufficiency and to a steadily increasing domestic demand, Derby's Silk Mill appeared in the early part of the eighteenth century, the first textile mill ever, a large building housing hundreds of employees to operate complex power-driven machinery. Later came Jedediah Strutt's improvement of Lee's stocking-knitting frame to produce the 'Derby Rib' stocking. The next few years saw the successful mechanisation of the spinning of cotton, by James Hargreaves and by Richard Arkwright, and John Kay's speeding-up of the weaving process with his flying shuttle. All this happening within a period of about fifty years created great changes within the lifetime of individuals. In Derbyshire people who had been self-employed, or who had been outworkers in their own houses, found themselves living in new villages like Cromford, and working in large 'mills' for a single large-scale employer such as Arkwright, Strutt, or Thomas Evans and his sons.

So great were these changes, initially within the textile industry, that to many they appeared to be revolutionary, and they were referred to as the Industrial Revolution. This has had the unfortunate and unintended effect of creating a widespread impression that until that time England was an entirely rural country, with no industry and no technology; yet as we have seen, important developments on which this further expansion was based had been in process since the sixteenth century at least. Derbyshire people and Derbyshire places played a prominent part in this Industrial Revolution, and

we have already seen how much they were concerned with the earli
developments. The availability of water power and of industrialise
yet docile and non-organised labour were among the reasons whic
led to the establishment of the textile mills in the Derwent valle
but the influence of Sorocold must not be overlooked. The subse
quent application of steam power to textile factories enabled Lan
cashire to recover its traditional position in the cotton industry, an
Derbyshire lost its important place. One fortunate outcome was th
the county did not suffer the headlong expansion of the nineteent
century and the ensuing recession, experienced elsewhere. It is largel
due to the absence of expansionist pressure to use existing space tha
so many relics of the old textile industry have survived, although som
of the finest examples have disappeared within the past few years.

The spinning of wool and from about 1600 of 'cotton wool' ha
always been cottage industries, as too had been the weaving of cloth
the methods going back to prehistoric days. Indeed, the greates
technical progress made was the application of water power to th
fulling of cloth, probably in the fifteenth century.

Hand-knitting was introduced into England from the continent i
the sixteenth century. In a remarkably short space of time the process
was mechanised by the invention of the hand-frame knitting machin
of William Lee, in 1589. This isolated act of genius was, however
to remain unimproved for 170 years. Lee received little encourage
ment in England and took his invention to France, but with no mor
success. Later, fashion played its part, and the growing demand fo
finely-knitted silk gloves and clothing, which had formerly been imported from Spain, led to Lee's machine being taken up in London
in the latter half of the seventeenth century. A silk-knitting industry
was established by Huguenot immigrants at Spitalfields, but spun
silk thread had to be imported from France and Italy.

The desire to become self-sufficient led to attempts to spin silk
in this country, and Derby's Silk Mills were the result. At about the
same time, to obtain cheaper labour and to avoid the restrictions of
the London guilds, much of the hosiery trade moved to the Midlands.

Nottingham became the centre for the cotton hosiers, who used cotton spun by hand in Lancashire, Leicester was occupied chiefly with woollen hosiery, and Derby with silk.

By the early eighteenth century the textile industry had become organised on capitalistic lines. In Lancashire two brothers employed 2,400 spinners and 600 weavers as out-workers.[1] In Nottingham in particular the hosiery trade was similarly organised, a small number of increasingly wealthy men letting out knitting frames to large numbers of artisans who worked in their own homes. This expanding trade and the weavers' adoption of Kay's flying shuttle in 1733 increased the demand for cotton thread and provided the impetus for further developments in methods of spinning. Researchers are still investigating the relative importance of the contributions of Wyatt and Paul, Hargreaves and Arkwright. Whatever the outcome, it is to Arkwright that the credit must go as the great driving force behind the 'revolution'. It is unlikely that even he would have succeeded had he not found in Nottingham and in Derbyshire the people, the money, and the technology for his purpose.

After the erection of Sorocold's Silk Mills for Cotchett and the Lombes, Smeaton made great improvements in waterwheel design about 1759. Many large mills were built during the last quarter of the century, and heating, ventilation and fire-resistance were developed, notably by William Strutt. At this time too came the direct application of steam power to rotary motion for driving machinery, the first installation being at Papplewick in Nottinghamshire in 1788. Bringing together hundreds of workers in one building in sparsely populated areas led to large-scale housing developments (Chapter Six). The Derbyshire pioneers were careful of the wellbeing of their employees. Arkwright advanced loans to those wishing to buy a cow; Strutt established farms for the provision of fresh green vegetables and milk; Oldknow went further and became actively interested in agricultural improvement. All these men set up schools for the children of their employees, and they built churches and chapels. Arkwright, Strutt, Evans, Hollins, Oldknow, Newton of Cressbrook and

others represent a side of the coin too often disregarded by writers
who base their knowledge of the factory system on John Brown'
Memoir of Robert Blincoe. In the words of C. R. Fay, 'We know most
of those who fared worst.'[2] The early enlightened efforts have been
overshadowed by the malpractices of some of the later cotton masters
of Lancashire and of the notorious Needham of Litton Mill, whose
deeds have been recorded in lurid detail.[3]

Although Derbyshire lost much of its silk trade to other parts of
the country, and most of its cotton-spinning to Lancashire, the textile
industry has continued to develop, and it still occupies an important
place in the county's economy. Much fine woollen knitwear is made
in Derbyshire, eg in Derby, Alfreton, Matlock, Lea and Belper
Nylon stockings are made in quantity, while Derby and Wirksworth
have an important narrow-fabric output and Derby has a leading
manufacturer of elastic fabric. At Ashbourne, in a century-old mill
tapes are made in a wide variety of fibres, including glass, and there
is a large corset manufactory.

About eighty years ago machine-lace making moved from Nottingham to Long Eaton, which in consequence has grown from a
small village into an urban district with a population of over 30,000.
There was an important lace factory in Derby itself from the early
nineteenth century until 1958.

WOOLLEN MANUFACTURE

Although it had little influence upon the later industrial developments in the county, mention must be made of the traditional textile,
wool. Glover in his *Peak Guide* (1830) summarised the industry
briefly. With wide areas of the county suitable only for sheep rearing,
it is not surprising that Chapel-en-le-Frith had an important wool
fair. Long before the Silk Mills were built on By-Flatt in Derby
there had been three fulling mills there, and in the 1820s there were
others at Glossop and at Simmondley.

During the eighteenth century the woollen-weaving industry expanded at Glossop and in the neighbouring villages of Chunal, Hayfield and Simmondley. Many of the mills were later converted to cotton manufacture, but that at Gnathole remained a woollen mill, and it has now been skilfully converted into dwelling houses. Brassington had a bleach-works for blankets. Worsted for stockings was spun at Litton, Lea Wood, Melbourne, Tideswell and Derby. The important woollen firms surviving today belong more strictly to the hosiery industry.

Although the growing of flax, and linen manufacture, did not expand in Derbyshire, the industry has its place because of its connection with the brothers Dakeyne, who invented the unusual water-pressure engine mentioned on page 102. Their flax-spinning Ladygrove Mill, at Two Dales, which was established in 1826 and is now used by Johnsons for cattle foods, has a beautiful chain of dams which give a vivid impression of the scale of this enterprise.

HOSIERY

The stocking frame invented by Lee in 1589 has been described as the most complex machine in industrial use before the eighteenth century,[4] with 3,500 different components, requiring fifty days for their making, and twelve more for their assembly. It is unfortunate that little is known of the manufacture of these machines, save that most villages had their frame-smiths. Lee's frame was improved in 1758 by Jedediah Strutt of South Normanton to enable a ribbed and much better-fitting stocking to be made—the 'Derby Rib'. A later development enabled gloves and mittens to be knitted.

With the exception of the factory erected in Nottingham by Samuel Fellows, who moved there from London in the 1720s, the hosiery industry remained essentially one in which master hosiers owned large numbers of frames, which were let to out-workers for use at home. Work rooms were added to private houses, either as attics,

L

usually provided with additional windows, or as lean-to buildings. The whole family including quite young children would work at the machines, and sometimes the attics would be opened up along a whole row of cottages. This was done in the two rows of houses comprising North Street, Cromford, which were built by Arkwright in the 1770s. Perhaps the finest example of a stockinger's house in Derbyshire is that still to be seen in Crich, but there are buildings standing in Derby in which the stockingers' attic windows have been bricked up. A lean-to stockinger's shop which survives at Duffield was in use for its original purpose until about fifty years ago.

One of the largest hosiery firms was established in Belper in 1803, and it still flourishes. In 1802 William and John Ward came to Belper and in the following year came George Brettle. They combined as Ward, Brettle & Ward, and established a large organisation of out-workers over a 20 mile radius, with a big export trade. This firm claims to have made the vest worn by Lord Nelson at the battle of Trafalgar, and silk stockings for George IV and for Queen Victoria for her coronation. According to Glover, in 1829 the company had about 400 frames for silk hose and gloves, and 2,500 frames for cotton hosiery, producing a total of 100,000 dozen pairs of stockings annually. At about this time small workshops were built at Belper, Bargate, Holbrook and Derby, which can still be seen in a more or less dilapidated state. In 1833 William Ward's death caused the partnership to be dissolved. George Brettle continued independently, and he built the dignified buildings with imposing stone frontage which are still to be seen complete with horse-mounting steps on the west side of the main A6 road through Belper. John Ward formed another company which became Ward, Sturt & Sharp, occupying the original buildings to the south of Brettle's new ones, and erecting those across the road which are now occupied by Dalton's oil refinery. The two companies were reunited after the first world war.

Meanwhile firms in Derby were setting up manufactories, amongst them Longdons (probably in 1802), today well-known for its large production of knitted elastic fabric in all widths from a fraction of an inch to a yard or more. The firm's first factory produced surgical bandage, and elastic hosiery, which was invented by Thomas Parker Tabberer in collaboration with Robert Longdon. The premises occupied by the firm today, in Agard Street, are strongly evocative of the early nineteenth century, with their quietly dignified entrance hall, their board room, and the book-lined office of the managing director. The atmosphere is intensified by the fact that at the time of writing Longdons still employed four hand-frame knitters to make special sizes of elastic hosiery. The ages of these four workers then totalled 278 years, and the most senior of them, Mr George Holdsworth, eighty-five years old, still focused the light on to his work by the traditional glass globe filled with a weak solution of blue vitriol, put in position by his father (plate, page 126). This persistence of tradition is the more striking because of the fact that from adjacent machinery of more recent date the company achieves a rate of output not exceeded anywhere.

A more exotic application of the warp-knitting machine was to the production of knitted silk goods, ornamented with figures and flowers. According to Pilkington there were eighty knitting frames in Melbourne in 1789. In 1812 Thomas Haimes, born in Melbourne in 1780, began as a warp knitter and was soon making figured silk shawls equal to the best French products. In 1822 he used an endless canvas belt with small pieces of leather glued to it, instead of the usual Jacquard punched card. Haimes died in 1825 of 'a brain disorder', and his son Thomas carried on the business, developing an elastic velvet fabric, the Royal velvet glove and a double-knitted fabric. By 1850 the firm had 1,100 employees, and in about 1857 the Castle Mills were erected. The present frontage, however, is of 1933 date, following a fire which damaged the old buildings. In 1880 the company sold four warp-knitting machines to Clarke of Nottingham, who emigrated to the United States, there to establish the industry.

Another establishment for warp-knitting of fine milanese and glove fabrics was set up in Ilkeston by William Beardsley in about 1820. The original building stands in a quiet backwater, still operated by

W. Beardsley & Sons Ltd for the manufacture of warp-knitted fabrics, nets, veilings, laces and milanese. About five years later W. Ball & Son started in the same line of business, also in Ilkeston, and today has a complex of buildings of roughly contemporary date, the largest having a typical pedimented brick frontage of four storeys and nine bays.

Knitting of woollen garments, too, has long been a staple industry in the county. Nightingale's cotton-spinning mill at Lea was changed over to hosiery manufacture by Thomas Smedley, whose son John in about 1840 introduced modern machinery. This company is still renowned for its fine woollen goods, made in buildings which form a complex of sequential dating presenting an interesting picture of cautious and continuous expansion over a period of about 180 years. In Heanor, the large knitwear and hosiery factory of I. & R. Morley Ltd is interesting as an example of a late nineteenth-century building.

Of much later date, but still in the good architectural taste of Derby mills, are the Britannia Mills built in 1912 by Moore Eady and Murcott Goode for fine knitwear, on the site of a much older mill, one of the highest on Markeaton Brook. The entrance block of cylindrical form, and the dome carrying the figure of Britannia, are unusual features.

THE SILK INDUSTRY

The important work of George Sorocold in the engineering of the textile industry has already been mentioned. Thomas Cotchett's contribution to the establishment of the factory system may have been too little appreciated.[5] The romantic circumstances allegedly surrounding the journey of John Lombe to Italy, his 'stealing' of the secrets of the silk-throwing machine, and his early death in suspicious circumstances, have diverted attention from the pioneer work of Cotchett and Sorocold. The situation has not been helped by the inaccurate and denigratory account of the 'historian' Hutton.

Cotchett was born in Mickleover in 1640 and was admitted a barrister at Gray's Inn in 1661. In 1702 he built a silk mill on the Derwent in Derby, adjacent to the corn mills which were situated where now stand the offices of the East Midlands Electricity Board in Sowter Road. Sorocold was the engineer. The mill was 62 ft long, 28 ft 5 in broad and 35 ft high, with three storeys. It was well-lighted by windows, and had accommodation for forty-eight doublers. Its waterwheel, 13½ ft diameter with twenty-four ladle boards, drove four machines in each of the two lower storeys, by shafting and gearing. Each mill had 148 spindles, and in total there were 1,340 spindles, '56 reels, 69 toats (sic), 56 lantherns, 116 stars, 8410 bobbins, and 2340 leads'.[5] This mill has a good claim to the title of being the first factory, in the sense that it was a single establishment with complex machinery, a source of power, and accommodation for a number of workers.

It was certainly of sufficient importance to attract the notice of Sir Thomas Lombe, a wealthy silk merchant of Norwich and London, who had a clear idea of the value of spun silk to the economy of the country. He had his younger half-brother John apprenticed to Cotchett. Probably knowing well the advanced state of the art in Italy, whence silk thread had been imported for many years for the Huguenot silk weavers of Spitalfields, he sent John there for two years to learn the secrets of the machinery. Sorocold, however, may already have been familiar with Zonca's book *Novo teatro de edificii et machine* of 1607, which contains a description and drawings of the Italian machine (see page 182). Significantly, it was to Derby and Sorocold that John Lombe returned. Extensive additions were made to Cotchett's mill, which became known as The Old Shop, again with Sorocold as engineer. The Old Shop and its Dutch machines remained in use, in 1802 being included in a bill of sale for the whole establishment, by which time it had a 3 hp steam engine, of which the short square chimney still stands.

F. Williamson has reproduced a detailed description of both Cotchett's mill and Lombe's additions of 1717–20. (The description had

Italian silk-throwing machine. (Zonca's *Nova Teatro de Edificii et Machine*, 1607)

been prepared by William Wilson who, with Samuel Lloyd, bought the works from Sir Thomas Lombe's widow in 1739.) The Lombe mills were much greater in size and in overall concept than Cotchett's original mill, the largest building being 110 ft long and 39 ft broad, with five storeys. At a rough estimate, the total floor area of the whole establishment was about 40,000 sq ft. As in Cotchett's earlier mill, care was taken to provide adequate lighting, and the large five-storey shop had room for 306 doublers. This venture established for all time the pattern of textile factories, which are still referred to as mills because these early ones were powered by water. The plate on page 143 shows the Silk Mill as it stood for nearly two centuries, before a series of mishaps befell it. In 1890 a part collapsed through the piles having rotted, and in 1910 fire caused further extensive damage. The present structure still gives a rough impression of the large shop and the tower, but it has only three storeys in place of the five of Lombe's mill. Some of the stone foundation arches built by Sorocold for Lombe's mill can still be seen. The repaired tower is slightly modified from the original, but the bridge and the gateposts are as they were.

The mill passed through many different hands. In the 1790s the Old Mill was occupied on a short lease by Brown & Mawes for marble-sawing and polishing. In 1916 the present building, then called the Riverside Works, was used by F. W. Hampshire & Co Ltd, manufacturing chemists, who produced amongst other things those fly-papers which were rendered near-obsolete by the aerosol spray. The elegant wrought-iron gates, made by Robert Bakewell at his shop in Oakes Yard in about 1722, were renovated in 1905. In 1934 they were removed to their present site adjoining the Borough Library in Wardwick. A plaque indicates that Derby became troubled by those industrial disputes from which the town had been remarkably free earlier:

Derby Silk Strike Centenary
1834–1934
Erected by
Derby Trade Unionists,
and unveiled by the
President of the Trade Union Council (Mr A. Cowley)
To commemorate the First 'Derby Turn Out', when the silk workers, supported by their colleagues in other trades, left work from Nov. 1833 to Mar. 1834 to defend the right to combine in a Trade Union.
'They pioneered the way to freedom.'
'The liberty is yours.'

March 17, 1934.

On the lapse of Lombe's patent in 1732 many silk mills were erected, in Derby and in other places, but notably in Stockport and later in Macclesfield. In 1789 Pilkington reported twelve silk mills in Derby, employing 1,200 people, but by 1761 in Macclesfield 2,500 people were already employed in the industry, and in 1768, according to Farey, there were six silk mills in Stockport. By a date which has not yet been established, but about 1760, Jedediah Strutt had a silk mill in Derby, on the Markeaton Brook, in what is now Albert Street. Later he had one in Morledge, but both have vanished. A number of mills erected originally for silk throwing, and for the weaving and knitting of narrow fabrics and trimming are, however, still to be seen in the town. The large and imposing buildings in Brook Street and Bridge Street erected by Peets and by Bridgetts from 1823 onwards were set up for the manufacture of narrow fabrics, still being made there by Rykneld Mills Ltd. This complex of five-storey and seven-storey brick buildings of excellent proportions is today much better appreciated since the demolition of surrounding property in preparation for the Inner Ring Road. It is endowed with special character by the small-paned cast-iron windows and the combination of hipped and pedimented roof lines. The Green Lane Silk Mill, now a furniture store, and with its frontage much altered, is almost certainly of eighteenth-century date, since it was advertised for sale in 1802. Its rear view, seen from Oakes Yard in St Peters Street, gives a good impression of its original appearance. In 1827 it was taken over by

G. B. Unsworth, whose family held it for about 100 years. The Unsworths had another mill in 1831, in Devonshire Street. This still stands and can be identified by the short chimney of its first boiler furnace.

Pigot in 1828 listed nine silk throwsters in Derby. Several of these were in Agard Street, and their premises are now occupied by elastic fabric and narrow fabric firms. Several of them back on to the Markeaton Brook, which was formerly a complex of dams and leats, and which later provided water for the early steam engines. Many of the modest chimneys of these engines still stand. In 1854 the large brick building in Siddals Road which is now used by ICI Ltd, Dyestuffs Division, as a colour works, was erected by T. Mitchell. It backs on to the Derby Canal, and it produced silks for hosiery, embroidery, knitting, etc, and later for electrical insulation. The silk industry continued to prosper in Derby and in 1874 Charles Dould & Son built the Spa Lane Mills for the manufacture of gimp trimmings, furniture trimmings, fringes and tassels. By 1916 they were using artificial silk.

In his third volume Farey included seven silk-spinning mills in Derby and one in Chesterfield. This last, in Beetwell Street, was possibly the oldest surviving example of a water-driven silk-spinning mill until its demolition in 1967. Little is known about it, and research is needed to fill the gaps in its history. It was a compact building in brick, five storeys high, seven bays wide and three bays deep, with a low-pitched hipped roof. A stone embodied in the brick structure bore the date 1737, but this may have been removed from the adjacent bridge when it was modified; a reference by Dr S. D. Chapman[6] to John White's factory in Chesterfield may, however, confirm this date.

White (1857) copied Bagshaw (1846) in including 'a silk mill' in the list of Chesterfield's industries, but the unnamed author of *The History of Chesterfield*, 1839, in a sorrowful commentary on the lack of industrial initiative in the town, complained: 'Chesterfield may boast of having a silk mill, carried by water, for a great number of years, yet nothing worth naming is done in this trade, though it would, perhaps, puzzle any one to advance a plausible reason why the manufacture of silk could not prosper as well here as in Derby.' Today, no silk throwing is carried on in the county.

THE COTTON INDUSTRY

Its identification with the Industrial Revolution has resulted in the early cotton industry receiving much attention from economic historians, and it has an extensive literature. All who are concerned with the successful prosecution of industrial enterprise will find it rewarding to study the different approaches of Richard Arkwright and of Jedediah Strutt. These have been described in detail by Fitton and Wadsworth,[7] whose work must long remain the standard reference. On the one hand Arkwright, inexperienced in industry, but a man of great initiative and drive, made a fortune of half a million pounds in only twenty-three years, from his patents and by his expansionist policy of building mills in a large number of places in Derbyshire, Lancashire, and Scotland. On the other hand Strutt, who already had fifteen years' industrial experience, believed in consolidation and concentration. His was in the long run the more stable business, and he and his sons contributed more than Arkwright to the industrial innovations of the day, notably in building construction, housing estates, and public works.

Little is known about Arkwright save that he was born in 1732 at Preston in Lancashire, moving to Bolton in 1750. He was a barber and peruke maker, with a clientele 'of the better sort', and he had a great interest in mechanical devices. His journeys to buy hair for wigs would keep him aware of the developments of the times, and in the 1760s he became interested in developing a roller spinning machine. James Hargreaves was working on his spinning jenny at Blackburn at the same time. He and Arkwright moved, independently, to Nottingham in 1768,[8] both for the same reason, the dread of the machine-wreckers in Lancashire, who had already broken up Hargreaves's machines. Arkwright took out the patent for his 'water frame' roller spinning machine in 1769, while in Nottingham, and he had financial assistance from Ichabod Wright (1700–77), a timber, iron and hemp merchant of Nottingham who founded a bank in 1759 and whose grandson John was one of the partners of the Butterley Company. Shortly afterwards Samuel Need took over the financial support of Arkwright, and called in his partner Jedediah Strutt, who was by now well-established as a silk throwster and hosiery manufacturer in Derby.

Strutt was of course familiar with the Derby Silk Mill, and since 1760 had had his own silk-throwing mill on the Markeaton Brook. Arkwright's first cotton-spinning mill in Nottingham had used horse power. The reasons for his choice of Cromford for his first water-powered cotton-spinning mill erected in 1771, have aroused speculation and his modest start, using the water from Bonsall Brook and Cromford Sough, seems at first surprising. The site may, however, have been selected for no other reason than that it was available, in an area with which Arkwright was already familiar, with ample female and child labour to be had from Wirksworth, 2 miles away. Moreover, as Dr S. D. Chapman has pointed out, Cromford was comfortably remote from busy towns, with the risk of industrial unrest.

For his first mill at Cromford Arkwright carried the water from Cromford Sough over and across the road in a wooden launder, which was replaced fifty years later, in 1821, by the present cast-iron one. A sizeable wheel must have been turned, as indicated by the height of the launder. The remains of this first mill of 1771, which lost its two upper storeys by fire, are barely recognisable. Still less is to be seen of the second mill of 1777, and most of the records have been lost, but a conjectural study of the site has been made by Dr K. Swindin.[9] From a passing reference by Fitton and Wadsworth, it appears that Arkwright installed a Boulton & Watt steam engine of 8 hp, in 1780. This must ante-date by eight years the installation at Papplewick, although this earlier application of steam power was indirect, to raise water to work a wheel, which provided the rotary motion.

As soon as the second Cromford Mill was finished Arkwright built in quick succession mills at Cressbrook (1779), Ashbourne (1781), Bakewell (1782), Wirksworth (1783) and Masson (1784). The old mill at Cressbrook is still visible by the side of the stream behind the large building of 1815, and is identified by reference to contemporary drawings. The Ashbourne mill was taken over by J. D. Cooper, a son-in-law of Jedediah Strutt, and was replaced in 1865 by the present Alrewas Mill of M. Bond, whose company still operates it a century later. The mill at Bakewell was burnt down in 1868, and its site is occupied by the present works of the DP Battery Co Ltd. Which of the Wirksworth mills was Arkwright's has been in doubt, but it is now reasonably established as the Speedwell Mill.[10] Masson Mill is the only one to have been located on a large river, the Derwent, and the unusual down-curved weir here may possibly be due to Arkwright's limited knowledge of water power. On the other hand, it is known that Arkwright had bought existing corn and paper mills from Shore of Snitterton and White of Winster (two men who were operating lead mines in Cardiganshire, at Llwyn Llwyd, in the 1780s) and it may be that they were responsible for the 'wrong' design of weir, which has persisted to this day.

In 1781, on the death of Need, the partnership between Arkwright and Jedediah Strutt was dissolved, possibly because the two men wished to develop their businesses along different lines, at different rates. Strutt retained the Derby Mills, the Old Mill which had been built at Belper in 1778, and the Milford Old Mill of 1780. He continued to expand these until 1827, as follows:

1778	Belper Old Mill (D)
1780	Milford Old Mill
1786	Belper North Mill
1790	Milford Bleaching Mill
1793	Derby Mill (demolished about 1876) (F)
1793	Milford Warehouse (F, D)

1795   Belper West Mill (F, D)
1803   Belper North Mill destroyed by fire
1804   Belper North Mill rebuilt (I)
1806   Milford East Wing. Lit by gas (D)
1808   Belper Reeling Mill (I)
1810   Belper Old Mill demolished
1812   Belper South Mill built on site of Old Mill (I, D)
1813/16 Belper Round Building (D)
1817   Milford Mechanics Shop (D)
1827   Milford Old Dye House
    F = 'fireproof' mills   I = iron-framed mills, fireproof
            D = demolished during recent years

In 1789 the Strutts were employing 600 people at Belper, and by 1802, 1,200–1,300; by 1815 the total was 1,500, and by 1833, 2,000. In 1818 there were 700 employees at Milford. The accompanying rapid growth of population was met by a vigorous programme of house-building by the Strutts, at Belper, Milford, and Hopping Hill.

The Strutt mill buildings have attracted much serious study. The papers of Professor A. W. Skempton and Mr H. R. Johnson,[11] which describe in minute detail the development of the successive buildings of William Strutt, son of Jedediah, at Milford and at Belper, are classic examples of industrial archaeological recording. The fireproofing, the iron-framed construction, and the machine drives were more ambitious than anything done by Arkwright. In fact William Strutt was the first man to design and build multi-storey fireproof buildings, and although his friend Charles Bage built the flax mill at Shrewsbury with cast-iron beams instead of the earlier plaster-covered wooden ones in 1797, seven years before Strutt's iron-framed Belper North Mill, he received a good deal of help and information from Strutt.

The first 'fireproof' building, the Derby cotton mill of 1793, was six storeys high, 115 ft long and 31 ft wide. The walls were load-bearing, and the floors consisted of brick arches of 9 ft span, springing from wooden beams supported by cast-iron columns. The ceiling of the top storey was made of hollow earthenware pots built into arches, cemented together with gypsum plaster. Typical pots are $4\frac{1}{2}$ in diameter, $5\frac{1}{4}$ in long, $\frac{3}{8}$ in thick, with a loose lid $\frac{1}{4}$ in thick. A more advanced design is that of the Belper North Mill, 1803–4. Five storeys high, with an attic which was used as a schoolroom, it is iron-framed throughout, with iron beams as well as pillars, and brick arches. It is built in mellow brick and is 127 ft long, 31 ft wide, 63 ft high, with a wing 41½ ft × 34 ft projecting from the centre of the north side. The drawing made by John Farey Jr for his article on Cotton in Rees's *Cyclopaedia*, 1819–20, shows the huge waterwheel, 18 ft diameter and 23 ft wide, and the bevel-gear shaft drives to the four working floors. This wheel, which was under the wing, has disappeared. In the basement can be seen how the massive stone blocks which form the bases for the iron columns were carefully levelled with iron wedges (figure opposite).

The demolition in 1964 of William Strutt's classic mills at Milford is adequate justification for industrial archaeology. A comprehensive photographic record of these mills, and of those at Belper which were demolished earlier to make way for modern structures, has been made by Mr A. N. Smith.

Only visible in winter, when the creeper has died back, are the gun embrasures in the footbridge over the road at Belper. These were evidently thought advisable following the destruction of Arkwright's mill at Birkacre, near Chorley, in 1779, and in anticipation of trouble from the Luddites in 1811–12. Fortunately, they were never needed.

For many years a large portrait in oils of William Strutt lay forgotten in the attic of the Derbyshire Royal Infirmary, for which he designed the original building. The portrait was recognised by Professor Skempton, and it has been restored and lent by the Infirmary authorities to the Science Museum (see frontispiece).

Thomas Evans, owner of lead mines at Bonsall and of the iron and copper rolling and slitting mills at the Holmes, Derby, was a partner in the Crompton Evans bank in Derby. In 1783 he and his sons Walter and William built a cotton-spinning mill at Darley Abbey, and paper mills on the right bank, opposite. The cotton mill was burnt down in 1788, but was rebuilt immediately and became well-known for its Boars Head sewing cotton. The brick-built mills,

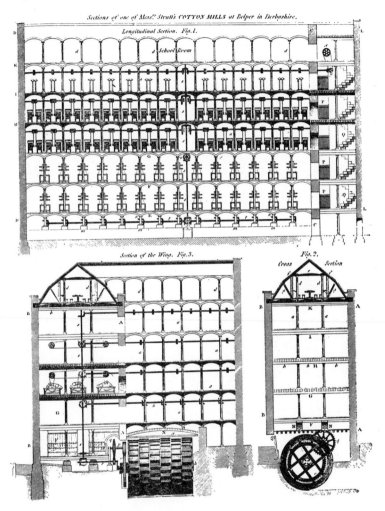

Belper North Mill, 1804. (Rees' *Cyclopaedia*, 1819)

with many original windows, a noble and very wide weir, and a toll
bridge over the river, are still in use, although the waterwheels have
been replaced by water turbines. Like the Arkwrights and the Strutts,
the Evans family was benevolent, and built a considerable village,
which forms a well-preserved and picturesque corner off the main
Derby road (see Gazetteer).

Meanwhile in 1785–6 John Gardom, who as a yarn and cotton
merchant of Bakewell had been a supplier to Strutt's hosiery factory

Girls at work in Evans' mills, Darley Abbey. (*The Illustrated Times*,
26 July 1862)

at Derby, entered into partnership with John Pares and built a cotton-spinning mill at Calver, under licence from Arkwright. The mill, which was at one time wrongly thought to have been Arkwright's work, was burnt down in 1802, and was rebuilt in its present form in 1803–4. It is an imposing stone building of six storeys with a pedimented frontage best appreciated from the hills to the south, and square staircase turrets at the rear (plate, page 143).[12] The external structure of this fine building has been preserved by the present owner, who uses the premises for the manufacture of stainless-steel holloware. The wheel-house, erected in 1834, is a solidly built stone structure of good appearance. The flow of water which formerly operated two wheels of 22 ft diameter, producing a total of 160 hp, gives a vivid impression of potential power.

In about 1783 two cotton-spinning mills were erected at Tansley by Samuel Unwin, who had mills at Sutton-in-Ashfield and Mansfield in Nottinghamshire, and by James Heygate. Much altered, they are now used for joinery, but there is an interesting stone wall, with through arches, carrying a large water pipe from the dam to the wheel. The Tansley Wood Mill was built probably in 1799 as a large bleachworks, fed by water conducted through siphons. It is now operated by F. H. Drabble & Sons Ltd.

Little remains of the original Litton Mill, built in 1780 by Ellis Needham and the scene of the tribulations of Robert Blincoe, as recounted by John Brown. The first mill on the Derwent is that at Bamford. The oldest part of this spinning mill was built in 1780, and it was still doubling cotton when it was shut down in 1965. Fortunately it is being preserved (see Bamford in Gazetteer). Smaller mills were opened at Eyam and at Edale for the spinning of cotton thread for lace-making. At Lea, Peter Nightingale built his first cotton mill in 1784, and this may be the small mill which still stands upstream of the later Smedley complex.

At the eastern boundary of the county, in Pleasley Vale, stands what is probably the most beautifully situated textile manufactory in the industry, that of William Hollins & Co Ltd.[13] The first mill

M

was built in 1784 on the site of Pleasley Forge on the river Meden, which forms the county boundary with Nottinghamshire. The mills expanded, but were destroyed by fire in 1840 and in 1844, and the present buildings date from about this period. Today the company has widespread activities, including the garnetting mill in Via Gellia, whence the trade name of its proprietary fabric Viyella was taken in 1894. (Garnetting is the processing of textile waste.)

J. D. Cooper, who took over Arkwright's mill on the Dove at Ashbourne, also worked a small spinning mill at Woodeaves, near Tissington. This was established probably in 1784. Its long narrow dam, which did double duty as a short canal, has already been noticed. There was a steam engine of 16 hp. Only traces of this mill remain amongst the present farm buildings, but the manager's house still stands.

Except where stated, all the sites mentioned are still in use for textile manufacture, or have only recently been abandoned. They represent industrial locations which are in the main between 150 and nearly 200 years old and which were determined by the river Derwent and its tributaries.[14]

In north-western Derbyshire developments followed a somewhat different pattern. The area is full of industrial interest, set amongst dramatic scenery, and it offers great scope for the industrial archaeologist.[15] The pioneer here was Samuel Oldknow, nephew of Thomas Oldknow, Mayor of Nottingham in 1773–4 and again in 1778–9, and a partner of Henry Hollins and others who established the mills at Pleasley Vale. When Samuel Oldknow, who had been muslin-weaving in Stockport, built his great mill at Mellor in 1790–1 it was situated in Derbyshire, but due to boundary changes the site is now in Cheshire. Oldknow received financial assistance from the Arkwrights, who took over the mill on his death in 1828. He was the moving spirit in promoting the Peak Forest Canal, interested himself in agriculture and in the lime business, and he treated his apprentices well. He is reputed to have employed Derbyshire lead miners to build the Mellor mill, his decorative lime kilns, and other structures, being appreciative of their skill in working in stone. The mill was still being worked by the Arkwrights when it was burnt down in 1892. Now, only indications of the complicated water sluices which were formerly underneath it can be traced amongst the bramble-covered ruins.

It was the fortunate discovery, in 1924, in a derelict building on the site, of forgotten and sodden but still legible papers that enabled Professor George Unwin to build up his instructive account of *Samuel Oldknow and the Arkwrights*.[16] A coloured engraving of the 'West View of Mellor Mill', made by F. Jukes from a painting by J. Parry shows that the west front had three staircase turrets (plate, page 144). A mystery which puzzled Unwin was that the completion date of the mill was established as 1791, yet the large oval stone plaque found amongst the ruins, which is now preserved in Marple Park, carries the date 1790, along with a reproduction of a shuttle. The engraving clears this up, showing two small buildings flanking the mill proper, each carrying a plaque, one with date 1790; these lesser buildings may well have been completed before the larger central one.

The developments in Glossop, Hayfield, and along the river through Birch Vale to New Mills took place during the early part of the nineteenth century. The first mill at Wrens Nest in Howard Town, Glossop, was built in 1816, and considerable extensions were made soon afterwards. With the encouragement of Bernard Edward Howard, 12th Duke of Norfolk (d 1842) and his son Henry Charles Howard, the 13th Duke, Glossop grew extremely rapidly. The mills, the Market Hall of 1838, the railway station of 1847, and the gasworks of 1845, are worthy of preservation in their entirety as an unspoilt example of a 'new town' of that period. At Dinting, Edmund Potter opened a large calico-printing works in 1825, and this and the railway viaduct, though now strengthened and modified from its original form, are impressive period pieces. Ruins of mills can be seen at Little Hayfield: one, of which nothing remains but a flued chimney apparently growing out of a field, was a buckram mill.

Down the valley of the Sett from Hayfield is a chain of large calico-print works, now operated by the Calico Printers Association. Each has its dam, but now they all depend upon steam power. The chimney of the Birch Vale Print Works, which carries the date 1851, has a massive pedestal close by the roadside. The mills at Thornsett and New Mills are of earlier date, the Salem Mill probably being the oldest.

Of the early textile machinery, little remains in the mills themselves. TMM (Research) Ltd has preserved some of the early machines of Arkwright, in old mill buildings at Helmshore in Lancashire. These machines had been acquired by Platt Brothers & Co Ltd of Oldham, from the Cromford Mill. TMM (Research) Ltd has also made a replica of Hargreaves' original spinning jenny, and there are examples in the museum of later ones. In the Science Museum in South Kensington is a carding machine of about 1775, and a water frame of about the same date, both from Cromford, and from Milford a carding machine of 1800–30. It is more than likely that old textile machines, as well as machine tools for their manufacture and repair, still lie in forgotten corners. The Confederation of British Industry and the Ministry of Works are hoping to bring some to light.

The story of Samuel Slater, the Strutt ex-apprentice who left Belper for America in 1789 at the age of twenty-one, to help found the cotton industry there, is well known. Ruins of his home, Holly House Farm, stand in the grounds of Holly House, Blackbrook, near Belper. He died in 1833 and is buried at East Webster, Worcester County, Massachusetts. The way in which Slater's Mill at Pawtucket, Rhode Island, has been preserved is an example of what can be done.

THE LACE INDUSTRY

The making of lace-net by machine was a logical development from knitting hosiery by machine. In the period 1760–70 efforts were made, in Nottingham and elsewhere, to mechanise the making of lace-net along the lines of the stocking-frame. Eventually, in 1808

John Heathcoat, who was born in 1783, the son of a Duffield farmer, patented the bobbin-net machine which, using a twisted thread of cotton, successfully simulated hand-made lace. At this time he was living in Long Whetton, near Loughborough. His enterprise, a partnership with Lacy and Boden, was beset by the Luddites, and in 1816 he moved his factory from Loughborough to a vacant wool mill, with water power available, in Tiverton, where his company still operates. Offered the opportunity of assisting his new venture, about 100 of his people in Loughborough walked to Tiverton to enter his employ there. John Boden left the partnership and set up a factory in Derby.

Nottingham, the traditional centre of hand-made lace, accepted the new lace-net, and a large industry developed, many thousands of women being employed to embroider patterns on the net. John Leavers, a frame-smith of Sutton-in-Ashfield, moved to Nottingham, there to construct point-net and warp lace machinery, and in 1813 he brought out an improvement to Heathcoat's machine. This, and many inventions which followed it, are described in detail by Felkin.[17] Rapid development of lace-making followed in the area in and around Nottingham. The adoption of steam power in place of water power led to an increase in the size of machines until they were 40 ft long, and this determined the pattern of the factory buildings—very long multi-storey buildings with a width-module adapted to the machine length.

Derby, which was on the perimeter of the machine-lace area, occupied for a time an important position. John Boden, who had been a partner of Heathcoat in Loughborough, joined with William Morley to set up in 1825 the largest lace factory of its time in Castlefields, Derby. It had 170 machines at work, and in the precincts a pleasance of lawns, gardens, a lake, swings and a maypole for its employees. This company closed down its Derby factory in 1958. In 1828 Pigot listed eleven lace firms in Derbyshire, which included William Beardsley (1820) and W. Ball & Son (1825), both of Ilkeston, and Edward Fletcher, who set up a factory in Heanor in about 1845 (see Gazetteer).

John Leavers' improvement to Heathcoat's machine enabled fancy patterns of lace to be produced, and there followed a big expansion of the industry in Nottingham. When in 1841 the Jacquard punched-card system was combined with the Leavers machine an infinite variety of fancy lace patterns became possible; supply, and the demand resulting from the popularity of lace curtains, led to a boom. Derbyshire was little affected by this further expansion in the industry until the 1870s brought a movement of lace-making firms away from Nottingham under the pressure of the increasingly active trade unions, serious industrial disputes having arisen in 1873–4 and again in 1889. The migration led to a rapid and large-scale increase of business, especially in Long Eaton. Profiting by experience, a number of large factories were built, designed to accommodate the latest lace machines. In order to house a large number of small firms, each of which owned relatively few of the big machines, weighing up to 20 tons, 40 ft long and 8 ft wide, especially big 'tenement factories' were built at Long Eaton, Sandiacre and Draycott, each with a common source of steam power. One of these factories, the Harrington Mills, is in Leopold Street, Long Eaton. Erected in 1885, it is a four-storey building, about 700 ft long. The staircase turrets, which housed the workers' lavatories, are a distinctive architectural feature. Another similar building is the Victoria Mills, Draycott. Its narrow end fronting on to the main road is unremarkable, but its side elevation is impressive, of four storeys, with 228 windows along one long side. It resembles the Harrington Mills in having turrets along one side, to leave the floors clear for the long machines. The final extension was completed, and the clock started, on 16 September 1907, when it was claimed to be one of the largest lace factories in the world.

The Springfield Mills in Sandiacre were built in 1888 by Terah Hooley, father of E. T. Hooley the financier, of Risley Hall. The whole building was said to have rocked alarmingly when all the machines were working. This may account for the fact that a feature of it is the large number of transverse ties, each ending in a fancy cast-iron plate bearing the monogram T.H. The mill, which backs on to the Erewash Canal, has a pediment with a clock in the centre of one long side. Lace is still made there, and J. C. Groves Ltd, the principal occupier, has Leavers machines built by Wallis Longdon & Co Ltd of Long Eaton in 1914, and some of the latest German machines. The steam engine which supplied power has been replaced by electricity.

SMALLWARES—TRIMMINGS, TAPES AND WEBS

According to Glover, the weaving of tapes, ferrets (stout tape of cotton or silk), and smallwares (eg bindings and braids) was introduced into Derby in 1806 by Riley, Madeley, Hackett & Co at the Haarlem Works, between Kensington Street and Talbot Street. This was the beginning of an industry which has expanded until today the companies in Derby, Wirksworth and Ashbourne comprise probably the biggest concentration of tape and webbing manufacture in the country. At first silk ribbon, gimps and trimmings were made, Derby for a time rivalling Coventry, the leading ribbon-manufacturing centre. The motor car created a new and steadily increasing demand for bindings for upholstery, and webbing for hand rests and now for safety belts. Two great wars created a need for stout webbing for soldiers' kit and for parachutes.

Hackett opened a mill at Wirksworth, giving it the same name as his mill in Derby—Haarlem. This was taken over by Jeremiah Tatlow and later by Joseph Wheatcroft, who was running the Speedwell Mill. Wirksworth became traditionally the centre for the weaving of 'red-tape', used for tying bundles of documents.

In 1823 a large works was erected in Derby by Messrs Peet, for weaving silk ribbon and trimming. This, and the silk piece-goods mills of Thomas Bridgett & Co, set up about the same time, may have been the original enterprises of the large complex which is today occupied by Rykneld Mills, in Brook Street and Bridge Street, for the weaving of tapes and bindings. The lofty buildings (see Gazetteer) are of about this date, with cast-iron stanchions and brick-arched floors of the period.

Today there are several large tape mills in Derby. J. Bonas & Son Ltd came to Derby from Tamworth in 1883 and has works in Lynton Street; C. Lilley & Sons in Boyer Street, and H. Lilley & Son in Parliament Street, occupy buildings of earlier and later dates in the area between Burton Road and Uttoxeter New Road, not far from the original Haarlem Mill, now vanished. Another large mill was operated by T. Mitchell, whose name can still be seen on what is now an ICI colour works in Siddals Road. In 1916 Alan Turner took over the building which had previously housed the Phoenix Foundry to make tapes for cars and carriages. Later this firm took over the Spa Lane Mills, which had been operated by Doulds.

In Ashbourne a large mill was built in 1864 by M. Bond of Alrewas on the site of Cooper's spinning mill (see page 188). Tapes in many materials are made here.

CHAPTER SIX

Industrial Housing

ONE of the many new problems posed by the rapid growth of the textile industry was that the many hundreds of people employed in the cotton mills had, with their families, to be housed, fed and educated, preferably nearby, since hours of working were long. From the last quarter of the eighteenth century onwards Arkwright, Strutt and Evans established large settlements of houses which were so soundly constructed and so well-designed that they are still sought after.

Arkwright built two rows of houses in North Street, Cromford, before 1777. He and his son Richard went on to build the great house, Willersley Castle and the church by the river. For the convenience of travellers wishing to see the wonderful new mills Arkwright built the fine Greyhound Hotel—of which the Hon John Byng wrote in June 1790 that it was cheap and pleasant, with good stabling. The houses on either side of the steeply climbing road to Wirksworth are possibly the first to have been built on a standardised plan. Many of them still have the original cast-iron window frames, with small panes and ventilation by means of a small sliding unit, hopelessly inadequate to allow exit in case of fire.

The Strutts were less ostentatious, their own houses not being in the style of Willersley Castle. Many workers' houses were built, at Belper, Hopping Hill and Milford. They are in gritstone, and Long Row, Belper (plate, page 144), is probably the oldest and the best example, with quite big gardens. Here too are the streets named after Jedediah Strutt's sons George, Joseph and William, and the Clusters—square blocks of four houses, back-to-back. At Hopping Hill the terraces built up the steep hillside are remarkable, the East and West Terraces being back-to-back. Many of these houses were built between 1793 and 1794. Across the river the curved row of Bank Buildings, and the chapels, are of later date, but they show the same sound architecture which characterises the mills.

Thomas Evans of Darley Abbey and his sons were not behind Arkwright and the Strutts in concern for the welfare of employees. Situated in a quiet backwater off the Derby–Duffield road and only 1 mile from the centre of Derby, Darley Abbey has become a living relic of the early nineteenth century, many of the houses having been pleasantly modernised. Here too are four-square blocks of houses, Four Houses, resembling the Clusters of Belper, but in brick.

Following the practice long-established in the cottage industries, where whole families worked at spinning, knitting and weaving, child labour was employed in the mills. The children were given the rudiments of an education on Sundays, certainly at Cromford and at Belper. In 1802 Joseph Lancaster visited Derby to advocate his system of 'mass education', and this may have influenced Strutt to provide a large schoolroom in the top storey of the rebuilt North Mill in 1804 (figure, page 191). Shortly afterwards he had built large schools 'on the Lancasterian principle' at the bottom of Long Row, Belper, and at Milford; the latter still stands. In 1826 Evans built the fine school to be seen at Darley Abbey, with its pedimented front and a house at each end for the schoolmaster and the schoolmistress.

Evans was followed by Richard Arkwright II, who built a substantial stone school in 1832 at the end of North Street, Cromford, with good houses for the schoolmaster and schoolmistress. The buildings have been slightly modified as regards the windows, but are still adequate for today's classes.

The mill owners in the more sparsely populated areas such as Mellor, Cressbrook and Litton employed numbers of child apprentices, mainly paupers brought in from other districts. Boarding houses were built for them, and although that at Litton has vanished, those at Cressbrook and at Mellor (Bottoms Hall) still stand, the former being fancifully decorated, and the latter being a substantial house in which the children were well fed and well cared for.

Regrettably, the standards of housing established by the Arkwrights, Strutts and Evans were not maintained by the cotton men who came later, especially in Lancashire, and by some of the iron and coal masters of Derbyshire. The county has many examples of industrial housing of all periods over the 170 years from the turn of the eighteenth century to the present day. It would be rewarding to study the factors controlling the fluctuations in the quality of the housing provided in different places, at different times. In one small area, for instance, there is the picturesque village-type settlement of Oakes Row, the straight William Street, Ironville, and the row of 'no-back' houses at Jack's Dale. These last, just over the county boundary, have their privies and their open-air wash-boilers facing the house fronts, across a muddy lane, and there is no obvious reason for the lack of a back door. The railway era had a great influence, especially in Derby, and a graduation in size of house can be traced, from those in Railway Terrace for the engine-drivers to the smaller ones farther from the station.

A town deserving detailed study is Clay Cross. When George Stephenson arrived to drive his tunnel and to establish George Stephenson & Company to exploit the coal and iron existing locally, only a few houses existed. Today, the first houses of 1837–40, rows of cottages to house the tunnellers, are being demolished. Many others will remain occupied for some years yet, such as Tunnel Terrace East, and a little farther afield the houses for the employees of the new company, such as Office Row, Elbow Row and Gaffers Row. This last shows that the outdoor privies were not something to which workers exclusively were condemned, as they were normal to the better-class houses too. They were not usually, however, as obtrusive as those at the two extremely unattractive housing estates at Arkwright Town and at Poolsbrook, which resemble nothing so much as the old barracks rows at Aldershot. They were not built until the last decades of the nineteenth century, and their minimum standard is all the more remarkable as they are contemporary with the enlightened plan of the estate at New Bolsover, only 2 or 3 miles away.

In studying workers' houses, especially those of the early period, it must be realised that most of them were, in their time, an advance on contemporary standards. Indeed, Derbyshire's industrial housing impressed Farey: 'The Cottagers throughout Derbyshire, are much better provided with habitations than they commonly are in the Southern Counties of England, and they generally keep them more neat and in better order, I think.' In referring to the beneficial influence of the 'vast numbers of neat and comfortable Cottages' erected by the Strutts, the Arkwrights and the Oldknows, it is greatly to be regretted that he saw 'no motive for enquiring for Plans or Estimates of Expense'.

CHAPTER SEVEN

Other Industries

EVEN that indefatigable recorder Stephen Glover found it necessary to terminate his detailed account of Derbyshire's industries with the words that they were 'too numerous to particularise'. It is only possible here to indicate briefly a few of the industries whose further investigation would be worthwhile. As is usual in Derbyshire, most of them have left concrete evidence of their past. The fact that they are indeed 'miscellaneous' means that they have been less well recorded than the major industries, but they are potentially no less interesting.

PAPER AND PRINTING

The making of paper from wood and rag pulp dates back to the fifteenth century. Water power was used quite early to break up the rags and wood by stamping, and water was needed in the subsequent processing. It was common therefore for corn mills to do alternate duty as paper mills.

Papermaking in Derbyshire is not well documented. Shorter[1] listed ten mills at the turn of the seventeenth century at places which retained connections with the industry, such as Duffield, Darley Abbey, Hayfield and Masson. According to Hickling[2] there were three paper mills on the Ecclesbourne at Duffield by 1700, and there were others at Peckwash and at Darley Abbey on the Derwent. The Darley Abbey mill was advertised for sale in 1713, and in the 1780s Samuel Evans was running the paper mill, and a lead and a copper mill here on what is now a sports ground on the Darley bank of the Derwent. In 1771 Robert Shore and George White, with lead interests in

Derbyshire and in Cardiganshire, were operating the paper mill at Masson, at what was to become the site of Arkwright's third mill.

In the latter half of the eighteenth century Thomas Tempest acquired the Peckwash Mill at Little Eaton, and in 1805 he had a charter of 1425 renewed; in addition he obtained the right to take up to 800 hp from the river Derwent, and began to erect the first of the extensive buildings. In 1821 he installed a Fourdrinier machine, thus establishing a connection with Bryan Donkin, whose firm was later to establish large works in Chesterfield (see page 134).

In France in 1799 Louis Robert patented his conception of a machine capable of producing paper of great size by continuous operation, but he experienced difficulty in converting it into a practical working proposition. The patent was taken over by Henry and Sealy Fourdrinier, who were the most important stationers and papermakers in Britain in the first decade of the nineteenth century. They engaged the firm of Hall of Deptford to develop the machine, where their 'young and zealous mechanist' Bryan Donkin worked hard on it for three years. Britain held this lead in papermaking for many years, and Donkin was encouraged by his success to launch his own concern in 1803. The firm of Bryan Donkin moved from London to Chesterfield in 1906, where it is today manufacturing equipment for the transmission, distribution and control of gases.

By 1850 Tempest had installed five large waterwheels at the Peckwash Mill. Some of these have left their mark upon the walls of the wheel wells. By this time it was possibly the biggest paper mill in the country. In 1889 it warranted a branch from the main railway line, crossing the river by a wooden bridge. The embankment of this railway still forms a barrier across the river terrace. In 1894 two large steam turbines were installed, in what can be seen as a massively built stone house. The tall chimney was built at the same time, but its smoke was a nuisance to people in the houses on the hillside: about 1905, an injunction was awarded to C. W. Catt, of Outwoods, restraining Tempest & Son Ltd from emitting smoke therefrom. In 1906 the mill ceased to make paper, and the chimney has not smoked since, although many other activities took place there until 1958. In 1854 Tempest, in partnership with Robert Harvey, was making paper at Brook Mill in Little Eaton. This mill is still operated by Dowdings Ltd, who took it over in 1906.

John Ibbotson established a paper mill at Whitehough, in Chapel-en-le-Frith, about the turn of the eighteenth century. This was owned later by the Slacks who still operate a paper mill at Hayfield. The Whitehough mill, which still has interesting weirs, produced news-print in large sizes, for newspapers and notably for the first issue of the *Illustrated London News*. It is reputed to have made the largest single sheet ever, in its time, about 1 acre in extent. Farey and subsequent directories mention a paper mill at Hathersage. This was in a remote spot, at Green's House, North Lees, beneath Stannage Edge; it produced brown paper and wrapping paper for shops. In 1857 it was run by Charles Marsden. One of the Matlock mills, too, produced paper. What was probably a very old paper mill was situated at Alport-by-Youlgreave, upstream of Johnson's corn mill, above the bridge. No trace remains today.

The paper manufactory which succeeded Tempests as one of the largest in the country, the extensive complex of Olive & Partington, at Turnlee, to the south of Glossop, is now being demolished. This enterprise was started in the 1830s, in mills which had formerly been used for cotton manufacture. It was taken over by Ibbotson, then by Castle, Petter & Galpin. In 1872 Edward Partington and William Olive bought the works and it was developed rapidly into a large and important concern, occupying the triangular site between the two main roads. Across the road the Dover Mills, formerly a woollen mill, a fine four-storey building, with dam fed by an underground leat, was incorporated in the enterprise. The works is, however, disappearing under a scheme to rationalise the affairs of the large consortium to which the company now belongs.

Developments in papermaking encouraged invention in printing, cylindrical and power-operated press printing being conceived between 1798 and 1804. Glover reported that Henry Mozley & Sons had introduced printing into Derby on a wholesale scale in 1815, and at the time of his *History and Gazetteer* (1829) nine other firms were in the town, including Bemrose.

Starting modestly in Wirksworth in 1826, then moving in 1827 to a works at the corner of Sadler Gate and Iron Gate, on the site now occupied by Lloyds Bank, Bemrose responded to the Midland Railway Company's demand for timetables and for pasteboard tickets. Moving to a site at the corner of Wellington Place and Midland Place in 1854, the firm expanded rapidly, occupying the Midland Place Works in 1865, while at the same time improving techniques until it achieved a high standard of letterpress, gravure and lithographic work. Bank cheques, high-class coloured calendars, illustrated books, and millions of wrappings for foodstuffs and consumer goods are amongst the present activities. The large complex of buildings near the Midland Railway station, which warranted its private spur from the Derby Canal, has had to be augmented by new premises at Borrowash.

COLOUR GRINDING

The minerals of Derbyshire have provided materials for a colour industry which has persisted over many years. Farey mentioned colour works in Derby and in Bonsall Dale. In Derby Joseph Mason was established as a colour grinder in 1800 and had a works in Derwent Street in 1835. A map of 1819 shows a large paint and colour mill on Markeaton Brook at the site now occupied by the mills of Moore, Eady Ltd. In 1827 this mill was being worked by Benjamin Challinor, and in 1846 it was in the possession of William Ellam, later in partnership with Robert Jones in Morledge. Also in 1827 Ratcliffe & Nutt was operating in Bridge Gate—a possible connection with Adshead, Ratcliffe & Co Ltd of Belper. Robert Pegg & Co was a colour, gypsum, cement and plaster manufacturer with a works in Uttoxeter Old Road and on the Morledge in 1835. Pegg,

Harpur & Co, and Ellam, Jones were both operating at the Morledge in 1857. These two firms eventually merged, and the company occupied a large works where today the Cattle Market stands (see figure, page 100).[3] Leech, Neal & Co had works at Spondon, now seen only as ruins by the side of the Derby–London railway, and in 1838 W. Hawley & Sons set up a colour works at the Upper Mill at Duffield. This is now working on a large scale, and has recently been taken over by Pegg & Ellam Jones Ltd—another example of Derbyshire industrial longevity.

The mills occupied by T. Mitchell in 1854, in Siddals Road, Derby, for his large silk-throwing and gimp and trimming weaving, are now operated by ICI Ltd as a colour works. The Bonsall Dale mills referred to by Farey may be the former lead-smelting works in Via Gellia, now the Via Gellia Colour Co Ltd. This industry has supported an important paint manufactory in Derby, the firm of Masons, founded in 1800.

CHEESE

Before the advent of the railways it was not possible to transport milk any distance from the farms. Accordingly the farmers in the rich dairy-farming districts converted their milk into cheese, which had better keeping properties. In 1730 London received 500 tons of cheese from Derbyshire, Warwickshire, Leicestershire and Staffordshire. Later, the canals played a big part in facilitating the expansion of production. According to White, in 1817 about 2,000 tons were shipped from Derbyshire alone, 8,000 tons in 1841 and 10,000 tons about 1856.

The railways made possible an increasing trade in milk, but efforts were still made to expand the cheese industry. Joseph Harding or Marksbridge in Somerset was the prime mover. He saw the value of standardisation, and he went all over the country lecturing, travelling also in Scandinavia, in the Dominions and in the United States,

N

where cheese-making had already been established on a factory basis in 1851. In 1870 the first cheese factory in England was opened at Longford, in Derbyshire. The simple wooden building carries a commemorative plaque.[4] By 1876 there were ten cheese factories in the county and one is still in operation at Hartington, producing Stilton cheese; the green-striped Derbyshire Sage cheese has recently regained popularity. A disused factory, at Grange Mill, a substantial grit and limestone building erected in 1875, has two foundation stones, laid by the Gells. Another cheese-factory building stands at Elton. These factories are not yet a century old, but they are interesting as the forerunners of today's large establishments for the processing of milk products, such as those at Ashbourne, Hatton and Mickleover.

HAT MAKING AND CLOTHING

'The Factory' at Fritchley, which has not been a works for a long time, is thought to have made hats; and, at Lea, some ruins about to disappear are those of a once-important hat factory. Here a variety of military hats and caps were made, including many for the Crimean War, when William Walker & Son ran the business. At Bradwell, the building where the felt hats worn by lead miners were produced has disappeared only recently. There is a story current locally that 'Bradder hats' provided the model for the soldiers' steel helmets or 'tin hats' of world war I, which were first made in Sheffield.

Involved in the making of military uniforms and livery is the firm of James Smith & Co (Derby) Ltd. This began as a tailoring business in Derby in 1840, and now employs over 600 hands, with a second works in South Wales. During the last war it produced two million garments for the forces. It would be interesting to find out when the firm adopted the methods which are regarded as well-established today by the multiple tailors.

Another type of garment industry, Coopers' corset manufactory of Ashbourne, started extremely modestly in a private house. The first works, 1864, is still visible in Crompton Street, as part of the large complex, the Excelsior Corset Works, which now extends almost to the railway station.

THE 'GAS WORKS'

Although the inflammability of coal gas had been known since the middle of the seventeenth century, it was not until 1792 that William Murdoch, Boulton & Watt's engineer, when working in Redruth, Cornwall, succeeded in lighting his office with it. In 1804 the firm of Philips & Lee was using it to light large cotton mills in Manchester, and three years later the first street in London was lighted, the Gas Light & Coke Company being formed in 1812.

The Strutts built their own gasworks in 1822 at Hopping Hill, near Milford, buying a gasometer from Isaac Horton of West Bromwich. The West Mill and the Round Building were lit by gas in 1824, and Strutts provided eight lamps to light the streets of Belper. Some of the 1,000 cast-iron pipes set down in 1822–3 may still lie below the surface of the streets. Belper's own gasworks was established in 1848, not far away from the Strutts' private works and near the first Belper railway station. Only derelict buildings now remain.

Derby was early in setting up a public gasworks, in Cavendish Street, in 1820; gasometers of early date still stand here. Chesterfield followed in 1826, Wirksworth in 1838, and Glossop in 1845. This last place has buildings of original date, and three gasholders of distinctly different periods. Other works followed, eg Alfreton 1848, Bakewell 1850, Buxton 1851, Long Eaton 1853.

Details regarding the development of techniques and structures in this industry are scarce, and the older works are being rendered obsolete by the grid, piped natural gas, and new methods of gas production. Often they occupy valuable land in towns, so that they must inevitably vanish. The remains of old works still standing, at

Matlock, Buxton, Wirksworth, Eckington and Glossop, to mention
a few, deserve study and documentation. Even small villages had
their gasworks, some of which, as at Smalley Common, have vanished
within the last few years. The demands which these gasworks imposed upon the local engineering industry would also provide a fitting
subject for research. In 1830 John Harrison, lock and clock smith
and engineer of Bridge Gate, Derby, was reported by Glover as
having made for the Nottingham gas company a tank 42 ft diameter,
18 ft 6 in deep, in wrought iron, weighing empty 36 tons, 'undoubtedly the largest ever made in this country'. Comparison with the
gasholder made for the Strutts at Belper only a few years earlier
shows how rapid must have been progress in this as in other contemporary industries.

WATER SUPPLY

The story of domestic and industrial water supply, from wells and
the use of river water, to dams for water power, and reservoirs for
human consumption, remains to be written, and Derbyshire would
be an appropriate area for study. At an early date the works of
Sorocold was providing a piped domestic supply; and even the
smallest streams have been dammed for water power. Long after the
wheels and mills have vanished the dams remain, nowhere more
impressively than along the Mossbeck Brook and at Ashford and
Two Dales.

Derby has an unusual waterworks at Little Eaton. It was established in 1848, to replace the by then inadequate works of Sorocold
on the Derwent, and is remarkable not only for what is, to our present
taste, the ugly Victorian architecture of the buildings, but also because it takes a part of its water from collecting tunnels of perforated
brickwork constructed in the gravels of the Derwent, nearby. This
method is used in only one or two other places in the country.

Finally, as the supplier of water to Nottingham and Leicester as well as Derby, from the great reservoirs of the upper Derwent, the county possesses one of the most striking series of dams and reservoirs in the country. The first of these, the Derwent and Howden dams, were begun in 1905 (see Gazetteer, Bamford).

MISCELLANEOUS

Many other industries have of course left their mark in the county. Centuries ago Derby was noted for its ale, which became known as 'Derby Canary' to indicate its wine-like quality. About twenty years ago over twenty of Derby's inns were still brewing their own beer. Today, only the Friary comes to mind as doing so, the seventeenth-century Seven Stars inn having stopped a few years ago. Malting was once a major industry, and old malthouses and one-time breweries are to be seen at, amongst other places, Little Eaton, Eckington, Bull Bridge and Shardlow.

The building of coaches and wagons was once an important activity. Holmes Brothers (now Sanderson & Holmes Ltd) built coaches of a quality claimed as 'the most celebrated in the kingdom'. Remains of several old 'bump' or candlewick mills can still be found. Tanneries are worthy of further investigation, the firm of W. J. Richardson, now of Sinfin Lane, claiming to be the oldest established concern in the county, having begun in 1624 at Holbrook.

Ropes were once required in great quantities by the lead and coal miners for winding, and by canal boatmen for towing. They were still being made by hand in 1967 with ancient and primitive machinery, in the Peak Cavern, Castleton (see Gazetteer, Castleton).

PART TWO

Gazetteer

DERBYSHIRE is rich in industrial archaeology, and this first survey must perforce be sketchy. It is to be hoped that the inevitable omissions will inspire readers to send in details to the author, so that as complete a list as possible may be prepared for the Council of British Archaeology's survey.

Parish boundaries pay little regard to the routes which are used most frequently by motorists, minor places lying on today's roads often being better known than the parishes to which they belong. Sites have therefore been listed under the best-known place name or under the place of most convenient access, cross-referenced as necessary. Ordnance Survey grid references have had the prefix Sk.27 omitted, as it applies to all places other than a few in the extreme north-west corner of the county, where the full reference has been given.

Unless otherwise stated, all sites have been visited during 1964, 1965, or 1966, but with change and demolition taking place so rapidly, this is no guarantee that they are still as they were. Mention of a site should not be taken as evidence that it is accessible without permission.

ALDERWASLEY

Wire works. 342.523. Established by Johnson Nephew & Co Ltd 1876, on the site of iron-smelting, forge and rolling mills existing in 1764. The works was operated by John & Charles Mold in the early nineteenth century, under lease from Francis Hurt, who in the 1780s built cold-blast iron furnaces, recently demolished. The tail race is in good order. A wharf on the Cromford Canal had access from the works across what was Hurt's private road, later a toll road, now the A6.

Sough. 328.554. A fine stone arch bearing F.H. (Francis Hurt) stands at the tail of Meerbrook Sough in the grounds of Ilkeston & Heanor waterworks (South Derbyshire Water Board). Flow is up to 17,000,000 gallons per day. See page 45. Nearby are traces of Milnes' extensive lead-smelting works, of Meerbrook Mine, of an old brickworks. See WIRKSWORTH, WHATSTANDWELL.

ALFRETON

This is a large urban district including much of industrial importance—coal mining, iron working and, today, textiles.

Forge and rolling mills. 443.513. Established by the Butterley Company in 1807, the Codnor Park works was producing wrought iron by the Cort process until July 1965, being demolished in 1966. The puddling process was filmed in 1964. A long masonry bank formerly surmounted by three 40 ft-high blast furnaces still stands. These were using hot blast in 1835, within two years of the Neilson patent. See page 59.

Industrial housing. Interesting examples at Ironville, eg King William Street. At Jack's Dale is a row of 'no-back' cottages with privies and wash boilers across a muddy lane facing the houses; at Riddings the Furnace Row housing is interesting.

Ironworks. The Alfreton Ironworks at Riddings, established by Ed Oakes, 1792, is now part of Stanton Staveley Ltd. Cast-iron pipes are the principal product. Picturesque domestic settlements are to be seen, eg Oakes Row, 435.529, some with slate roofs, some pantiled.

Petroleum industry. This began here after the occurrence of a flow of thick black oil in the New Deeps Mine, 435.524, in 1847. James Oakes informed his brother-in-law Lord Playfair, whose friend James Young refined the crude oil, in 1848 producing 30 tons per month. Later Young removed his refinery to the shale-oil area of Bathgate in Scotland. The mine closed in 1885, and nothing remains but waste heaps covered with large trees.

ALPORT HEIGHT

Stone guidepost. 304.516. Dated 1710, indicates 'Ashborne', Derby, Wirksworth.

ALPORT-BY-YOULGREAVE

Corn mill. 223.646. Picturesque mill with imposing weir on Lathkill 'where, by the mill is a pretty cascade' (Hon John Byng, 1790). Re-equipped late nineteenth century. Operated until recently by S. & E. Johnson Ltd for cattle, pig and poultry foods. A mill recorded here 1159–60.

Paper mill (? fulling mill *temp* Richard II) was above bridge on left bank. In use 1761 by Hall, in 1816 by Francis Kenworthy, now disappeared.

Lead-smelting works. 223.648. Ruins of large installation: an extensive complex of horizontal and rising flues, condensing chambers and chimneys. It was prospering in the 1850s, in the hands of the Barker family. Three parallel flues, now roofless, climb straight up the hillside to a 15 ft-square stone condenser formerly with two chimneys, only one remaining. See page 41.

Lead mines. Formerly a productive area. The Alport Mining Co in 1847 was worth £100,000. Noteworthy for hydraulic engines at local mines, including:

1. Wheel Rake, 229.648. Horizontal entrance intact by river Lathkill above Hawley's Bridge.

2. Crash Purse Shaft, on branch of Hillcarr Sough, 216.638, indicated by disturbed ground at the northerly end of Hollow Dam, was one of those, probably the first, at which Richard Trevithick's water-pressure engine of 1803 was installed. See page 101.

3. Guy Shaft, on Hillcarr Sough, 220.638, marked by a derelict coe and a stagnant pool, was the location of the famous Guy engine (376 hp) proposed by John Taylor, and improved by Darlington. See page 101. In 1963 Mr Johnson and his son were washing spoil

for fluorspar in a rocking-jigger by Luhrig & Co, London. This machine is still there.

4. Pynet Nest Shaft, close to Crash Purse, had a hydraulic engine built at the Milton Ironworks, 1845.

5. Broadmeadow Shaft, 223.643, visible as a mound from the lane from Alport to Priest Hill, was the site of the Blyth engine, built by William Fairbairn, 1836.

Many other shafts are still to be seen in this locality, eg Mawstone Mine, Blyth Mine, and they are being systematically explored by mining and caving societies. See YOULGREAVE.

AMBERGATE

This settlement owes its growth to George Stephenson. After following the Derwent valley up from Derby he planned the route of the North Midland Railway along the Amber valley to Chesterfield and thence to Rotherham, 1837–40. The line to Rowsley was opened 4 June 1849.

Ambergate and nearby Bull Bridge (qv) form a small area packed with industrial archaeological interest.

Railway station. 349.516. Platform and goods shed of original station of 1840. At south end of Toadmoor Tunnel stands elegant stone station rebuilt 1863 from material and somewhat in style of Thompson's original design, illustrated in Adams' *Gem of the Peak,* 1845, but of twinned V-form instead of single simple block. It was moved to present site when line from Derby was made continuous with line to Buxton. Present station, mainly of wood, 1876, is of rare triangular form, and straddles A610 road to Ripley. Until 1939 a train ran from Manchester to Nottingham using the northern platform, demolished in 1965. Interesting 'furniture' in cast iron can be seen—footbridge, drinking fountain, lamp posts, platform number plates, rustic seats etc.

Railway tunnel. 349.514. Toadmoor Tunnel, built by the NMR, 1839. Of unusual flat-arched section, designed to resist an early landslip of the steep hill of shale. Strengthened for part of its length at the southern end by steel hoops; 129 yd long.

Lime works. 353.519. Until mid-1966, Clay Cross lime works had an impressive curved bank of twenty kilns built by George Stephenson 1837–41, to burn limestone from Crich Quarries, using slack coal from Clay Cross Colliery. Started as eight kilns, increased to twenty in October 1841; see page 81. Stephenson also bought a narrow strip of land for access to the main railway line by a spur line and turntable, still visible. A 12 hp horizontal steam engine installed by him in 1841 for hoisting, in use until 1946, is preserved at Sheffield University.

Stephenson's incline. 352.524. A gravity incline from Crich tunnel to lime kilns, 1842. Two full wagons descending raised two empties up the incline, 1 in $5\frac{1}{2}/7$, with a passing loop half way. Large horizontal cable drum at summit was dismantled 1957 and rails taken to Talyllyn Railway. The line crossed the Cromford Canal by a wooden bridge reinforced by a warren girder, now badly buckled. Surviving wagons had cast-iron wheels with holes, not spokes, of the pattern used on the much earlier Fritchley tramroad. The upper terminus is now the site of the Tramway Museum Society's museum, at Crich (qv).

Hotel. 349.517. The Hurt Arms Hotel was built 1874 to replace the old Thatched House Tavern adjacent to original Thompson station, which had served railway travellers since 1840. Just north of the Hurt Arms was the turnpike, in use until the 1880–90s.

Railway bridges and embankment wall. 348.512. The bridges over the road and river, and the impressive gritstone walling on the east side of the A6 road, were constructed when the railroad was doubled in 1930–1, with a grant under a scheme to relieve unemployment. At the same time the tunnel at 347.508 was opened out into the present cutting.

Bridge. 347.515. Ha'penny Bridge, built 1792 by Francis Hurt for the use of his estate, to replace a ferry. Charged $\frac{1}{2}$d toll. Two main arches, five flood arches each end, spanning the Derwent and tail race from 'The Forge' (now the Wire Works) at Alderwasley; 18 ft wide roadway. The tollhouse ('Ferry House') at east end of bridge was demolished 1964.

Sawmill. 352.517. A square brick chimney marks the site of a steam sawmill built in 1856 by John Linacre.
See ALDERWASLEY, BULL BRIDGE.

ASHBOURNE

In 1334 the inventory of the Privy Wardrobe of the Tower of London itemised 'XX parvos cultellos de Assheborne', and the town contains much of industrial interest which is not apparent to through travellers.

Fishing-tackle maker. Foster Brothers have made fishing tackle since 1763. Remains of an original workshop to be seen at rear. Elegant Georgian frontage c 1820.

Clockmakers. W. Haycock & Son Ltd, North Leys Lane, is the surviving firm of the clockmaking industry of the town, which was begun by Joseph Harlow in 1740. Haycocks continued the Harlow business in 1826. The firm makes small gears for computers, meters, etc, and occasionally clocks, by modern machinery, but uses when appropriate a gear-cutting machine bought from Whitehurst of Derby (c 1855) which closely resembles the illustration in Emerson's book, 1758. See page 122 and plate, page 89.

Samuel Barton & Sons Ltd, North Leys Lane, also makes small gears for meters, computers, etc. This firm was founded by an apprentice of Harlow, 1844. Gears as fine as 264 DP are made by cutters shaped by hand. The shop contains old tools, eg bow drills.

Cotton mill. 159.455. The cotton-spinning mill established by Arkwright in 1781, and later worked by the Cooper family, related by marriage to the Strutts, was bought by M. Bond of Alrewas, 1864, pulled down and rebuilt in 1866 as the present Alrewas Mills, a building architecturally interesting of its time. Workers' cottages are now derelict but the manager's house is still occupied. Tapes and narrow fabric are produced in many materials, including glass filament.

Stay works, Compton Street. 181.463. The company was formed in 1855 by Richard Cooper and Charles Smith. The works, an unpretentious three-storey brick building still standing, was established in 1864, and has now expanded to 110,000 sq ft, with branches in other towns. In 1898 the firm introduced a revolutionary breakdown of the corset-making process into separate operations.

Railway station. 176.463. A small neat brick and stone building with twin-gabled bays and doublet-grouped Romanesque windows, erected 1852 as the terminal of the North Staffordshire Railway Co; replaced by a larger wooden station when the LNWR line was driven to Buxton in 1899. Lines closed 1954, rails removed 1964. Stations now derelict.

Railway engine house and goods shed. 176.462. A rectangular building of pleasing design in near-white sandstone found locally. Cast-iron windows with translucent panes, probably of early rough-cast rolled glass. Becoming derelict rapidly since closure of the line.

Gas lamp. 182.467. An ornate cast-iron lamp post, made 1864 and erected by the Ashbourne Gas Company at the foot of Buxton Road, was removed to its present site in Cockayne Avenue for safety. The names of Gas Company directors and an iron founder in Derby are cast on the base but are illegible.

Water pump. A highly decorated cast-iron water pump which was formerly in the Market Place still stands in Bellevue Road, with its handle missing. The original intention to preserve it should be supported.

Wheelwright's equipment. An old saw pit, old mortising machine and fello-ing jig still exist at sawmills in Bellevue Road.

ASHFORD-IN-THE-WATER

Marble works. 190.965. Being operated in 1748 by Henry Watson, who achieved a wide reputation for making ornaments in fluorspar and local 'black marble', this large water-powered works has been demolished by the North Derbyshire Water Board; see page 85. Polishing floor was of 80 sq ft. Only the weirs remain.

Coomb mill. Comb Mill, just downstream of the marble works, was operated by Rowland Holmes in the 1850s. Ruins and old pictures

indicate a single-storey stone building, 10 ft × 18 ft inside, with
large windows. Remains of 3 in-diameter wrought-iron shaft, and
cast-iron four-armed bosses for wooden spokes 6½ in × 3 in, indicate
an undershot paddle wheel about 9 ft diameter and 30 in wide. Inside
the building is a cast-iron flywheel 6 ft diameter, rim 4 in × 4 in,
six spokes.

Sawmill. 182.697. Formerly a bone mill. Two buildings, and two
waterwheels with cast-iron spokes, 13 ft × 4 ft 5 in, and 12 ft × 4 ft.
Adjacent building houses a wheel 8 ft × 4 ft 6 in, formerly used for
pumping.

ASHOVER

Once an important lead-mining centre, a Liberty outside the King's
Field. No traces remain of the important lead smelter at Kelstedge,
est 1702. Gregory Mine, at 345.618, is marked by waste heaps known
locally as White Hillocks, a square gritstone chimney, and the stagnant pools of the run-in shafts. Between 1758 and 1806 this highly
productive mine yielded an average of 511 tons of ore per annum,
and shareholders had a clear profit of £100,000 after spending
£23,000 on prospecting for a new vein. Several steam engines were
installed and worked by the Thompson family. See page 110. The
shaft north-west of Ravensnest House was 120 yd deep, that at New
Engine, west of Cocking Tor, 365 yd deep.

In the vicinity are Francis Thompson's Hill House, 1782; Overton
Hall, occupied by Sir Joseph Banks, 1780s; mine gear at Mill Town;
traces of Clay Cross to Ashover Light Railway, 1925–50.

BAKEWELL

Pack-horse bridge. 215.690. Over the Wye between Lumford Mill
and Victoria Mill.

Cotton mill. 213.691. Lumford Mill is now the Dujardin-Planté
battery works. On the site of Arkwright's third spinning mill, built
1777, which employed 300–400 hands, mostly women and children.
In 1789 it was being run by his son, and in 1829 by Robert and

Peter Arkwright. Burnt down in 1868. Later run by Lomas & Tun-
still, 150 hands, 6,000 mule spindles, 5,750 throstle spindles, 100
looms. Taken over by the DP Battery Company 1898. Until 1955
the mill was powered by two waterwheels fed from the beautiful
Ashford Dam. See page 102.

Gasworks. Adjacent to Battery Works, established 1850.

Corn mill. 217.685. Victoria Mill is a three-storey gritstone building, probably mid-nineteenth century, with trap doors for hoisting
sacks of corn in upper storey. Was the Duke of Rutland's mill, later
sold to Bayleys. In 1960 had a wheel 16 ft diameter × 14 ft wide.

See ASHFORD.

BAMFORD

Cotton mill. 205.834. A large spinning and doubling mill on the
Derwent, erected by Christopher Kirk c 1780 on 'a construction very
different from that at Cromford'. The original mill probably had four
storeys, seven bays; destroyed by fire 24 October 1791, it was rebuilt
by H. C. Moore, the present weir being constructed with rocks from
Bamford Edge and with yielding weir boards 4 ft high. The mill
now has thirteen bays and a large house for the manager. Waterwheel
of 30 ft diameter × 22 ft wide. In 1857 S. M. Moore & Son had a
60 hp steam engine and employed 230 hands. The mill was sold in
1885 to Hamilton Cash of Mansfield and in 1902 to Fine Spinners
& Doublers Ltd. In July 1965 it was closed down by Courtaulds
when employing 120 people. Fortunately much is being preserved
by Carbolite Ltd, now using the mill for the manufacture of electric
furnaces. The wheel was replaced by turbines by Gilbert Gilkes &
Gordon, removed from Edale Mill, 75 hp, driving a dynamo by
McClure & Whitfield, Stockport.

Principal motive power was a magnificent tandem-compound
piston-valve steam engine, 1907, by John Musgrave & Sons Ltd,
Globe Iron Works, Bolton, 140 psi, 102 rpm. The mahogany-lined
flywheel-pulley had a square-rope drive to all floors. See page 118.
The engine house has decorative cast-iron beams and a spiral cast-

o

iron staircase. There are five Lancashire boilers. The well-equipped millwrights' shop has an old radial drill by Jones & Shipman, Leicester, a 22 ft-long lathe by Leckenby Benton & Co, Halifax, and a shaper by J. Buckton & Co, Leeds. Formerly the mill generated its own gas from shale oil from Scotland—Patent Paraffin Gas Lighting Co Ltd, Glasgow. Doubling machines were by Burroughes, 1897, and gassing machines by Arundel & Co, Stockport, 1904. The clock tower is reputed to have the only four-faced clock in Derbyshire. This complex was a fine example of a self-contained unit kept in excellent order until its closure. It deserves the sympathetic treatment now likely.

Reservoirs. Bamford is the nearest village to the magnificent chain of reservoirs which extends up the Derwent Valley. First to be made were the Howden and the Derwent reservoirs, by the construction of two great masonry dams. Howden Dam, 170.924, begun 1905 and finished 1912, is 500 ft between the towers, a total width of 1,080 ft, and 117 ft high above the river bed. Derwent Dam, 173.897, finished in 1916, is 600 ft between towers, 1,110 ft wide and 114 ft high. Both dams are 178 ft thick at the base, tapering to 10 ft at the crest. Stone from the Grindleford quarries was used, over 1,250,000 tons being transported by a special railway running up from Bamford. To meet the increasing demand for water the Ladybower Dam, 198.855, was built to impound the waters of the Ashop as well as the Derwent. It was opened in 1945, the rising waters submerging the village of Derwent, 185.885, of which traces may be seen when the water level is low. The capacity of the reservoirs is: Howden, 1,980,000,000 gallons; Derwent, 2,120,000,000 gallons; Ladybower, 6,300,000,000 gallons. During the periods of dam construction the upper Derwent Valley must have been reminiscent of the railway age. Over 1,000 people, workers and their families, were housed in a temporary village at Birchinlee, 167.914.

BARGATE

Silk factory. 363.462. So indicated on OS map, a red-brick annexe to a dwelling house, with typical long windows.

BARLOW

Ironworks. 351.754. Barlow Brook is the location of an ancient ironworks. Iron forge 1578; new furnace 1605, probably shut down by the end of the seventeenth century. In 1951 Dr R. A. Mott reported that the ruins of a charcoal iron furnace were visible, but these were bulldozed away when slag heaps were removed. Ancient slag heaps remain, and a rank of beehive coke ovens, and ruins of later blast furnaces whose provenance has not been traced.

BELPER

The town is especially important in the history of the textile industry, but its earlier connection with the iron industry has been maintained.

Nailers' shops. A number of these small stone buildings still exist throughout the town, as in Joseph Street. The industry was first recorded in 1313, and was active in 1700 with a large export trade to the American colonies; it died out in the middle of the nineteenth century.

Cotton mills. 345.480. A very early cotton mill was worked by two horses in Paddlewell Yard, c 1730, by Joseph Robinson, spinning raw cotton brought from Manchester by pack horse. The impressive complex of the Strutts' spinning mills (now English Sewing Ltd), by Belper Bridge, is of historic importance. Note the fine weir and flood controls; North Mill, 1804 (figure, page 192), is the oldest remaining, and is scheduled for preservation. West Mill, 1798, South Mill, 1812, and Round Mill, 1813, were demolished during the past few years. Gun embrasures were built in the bridge over the road, for defence against the Luddites. See page 190.

Industrial housing. 348.478. The Strutt family was mindful of the welfare of its employees. See especially Long Row (plate, page 144), where to celebrate George IV's coronation a tea-drinking was given by the Strutts on 13 July 1821, followed by ale-drinking and music on the lawn of Bridge Hill House. The ale at Belper cost £16 19s 6d, and at Milford £12 0s 7d. See also the streets named after Jedediah's sons (page 201) and 'The Clusters'.

Hosiery warehouses and factories. 346.473. Ward, Brettle & Ward had a warehouse on the site of Dalton's oil refinery on the east side of Chapel Street. On the dissolution of the company Brettle built a factory on the west side, a red-brick building with large stilted iron windows, 1834, and a dignified gritstone frontage with horse-mounting steps. John Ward built the gritstone building to the south, retaining the warehouse on the Dalton site. See page 178.

Gasworks. 347.464. Erected 1848, ruins by site of old railway station. The Strutts had their own gasworks, lighting the West Mill and the Round Building on 5 October 1824, and Belper having eight street gas lamps in autumn 1825. Gasometer was 49 ft diameter × 12 ft deep, weighed 9 tons, by Isaac Horton. See also page 212.

Holly House Farm. 332.481. The home of Samuel Slater, who left Strutts and founded the cotton industry in the United States, 1789. The house is now in ruins in the grounds of Holly House.

Strutts' farms. At Wyver, 340.495, at Black Brook, 337.478 (Cross roads Farm), and at Moscow Farm, Milford, 346.445; they provided fresh vegetables and milk to the workers at cost. Built c 1811–12. Dignified stone buildings, in excellent repair.

Turnpike road. Private road built by Strutt, Hurt and Arkwright from Belper northwards. Opened 1 July 1818 as a turnpike as far as Cromford. Now the A6.

Railway. An impressive cutting runs right through the town, over a mile long, lined with masonry walls of good workmanship, with ten bridges. This was one of the popular sights when the railway was opened, 1840. The original station (replaced by the present station in 1877) was at the west side of the main road where the railway crosses it south of the town, 347.467. The platform and goods shed remain, and a 10 ton crane by John Stevenson, Canal Foundry, Preston.

Ironworks. 349.465. The Eagle Iron Works of Smedley Brothers Ltd was established in 1855, a manufactory of edge-runner grinding mills, steam engines, boilers and heavy castings. An unusual pictorial advertisement is painted in white on the brick exterior; elegant ironwork in the works yard. Adjacent is Park Foundry, established by one of the Smedley brothers who left the partnership. Deteriorated style shown by Victorian entrance arch, 1899. Now Radiation Parkray.

Inn. At the foot of Bridge Hill, the Talbot Inn was 'baiting place' for higglers and their teams who carted coal from Kilbourne, Marehay and Ripley collieries to Ashbourne until the North Staffordshire Railway from Uttoxeter brought coal from Staffordshire, 1852. Forty or fifty carts could be seen there at one time.

BIRCHOVER

Once an important lead-mining area, with the famous Yatestoop mine at 245.615; see page 113. Important gritstone quarries at 242.623.

BOLSOVER

Formerly noted for spurs and buckles of wrought iron, 'steeled' by carburising the surface to take a high polish.

Corn mill. 478.707. Picturesque, in magnesian limestone, with pantile roof; had a steam engine 1845. Dilapidated.

Quarries. Stone for the Houses of Parliament came initially from adjacent quarries, but later from Yorkshire.

Industrial housing. 465.703. At New Bolsover. With gardens, trees and village green, built 1890s, this contrasts favourably with that at Poolsbrook and at Arkwright Town of similar date.

See STAVELEY, DUCKMANTON.

Railway tunnel. 2,629 yd. Of Lancashire, Derbyshire & East Coast Railway, driven 1897, closed 1951 through mining subsidence.

BONSALL

An ancient lead-mining centre.

Smelting works. 278.573. The Via Gellia smelting works now belongs to the Via Gellia Colour Co Ltd. Ruins of lead-condensing flues go steeply up the hillside. Others, higher up the hill, follow a zigzag plan, originally 52 in wide, 30 in high, trenched 6 ft into the ground, terminating in rectangular condensing chambers, now ruined. Incorrectly marked blue as for a stream on the 2½ in OS map (see page 41). Worked by Saxelby & Co in 1808, by Alfred Alsop in 1852.

Textile waste mill. 284.514. Cromford Garnetters (Via Gellia) Ltd, a Hollins subsidiary, occupies the site bought by Hollins in 1890. Formerly a lead-smelting, red-lead and rolling mill, which also crunched bones for fertiliser (Farey). Bought by Thomas Elce 1807 and rebuilt as a cotton mill. A building of this date, with hipped roof, stands by the picturesque dam. Other mills downstream are milling gangue minerals—baryte, fluorspar and calcite. Upstream towards Bonsall are ruins of several water mills.

See CROMFORD.

BORROWASH

Cotton mill. 415.341. Built about 1800 on the Derwent, on the site of ancient corn mills. Owned by Earl of Harrington, later by John E. Swindell. Operated by John Towle & Co, 1857, cotton doublers with 250 hands. First storey is stone, two upper storeys are brick, with brick tower. Later a flock mill. Now tenanted by EMEB and threatened with demolition.

BRADWELL

Lead-miners' hats. The factory which made 'Bradder hats' for lead miners has now vanished; it was at 171.816.

Lead-smelting works. Overgrown mounds on the east side of the road south of the village are remains of a lead-smelting works. Underground flues were blown by a fan driven by a water turbine.

Ruined lime kilns are of late nineteenth-century date.

See BROUGH.

BRASSINGTON

Railway bridge. 225.557. At Longcliffe, the Cromford & High Peak Railway crosses the road by a cast-iron bridge, 1825, with timber decking, 19 ft span. See page 61.

BRETBY

Collieries. Opened at Stanhope Bretby in 1855 by Earl of Chester-field.

Brickworks. At Newhall, near Bretby, 280.215, the Bretby Brick & Stoneware Co Ltd has extensive clay pits and bottle kilns.

National Coal Board. Central Engineering Establishment, opened 1954.

BROUGH

Cotton mill. 182.824. A lace-thread doubling mill in 1846, this was operated by Pearson & Co. In 1860 Robert How Ashton enlarged it and converted it into a lead-smelting works. Today, Cooke & Stevenson Ltd makes springs, flap valves, diaphragms, etc, from heat-treated steel strip and wire. The attractive old stone buildings have been surrounded by trees and flower beds.

BUGSWORTH (BUXWORTH)

Canal wharves. 020.822. Extensive basins and wharves (dried up) of the Peak Forest Canal, tracks of horse-drawn tramroads, ruins of lime kilns, and the large Crist Quarry (gritstone), indicate a once busy and important site. Now being studied in detail by Mr Brian Lamb.

Mill. 017.823. Britannia Mill, multi-ridged, stone-built, 'F. S. Cawthorne, 1851'. The wood-framed windows are unusual for the date. Now Britannia Wire Works Ltd and Meredith Spring Seat Co Ltd. According to Mr Brian Lamb, this replaced a much earlier cotton-spinning mill.

BULL BRIDGE

With adjacent Ambergate this forms an area of great industrial interest, with many remains, largely determined by its position as the 'port' on the Cromford Canal for the rich lime quarries of Crich.

Lime works. 359.524. Ruins of five kilns erected about 1780, probably by Ed Banks & Co. Taken over by Butterley Co and operated until about 1930, burning lime from Hilts Quarry, Crich.

Tramroad. The Crich or Fritchley Tramroad, c 1780, brought stone from Hilts Quarry, Crich, and an older one adjacent, to the Bull Bridge kilns. Many stone sleepers remain, some incorporated in steps at Lime Grange. Tunnels, cast-iron bridge (360.523), long high embankment walls. Brunton's Walking Locomotive was used on this line; see page 154. A derelict smithy near Lime Grange was for wagon, horse, and line maintenance.

Jaggers' hostel. Stables and sleeping quarters for pack-horses and jaggers (the pack-horse train teamsters) in grounds of Lime Grange, identified by present owner, Mr Gerald Crane.

Gunpowder magazine. In garden of Lime Grange—a small round stone house, possibly of 1827 date. Now a dovecot.

Canal. On the Cromford Canal, the wharf and limestone-wagon tipple location at end of the Fritchley tramroad is now partly filled in. A swing horse-bridge survives. The famous aqueduct of shale freestone, 200 yd long, 50 ft high, over lane, river Amber, North Midland Railway and A610 was built in 1793 by William Jessop. The destruction of the aqueduct at the main road crossing, to remove a traffic bottle-neck, is imminent, but the stretch of canal from Cromford to Ambergate, with fine views, will be preserved as a public amenity.

The embankment was pierced by George Stephenson for his railway, 1839. See page 163 and plate, page 108. Canal tunnel is 93 yd long. A barge-building yard was situated opposite Stevenson's Dyeworks.

Railway water tank. 359.522. Was formerly filled from canal.

Railway embankment wall. An impressive long ashlar wall on the Ambergate–Ripley road, possibly of 1839 date.

Malt House. 357.523. A low stone building below the canal bridge, working 1843. Some perforated bricks of the drying floor have been found. Now used as stores by Stevensons (Dyers) Ltd.

Corn mill. Vestiges can be seen at the lower car park of Stevenson's Dye-works.

Dyeworks. 358.522. Stevensons (Dyers) Ltd established in Belper 1893, moved here 1908. The 'Dylan' shrink-proofing process for wool was invented here, 1954. Today the works dyes large numbers of nylon stockings from Derbyshire hosiery firms.

BUXTON

Railway. 059.737. The stations of the Midland Railway, 1863, and the LNW Railway, 1899, stood as twins until the semicircular end wall of the Midland station was removed. The LNW station has an impressive roof with fine cast-iron columns. At the east end of the town, 064.735, is a high viaduct. Another crosses Dukes Drive, 066.724. Railway employees' houses are concentrated in Hogshaw.

Lime works. Extensive lime works mar the countryside south-west and north of the town. Huge heaps of lime ash at Harpur Hill and Dove Holes have accumulated since before 1789. At Dove Holes is a very large lime kiln of Perseverance Works, 091.768. Harpur Hill works of Buxton Lime Firms was one of the biggest in the country. It had a Hoffman kiln from 1872 to 1947, with a 170 ft chimney, reputedly the largest kiln of its type.

Railway. The Cromford & High Peak Railway passes west of the town. Tunnel, now closed, at 032.738. 'Barrel Bridge', 077.692, is, unusually, in engineering blue brick.

Railway tunnel. At Dove Holes is the longest tunnel on the Midland Railway, 2,984 yd, begun in 1865 and driven with difficulty through hard limestone.

CALVER

Cotton mill. 245.744. An impressive sight from south-west, with seven storeys and large central pediment at front, staircase turrets at rear. Present structure replaced original of 1785 in 1803–4. See plate, page 143. Exterior is preserved. Wheel house had two wheels of 22 ft diameter, each developing 80 hp. The flow of water indicates the latent power of the Derwent. Very fully documented by Mackenzie and Parker (see note 12, Chapter Five).

School house. 245.747. Incorporated in farm, with bell.

Soughs. At 245.744, the tail of Calver Sough has been incorporated into a garden rockery. At 239.741, the unusually decorative stone arch at the tail of Red Rake Sough is marked 'N.L. October 27 1851'. Century-old dressing floor nearby. The outlet arch of Brightside Sough is just visible at 245.743, in a water trough in the village street.

Engine house. 238.745. The ruins of Calver engine house are hidden by trees.

See STONEY MIDDLETON.

CASTLETON

Renowned for three centuries for its caverns and its Blue John fluorspar ornaments, now rare, although a small local industry survives. The steep track through Winnats Pass was originally the route of the turnpike road from Sheffield to Manchester.

Ropewalk. 150.827. In 1967 Mr H. Marrison (83 years old) was still making brewery ropes, clothes-line and sash cord in Peak Cavern. He remembered thirty people working there, where his family had made ropes for 200 years. The simple blacksmithed machinery is of great but unknown age. A ropewalk has been here for at least 400 years.

Lead mine. 135.835. No confirmation has been found for the oft-repeated surmise that Odin Mine's name indicates Saxon working. A good example of a horse-operated ore-crusher lies on the site, below the road to Mam Tor, probably of early nineteenth-century date. Cast-iron track, 18 ft OD, 15 in wide × 2 in thick, formed of eight segments, with strap plates and 1 in diameter studs cast in. A 70 in diameter wheel of coarse grit with an iron tyre 75 in OD, 12 in wide, 1¾ in thick, which is now detached but was formerly fixed by wedges in lateral grooves in the rim of the wheel. The wheel has been mounted on a wooden beam passing through a 12 in-square central hole (see plate, page 17).

Cotton operatives' route. 137.845. Castleton girls working at Edale spinning mill walked 2 miles via Hollins Cross, seen on skyline, a climb of 650 ft, to a height of 1,250 ft.

CHAPEL-EN-LE-FRITH

Cotton mill. 061.807. New Hyde Mill, a two-storey building, with a low square stone chimney, vestiges of water power. In 1846 it had a 24 hp steam engine, and John Ashton was spinning cotton. In 1857 a 30 hp engine was at work, and the mill was operated by the Misses Alice, Nancy and Sarah Ann Bennett. Later a wadding mill, it is now a shirt factory.

Foundry. 065.809. Town End Foundry is a large stone building with lantern roof, now a crane manufactory.

Ferodo Works. 057.812. A huge modern works started as a small garden shed at Combs, 1897; moved to Sovereign Mill (1777) in 1903, on site of works car park. Frood's shed is preserved. See page 103.

Tramroad. Some stretches of the Peak Forest Tramroad track can be followed. A portion is used as a track for motor-car braking tests by Ferodo Ltd.

Railway tunnel. 088.837. The Midland's Cowburn Tunnel, driven 1894, is noteworthy as having only one single air shaft in length of 3,702 yd: a square stone structure, 22 ft × 20 ft high, visible for many miles, eg from Castleton Road, A625. Nearly 800 ft deep.

Colour works. 022.799. Now a barn, Cadster Mill was a paint and colour works with a 16 hp steam engine, operated by Charles Robe in 1857. Opposite are traces of a small coal mine, now completely grassed over.

Paper mills. 045.822. Glover reports John Ibbotson producing at

Whitehough Paper Mills one single sheet of paper 1,000 ft long and 7 ft wide, c 1827. Taken over by Slacks of Hayfield (see page 207). Purchased by J. J. Hadfield as nucleus of the present large works. Old dams and weirs remain.

Reservoir. 037.796. Combs Reservoir was constructed by Outram as a feeder for the Peak Forest Canal, 1794–1800. It is crowded at weekends with sailing craft.

CHESTERFIELD

The second town in the county, but although surrounded by rich lead, coal and iron fields, Chesterfield was slow to become industrialised. It may have preferred to retain its status as a market, established in the days of intensive lead mining. Pilkington in 1789 reported it as 'very flourishing', and mentioned especially the new Griffin Foundry of Smiths and the potteries, but according to Davies, 1811, it was 'not a place of great trade, nor is there any considerable manufacture carried on in it'. Nevertheless it supported a wide variety of small industries, which have been poorly recorded and which offer scope for research. Its larger enterprises though few in number have achieved considerable prominence in their time. The disturbed ground at Hady, near Central station, is evidence of early iron mining. The oldest industrial building is perhaps Walton Corn Mill, 365.706, ascribed by Pevsner to the thirteenth century. Other points of interest are:

Silk mill. 382.708. Markham Road. The Old Silk Mill, a four-storey brick building of seven bays, has an older smaller portion; see page 185. The mill seems to have lain idle for long periods but in 1846 George and Charles Tucker were silk throwsters (see page 185). Demolished 1967.

Hipper Street. 384.708. A row of old buildings here may have housed the companies concerned with ginghams and checks, and candlewicks, in the 1850s. More research is needed before the buildings disappear.

Potteries. 383.733. Pilkington, 1789, reported three coarse-earthenware potteries. Today the largest is Pearsons, at Whittington Moor, making stone bottles, refractory bricks etc. Established in 1810, this firm is still using bottle kilns.

Foundry. Robinson & Sons Ltd, makers of surgical bandages (*Pill Boxes and Bandages* is the title of a book describing firm's history), occupy the large works located on the Hipper at the west end of the town, on the site of the Griffin Foundry; and some of the original buildings, with cast-iron stanchions, are still in use. The Griffin Foundry of Ebenezer Smith & Co was established 1775. (See page 128.) It played a big part in the activities of Francis Thompson of Ashover, casting the cylinder of the engine built by him and now preserved in the Science Museum. Mr Philip Robinson has written the history of this enterprise, and has restored the Cannon Mill, 376.709, with its plaque showing the cannon and cannon-balls produced during the Napoleonic Wars, and dated 1816 (see page 129). Outlets of wheel races still exist, one leat having an unusual triangular overflow.

Canal. Brindley's early Chesterfield Canal of 1777 has been little used in the county since the collapse of the Norwood Tunnel in 1908. Its dried-up course can be traced, with locks, bridges and dilapidated warehouses, from Chesterfield through Killamarsh.

Railway stations. The Midland station is much altered, but a dark stone building bearing the NMR crest may have been the executive engineers' office, erected 1837. The GC, later LNW (Central) station, 1892, near the Midland station, is of simple wooden construction, bridging the now-disused Chesterfield loop line. West Park station, terminus of the Lincoln branch of the LNER, 1896–7, is now a paint stores.

Railway viaduct. The two-tier Horns Bridge, now partially demolished, was a most unusual viaduct, 1897, 700 ft long, 63 ft high, with a variety of steel and brick spans over the Midland Railway, GC, Chesterfield loop, and A617 road.

George Stephenson. Settled in Chesterfield, at Tapton House, 393.722. The Borough Library contains many Stephenson relics.

Later engineering. In 1855 the Sheepbridge Coal & Iron Company was founded. Its blast furnaces are now gone, and the site is partly occupied by Sheepbridge Engineering Ltd, and its subsidiary Sheepbridge Stokes Ltd. In 1889 Markhams took over the foundry and engine-building firm of Olivers (established 1860). Bryan Donkin, founded in 1803, came to Chesterfield from the south in 1903. The Chesterfield Tube Company was established in 1906.

CHINLEY—see CHAPEL-EN-LE-FRITH

CHURCH GRESLEY—see SWADLINCOTE

CLAY CROSS

Owes its present size to George Stephenson who realised the importance of the large deposits of good coking coal discovered when driving the railway tunnel; he founded George Stephenson & Company, 1837, which became the Clay Cross Company about ten years later.

Early tramroad. 420.665. Joseph Butler's Lings–Ankerbold railway of 1788 is traceable along the track of the 'zig-zag railway'. The incline down to the vicinity of Clay Cross station is prominent, 405.655. Stone sleepers are found occasionally, typically 20 in × 23 in × 10 in, two holes 1½ in diameter, 4 in deep, 7 in centres. Rail 3½ in wide, recessed into sleeper 1 in deep.

The route of Butler's line from Old Tupton to the early coke iron furnace at Wingerworth, 1780, can also be traced, but is threatened by new housing developments, 385.656.

Railway tunnel. 1,784 yd of difficult driving through wet shale. Oval section; the northern entrance arch is embellished with castellated circular towers to resemble a Moorish gateway, similar to that at Red Hill (plate, page 125). Ugly brick airshafts.

Railway station. 402.652. An interesting engine shed is now used as a store for surplus museum relics. It has twinned round-arched cast-iron windows. Sand hole at foot of chimney. Iron lamp-oil tank has tap handle fitted with padlock.

William Howe. For thirty years head engineer to Clay Cross Company, he died 17 January 1879 and is buried in Clay Cross churchyard. In the church a stained-glass window, erected by his friends, carries a diagram of his link motion.

Industrial housing. With its extremely rapid expansion during the 1840s, the town has interesting examples of housing, from the row near the south end of the tunnel, built for railway navvies, now being demolished, to Office Row and Gaffers Row for the staff of the Clay Cross Company. West Tunnel Terrace on the main road has vanished, but East Tunnel Terrace, which faced it, is still occupied. See page 203.

CODNOR PARK—see ALFRETON

COMBS—see CHAPEL-EN-LE-FRITH

CRESSBROOK

Cotton mill. 173.728. Twelve bays, with four-bay pediment, four storeys, a hipped roof, a cupola, and cast-iron columns but wooden beams. Built by William Newton 1815 to replace the smaller mill of Arkwright, 1779, remains of which stand at the western end, by the river. Behind is the apprentices' house, with false end in Gothic style; 200–300 orphans were employed and were well treated. McConnel Brothers had the mill from 1835 to 1857. Dams at 174.726 and 171.728. Imposing cliff-girt dam is upstream, behind mill. Mill out of use 1965–6.

CRICH

In the village is a three-storied stockinger's house. A high stone viaduct by George Stephenson on the Crich tramroad, 1842, can be seen, and close by is Hilts Quarry, used for over a century by the Butterley Company to supply its lime kilns at Bull Bridge.

Quarry. Situated below the imposing cliff, Crich Quarry was worked by George Stephenson for the twenty lime kilns at Ambergate, 1840 (see page 81). Quarrying ceased 1962, and the Tramway Museum Society is now putting the site to effective use, the cliff reflecting the nostalgic clangour of electric streetcars which run on the recently laid track.

Lead mines. Old End Mine, 346.558, has a stone beam-engine house, in ruins. A large oval winding shaft and a 30 in climbing shaft with stemple holes are filled in. The mine was 912 ft deep; 20 in square wooden beams and huge dressed stones for engine beds are to be seen. At Wakebridge Mine, 339.558, the engine house has lost its upper storey, but its original use for a beam engine is obvious because of the 5 ft-thick end wall for beam support. The two shafts are protected by iron fencing. The engine shaft was 660 ft deep, worked by E. M. Wass & Co, 1857. The engine was removed to either Bonsall or Portaway Mine. Traces of slag are to be found amongst the debris of the old crushing floor. There was smelting here in 1580. Three old dams are visible.

CROMFORD

A place of great importance in the history of the Industrial Revolution, and an early example of planned industrial development—the first water-powered textile mill, with Arkwright's well-laid out village, and the Cromford Canal, little changed since the late eighteenth century.

Soughs. Longhead Sough, very early, driven 1629–36, had an outlet at 294.566, recently filled in. The Cromford Sough, driven in 1673–82 to unwater the Dove Gang Mines, has its outlet still visible behind a shop in Wirksworth Road at 297.569. Water from this sough was used by Robert Shore of Snitterton and George White of Winster to drive a paper mill, while earlier a corn mill stood nearer to the Derwent (see below).

Arkwright's Mill. 298.569. In 1771 Richard Arkwright bought the corn mill, with a lease of land through which ran Cromford Sough and Bonsall Brook. In 1772 he erected his cotton mill, partly on the site of the corn mill, and worked it by a wheel turned by the water

of the brook and the sough, brought across the road in a wooden
launder (replaced 1821 by a cast-iron one). Water emerges from the
mill by a culvert under the roadway, into an open channel and thence
to the canal. The original mill was six storeys high, but it has lost
its two upper storeys, probably in the fire of 1890. A second mill
was built in 1777, adjacent to the first one, later almost completely
destroyed by fire.

In 1789 Arkwright employed 800 people, but this establishment
ceased work as a cotton mill in 1846. There is now a colour-grinding
mill, with the original water works still traceable; see page 187.

In 1811 the adjoining paper mill had forty employees, producing
writing paper from old rope and rags. Two men produced ten reams
per day.

Masson Mill. 294.573. Erected by Arkwright, 1783. The original
six-storey brick building is at the north end of the present complex.
Its frontage, with deep red-coloured walls and semicircular windows
outlined in white, is well known to travellers to Matlock. Less well
known are the impressive water works and the unusual down-curved
weir at the rear of the buildings, seen only, by permission, from the
left bank of the river. In 1846, 320 were employed. This mill was
sold to the English Sewing Cotton Co in 1897.

Industrial housing. Arkwright had built North Street by 1777—two
rows of substantial gritstone houses of three storeys, with attics com-
municating along the whole length, used as stocking-knitting rooms
by the families of employees. There are still water faucets in the
street, and a spring thought to be connected with Longhead Sough.
The houses on the Wirksworth road, with standardised rectangular
cast-iron windows, are of slightly later date. The school at the end
of North Street was built 1832, along with houses for the master
and mistress; the external windows have been changed but much
of the interior is original. Arkwright's own house, Willersley Castle,
was built 1788 onwards. William Thomas of London was the architect, but it was burnt out before it was finished, and was rebuilt
immediately, being finished after Arkwright's death in 1792. It occu-

P

pies the space where a large rock stood, which cost £3,000 to remove. The church, 300.571, was built by Arkwright, on the site of an earlier lead-smelting mill, and was consecrated in June 1797. The Greyhound Inn was built in 1788, and the right to hold a market here was granted in 1790. The handsome frontage of the inn is practically unchanged.

Corn mill. This, just above the lowest dam on Bonsall Brook, has been restored by Mr David Tye to drive a generator for his motorcycle business. The wheel is of 14 ft 7 in diameter, overshot, 30 rpm, with water conveyed through two iron pipes.

Canal. The Cromford Canal was opened 1793 by William Jessop, engineer. Wharves and warehouses to be seen at 299.570. Fed by Cromford Sough, the canal joined the Erewash Canal and so established connections with Derby and the Trent. The canal is carried over the Derwent by the Wigwell Aqueduct (316.556), 200 yd long, 30 ft high, built by William Jessop 1792–3. The arch over the river is of 80 ft span, with flanking cattle creeps. At the south end a short branch, Nightingale's Canal, 2½ furlongs, ran to Lea Mills. Now derelict, it was driven in 1802 by Peter Nightingale. At 319.325 a cast-iron aqueduct carries the canal over the Midland Railway, by Leawood Tunnel, 315 yd. Probably of 1849 date, the trough is of six or seven sections bolted together, with masonry supporting arch. Cast-iron railings and wrought-iron ties.

Cromford pumping engine, to raise water from the Derwent to the canal, is at the north end of Wigwell Aqueduct. It is a well-proportioned gritstone building, its chimney having an unusually wide parapet (because of valley downdraughts?). The present engine was built by Graham & Co, Milton Ironworks, 1849, and is a Watt-type single-acting beam engine, 5 ft bore × 8 ft stroke. The beam comprises two cast-iron plates 30 ft long, 4 in thick, spaced by bolts and distance sleeves. Journal of 13 in diameter. Octagonal cast-iron end pins. Parallel motion, and spherical end-sockets of piston- and pump-rods (5 in diameter) are machined all over. Pump is of displacement type, 3½ tons per stroke, 7–10 strokes per minute. Water hp = 71, hence steam hp of, say, 90. Outlet pipe to canal 4 ft 6 in diameter. In the engine house is a contemporary Bourdon pressure gauge. Steam at 40 psi was supplied by two Midland Railway locomotive boilers, replacing two earlier ones. Pump last ran 1948. The canal was abandoned under the LMS Railway Canals Act of 1944, and British Waterways took it over under the Transport Act of 1947.

Railway. Wharves on the canal at the foot of the Cromford & High Peak Railway are at 314.557. Workshops, engine shed, inspection pit, fish-bellied rails, forge with smiths' tools, signals of 1825, are all to be seen. West of the A6 road bridge a catch pit was installed in 1888, after runaway wagons had been flung over the road, the canal and the Midland Railway (see page 156). This installation may be preserved (plates, pages 107, 108).

Railway station. 303.574. The Midland Railway station is a gem of its type, French style, with matching villa for the station master, c 1860. The architect was probably G. H. Stokes, son-in-law of Paxton.

DALE ABBEY

Windmill. 438.398. The Cat & Fiddle post mill, of 1788 or earlier, had a stone round-house added in 1844. It is the last surviving working mill in Derbyshire, preserved by Stanton Ironworks Ltd (plate, page 71).

DARLEY ABBEY

An interesting backwater which preserves much of the atmosphere created by the Evans family.

Cotton mill. 354.386. On the east bank of the Derwent, built by Walter Evans. Original mill was burnt down 1788, but rebuilding started immediately, producing the well-known Boars Head sewing cotton. The fine weir still operates water turbines.

Industrial housing. There are picturesque streets of late eighteenth-century houses and 'Four Houses', similar to the Clusters of Belper but in brick; also a large schoolhouse and houses for schoolmaster and schoolmistress.

Tollbridge. Over the Derwent, and still maintained by the company.

Paper mill. Of 1713, on the Darley side of the river; only traces remain of the intake from the dam, by the present sports field.

DARLEY DALE

Lead mine. 260.625. Great waste heaps are left from Mill Close Mine, with remains of engine houses, eg Warren Carr Shaft, which housed the very large Cornish engine 'Jumbo', and Watts Shaft, c 1860.

Soughs. At 263.623 is the outlet of Yatestoop Sough, driven approximately 2½ miles to Yatestoop and Portaway Mines by Birchover and Winster, begun 1743. It took twenty-one years to build and cost £30,000. The stone-arched outlet of Hill Carr Sough, which is led to the Derwent by a short channel, is visible at 260.636 (plate, page 18). Begun 1766, it was driven under Stanton Moor, about 700 ft below the surface, for about 4 miles to Alport and Youlgreave; the twenty-one years' driving cost £50,000. The measured flow in January 1880 was 15,000 gpm.

Flax-spinning mill. 286.629. Two Dales Mill is on the site of a small cotton-spinning mill of 400 spindles working in 1785. A large three-storey gritstone building, it was erected probably 1826 by the Dakeyne family; see page 102. It is now occupied by Johnsons for cattle and poultry foods. The beautiful dams in the steeply rising narrow valley—Fairy Dam, Potter Dam—provided a 96 ft head of water for the water-pressure engine of 1827.

DENBY

Pottery. 393.475. Joseph Bourne moved here from Belper in 1808, but the pottery has been entirely modernised. Old clay pits at the rear are still used.

Earthenware works. 381.470. W. H. & J. Slater Ltd. The works was originally established about 1827 by Wm Drury-Lowe. Of the thirteen beehive kilns of up to 20 ft diameter, three are already converted to oil firing. The works has been operated by Slaters since

1874, making sanitary ware, sinks, chimney pots, etc. A Lancashire boiler by Galloways Ltd of Manchester, 1897, is of 6 ft 5 in diameter, with 2 in × 30 in flues. Large clay pits and adits.

Ironworks. The only surviving relic of the Denby Iron & Coal Co, established 1860 by Dawes of Elsecar, is a tall brick building about 70 ft high × 27 ft × 30 ft, possibly for a hoist for loading blast furnaces.

Tramroad. The track of a spur of the Little Eaton Tramroad passes Slater's Works to Belper Wharf, passing the site of Bassett Pit, 378.472, which used Newcomen engines until 1885.

DERBY

The county town has been the scene of pioneer industrial developments from those of Sorocold and Cotchett to those of Rolls-Royce. A remarkably large number of relics can still be seen, although current slum-clearance and road improvements threaten many. Much has been described in detail in the main text, and visible indications are merely listed here for ease of identification and reference, along the lines of the chapter headings already used.

Iron and steel. Examples of early cast-iron items are:

Mile posts by Harrison, eg in King Street; see page 64 and plate, page 36.

Windows, as in St John's Church, Bridge Street, built 1827; see plate, page 36. Fine examples of Handyside's single castings are in the windows of Fletcher's Mill, and Eastwood & Swinglers Foundry (both in Osmaston Road), the latter now a bus depot; others are in the Carriage & Wagon Works, London Road, and in many of the locomotive workshops.

Canal aqueduct, probably by Butterley for Outram's Derby Canal, 1795, under the road bridge in Cattle Market Road; see pages 61, 149, and plate, page 107.

Bridges. Handyside's finely decorated bridge for the GN Railway, 1878, is in Friargate; see page 64. His other, carrying the same line over the Derwent at Little Chester, 353.372, is of entirely different construction; see page 131. Carrying Cattle Market Road over the now-derelict Derby Canal is an unusual bridge, built in 1861 by Thomas Swingler, Victoria Foundry, Derby; see page 66.

Industry. Robert Bakewell's shop where he made his ironwork was reputedly in Oakes Yard in St Peter's Street. Decrepit old buildings were removed recently, but the gates to the yard (see page 184) may have been made by him early in the eighteenth century. He built the Silk Mill gates (see page 183) and those now at the Cathedral.

Eastwood and Frost had ironworks at 25 & 27 Morledge in 1852. Swingler erected the Cattle Market Bridge in 1861, and about 1864 Eastwood & Swingler was formed, occupying works on Osmaston Road and in Cotton Lane, on the site now occupied by the Rolls-Royce foundry and by the adjacent bus depot. Note the elegant cast-iron stilted windows and cast-iron lintel beams in this latter building.

James Haywood was working the Phoenix Foundry in 1846. The building, in Stuart Street, which is a good example of its time, brick-built with iron windows, three storeys and fourteen bays, has been subsequently an engineering works and a textile mill—in 1916 being occupied by the Derby Weaving Co Ltd, for the manufacture of small-wares and trimming, and later by Ernest Turner Ltd.

Leys Malleable Castings Co Ltd was established by Francis Ley in 1874 alongside the railway by the Osmaston Road bridge; see page 133. What are probably some of the original buildings remain.

Stone and Pottery

Marble works. Brown's works (see page 86), established 1802, can be seen in part behind Batterby & Heffords in King Street.

China works. The site of the original Crown Derby pottery is commemorated by a plaque at the beginning of Nottingham Road. W. G. Larcombe's small works of 1848 is now an antique shop in King Street. The kilns at the rear have recently been removed; see page 91.

The Royal Crown Derby Porcelain Co Ltd is now in Osmaston Road, in what was the workhouse of 1832; see page 91.

Engineering

Water power. The three great weirs on the Derwent, and those on Markeaton Brook, are of early but unknown date and would repay further investigation. See page 100.

Clockmaking. The old gabled shop now occupied in part by Haslams in Irongate was Whitehurst's works in the early eighteenth century. John Smith & Co Ltd, which succeeded Whitehurst in 1856, has a works in Queen Street, with old buildings at the rear; see page 121.

Industry. The site of the works of John and James Fox in City Road (see page 129) was taken over by Haslams in 1870, which was taken over in turn by Newton Bros Ltd (est 1899) in 1928. In 1860 George Fletcher started up his Masson Works in Litchurch Lane to specialise in the making of steam engines and sugar-processing machinery. The original buildings, with their customary tall cast-iron windows, are best seen from the train to Birmingham (see page 132). Fletcher & Stewart still makes sugar machinery here.

Communications

Canal. The Derby Canal is derelict and the Long Bridge which was used by horses to cross the Derwent just above the lowest weir was demolished in 1959. Underneath the Cattle Market Bridge is the iron aqueduct (1795) which carried the canal over the Cut; see page 149. Nearby are interesting wharf buildings, especially a warehouse dated 1820 which indicates the site of once important wharves.

Railways. The Midland station, the Midland Hotel, and adjacent buildings are basically of 1840–1. Although the front of the station was much altered in 1892, traces can be seen of Francis Thompson's original design, and there is still one bay of the three which comprised the 1,050 ft-long single platform; see page 160.

The locomotive workshops were built largely in 1841. An idea of their extent can be gained from Platform 6 of the station, but the original round house is hidden behind later buildings; see page 160. Mathew Kirtley, the locomotive superintendent from 1844 until 1873, lived at 22 Railway Terrace. This house has now gone, but others, presumably similar, remain. Nearby, in Canal Street, is a small building with semicircular cast-iron windows which was the hospital for the railway horses.

The Carriage and Wagon Works, probably the biggest workshops in their time, extend from Osmaston Road to London Road; see page 167.

The bridge over the Derwent north of the station, built 1839, and a popular subject for illustrations in contemporary publications, is best seen from the left bank of the river, where until recently was the extensive 'Signal Works'. The section of the road which was lowered by Stephenson to provide head room under his bridge for the North Midland Railway (1840) still exists—and floods—along the Nottingham Road.

Textiles

Silk mills. Lombe's Old Silk Mill disappeared finally in 1910, but the present structure gives a good impression of the larger of the two original buildings (plate, page 143), though with three storeys of roughly the height of the former five. The foundation arches, in stone, are probably original, and those at the north end of the building may be those of Cotchett's mill of 1702. The bridge over the leat is in its original form, and the tower is changed only in having fewer, larger, windows than the original one. The bridge gates have been restored and stand by the Borough Library in Wardwick. See page 183.

Silk mills of later date still stand in Green Lane (pre 1802, of five storeys, now the Greenhill Furniture Stores), and in Devonshire Street (a small four-storey building with cast-iron windows and a square chimney). See page 185.

Small-ware and tape mills. Originally a silk mill, Rykneld Mills, Bridge Street, now weaving narrow fabrics, is an imposing sight, with its seven-storey and five-storey blocks, with many small-paned cast-iron windows. Probably dating from 1823 (see page 199), these buildings have circular-section cast-iron columns, iron beams and brick-arched flooring, in the Strutt tradition. Banks's premises in Bridge Street, five storeys, eleven bays, with hipped roof, is also striking.

A number of smaller mills, originally thought to have been for silk throwing, are in Agard Street; see page 185. T. Mitchell's very large silk gimp and trimming factory, in Siddals Road and backing on to the Derby Canal, is now an ICI colour works. Derby, Ashbourne and Wirksworth together form the country's largest unit of tape production. The industry comprises a number of scattered factories, located in Wirksworth (see page 199) and in Abbey Ward, Derby. The Derby factories date in the main from the third quarter of the nineteenth century, and present an interesting phase in industrial development. See particularly the works of J. Bonas & Son Ltd, in Lynton Street—two blocks of three storeys and nine bays each, with a short square chimney; Garford, Lilley & Brother, Agard Street mills; C. Lilley & Sons, Boyer Street; H. Lilley & Sons, Parliament Street, with a mill in Olive Street dated 1900, and older ones behind; Rykneld Mills, Bridge Street, and G. H. Wheatcroft & Co Ltd at Markeaton Mills, which was formerly a colour works.

Bath Street Mills, built about 1848, is an early example of a tenement factory, three storeys and thirty-two bays and a typical central pediment. In Osmaston Road, Fletcher's Mill is a fine building of the late nineteenth century, with a T-plan form, and with exceptionally tall cast-iron windows, slightly arched. Originally making lace, it is now tenanted by a number of different businesses.

Indications of what may have been stockingers' houses are seen on an old half-timbered house in Bridge Street, in boarded-over windows at the corner of King Street and St Helens Street, and in Cheapside, at the building which has been occupied for 120 years by John Wallace the ironmonger.

Other industries

Paper and printing. At Midland Place is the large printing works of Bemrose & Sons Ltd, established here in 1854. The works had its own spur of the Derby Canal, of which the dried-up course can be traced under Siddals Road.

Clothing. The works of James Smith & Co (Derby) Ltd, in Drewry Lane, is unpretentious, but has played an important part in the supply of uniforms for the armed forces, the railways, the police. It was established here in 1856, as the firm expanded beyond the capacity of its premises in Cheapside, Bridge Street and Siddals Road.

Brewing. A fine Malthouse is in Manchester Street, and now houses a chemical manufactory. The Meeting House in St Michaels Lane, where John Wesley preached in 1765, was later a malthouse.

DETHICK, LEA AND HOLLOWAY

Mills. 318.565. Lea Mills is a large complex of textile-mill buildings producing the well-known Smedley merino-wool garments. Note the private footpath for employees.

Hat factory. 323.563. Now in ruins. William Walker & Sons made shakoes here for the army in the Crimean War, and 'fine hats for gentlemen' in Farey's time.

Lead-smelting works. 319.568. All that remains of the famous smelting works originally of Nightingale, then Alsop, then Wass, is a large spoil heap. The buildings were finally demolished 1948; see page 42.

DINTING—see GLOSSOP

DOVE HOLES—see BUXTON

DRAYCOTT

Lace factory. 442.332. With forty machines, 1842, behind the Toton Lace Co Ltd. Chimney dated 1850.

Tenement factory. 445.333. Victoria Mill is one of the largest lace factories in the world. Completed 16 September 1907, it bears the name Jardine on the clock. It is fifty-eight bays long, five bays deep, four storeys high; see page 198.

DRONFIELD

A prosperous iron town in the eighteenth century, and with a grammar school dating from 1575, Dronfield's long industrial history needs to be written. The works of Edward Lucas & Son Ltd, established 1790, makers of malleable iron castings, is on the main Sheffield road. Along Collywhite Lane are many engineering and iron works, some obviously of late eighteenth/early nineteenth century. In the grounds of the local Council Offices are fine cast-iron vases, typical of the products of Haywoods and Handysides of Derby in the 1840s. An interesting road bridge over the railway north of the station has cast-iron arched beams.

DUCKMANTON

Ironworks. The important Adelphi Ironworks of Ebenezer Smith & Sons, 1775–1836, has largely disappeared under the present railway complex. One remaining building, 428.715, partially converted into dwellings, of two storeys, with some cast-iron windows, may have been the joiners' (? pattern makers') shop.

Industrial housing. 180.467. Arkwright Town, an industrial housing estate, was built in the 1890s by the Arkwright Colliery Co. The parallel rows of back-to-back brick houses have no gardens.

DUFFIELD

Stockinger's house. The stone-built No 2 Holloway Road has a single-storey annexe which housed some of the last stocking frames in the village; working in the 1920s.

Railway. The NMR station is said to be by Thompson, the style being less pretentious than in others by him. The Wirksworth branch line starts here, opened 1 October 1867; it was originally projected to be continued to Rowsley in the event of the Midland Railway losing the lease of the Matlock line from the LNWR. Employees' cottages nearby had an ale house at the south end of the row. The present station-master's house was an office with weighing machine.

George Stephenson's 'Sighting Tower', 346.452, is a tall square gritstone building, 47 ft high × 21 ft square, on Chevin Hill on the line of the tunnel (plate, page 53). Roofless since fire in 1939. Chevin tunnel, 1839, has 'rich and handsome arched frontings', 346.455.

Colour mill. 335.438. The oldest part was built 1788, probably on the site of a Domesday mill. Taken over by W. Hawley & Son for colour grinding, when the firm, founded 1838, moved from Buxton; now owned by Pegg & Ellam Jones Ltd.

Canal dam. 353.425. Remains of reservoir above Peckwash Mill, used as feeder for Derby Canal at Little Eaton, by underground conduit, 1796.

ECKINGTON

Coal mining. The main road crosses over a disused mineral line called the 'Penny Engine Railway', from coal mines on Mossbeck Brook to the MR at Renishaw Lane End station. The Mossbeck Brook valley was rich in coal and iron and has been busy from the sixteenth century. Seldom Seen coal mine, 422.800, has an exceptionally large brick beam-engine house, about 75 ft to eaves, 40 ft × 20 ft, in ruins, the shaft headings having cross-ventilation tunnels (plate, page 53). Other coal-mine ruins are at 427.797, where a pillar-type beam winding engine was apparently replaced at some time by a horizontal engine.

Ironworking. 422.800. Traces of beehive furnaces, and ancient slag heaps are to be seen. Slitting Mill Farm, at Renishaw, 436.769, is probably the site of George Sitwell's mill of 1652. No traces remain of the ironworks of the Sitwell family, of 400 years ago, or of the foundry worked by Thomas Appleby in 1782 at the site (448.779) of the extensive basic and foundry pig-iron works of Appleby & Co Ltd.

Scythe and sickle industry. Along Mossbeck Brook were eight or nine dams in less than 2 miles, operating grinderies and forges for the scythe and sickle industry, which in the early 1800s had a large export trade. Birley Hay, Never Fear Dam, Bowercinder Hill, Fields Wheel Dam, Carlton Wheel, all broken, can be identified. Their history has been recorded in an excellent booklet by 'W.F.', entitled *Ridgeway Village* (1950). Ridgeway was an important centre for this industry: at 404.822 is the former reaping-hook factory of Websters, now derelict; at 403.822 is the Phoenix Works, now Garden Suppliers Ltd, makers of the 'Scythette'. In the yard is the inscription T. & J. Hutton, 1822. Behind is the old 'tedding shop', where teeth were put on to sickles. On the west side of the road down to Ford is the old factory of Taylors, which made handles for scythes, reaping hooks and knives. At 402.807, opposite Sloade Lane, are the buildings of Fox's factory. At Birley Hay, Ford (398.804) are the ruins of a once-important sickle factory, possibly pre-1757, with two large dams. Three small grindstones now serve as stepping-stones in the brook.

Corn mill. 429.798. Park Mill has vanished, save for weirs and water channels. A massive wooden wheel-axle lying on the site is eight-sided, 22 in across, with rectangular holes for inset teeth, $2\frac{1}{2}$ in × 1 in in two staggered rows $7\frac{1}{2}$ in apart.

EDALE

Lace-thread spinning mill. 134.854. A long low three-storey gritstone building with square chimney, possibly of 1795 date, when James Harrison, Robert Blackwell and Joseph Fletcher of Manchester enlarged the mill of 1790. Said to resemble Arkwright's mill at Cressbrook, it was in the Christie family 1816, 1846, 1857. Steam and water power 27 hp. Worked by Marslands in 1933. Future uncertain.

Railway tunnel. Large and unusual hummocks in an area striking enough for its landslips are spoil heaps from Cowburn Tunnel, whose eastern portal is at 104.844.

EGGINGTON

Canal. The Trent & Mersey Grand Trunk Canal crosses the Dove by Brindley's long aqueduct at Monks Bridge (268.269): twenty-three arches in blue brick, 13 ft high and 12–15 ft span. Total length 10 furlongs. Built in 1777.

ELDON

Leadworking. 120.815. A large lead-ore crushing circle, with track and wheel—unusually in limestone. Track 22 ft OD. Wheel 58 in OD, 14 in wide, 12 in square hole in centre, eight grooves for wedging the iron tyre, which is missing. Stump of centre post remains, about 10 in diameter.

ELTON

Cheese factory. 209.616. A small cheese factory, in stone, presumably post-1870.

Quarry. 218.615. Prince's Bury Cliff quarry exported grindstones to Alexandria for glass bevelling, to Sheffield for file grinding, and to the USA.

EYAM

Lead mines. The chimneys of Ladywash Mine, being worked for fluorspar and barytes, and of the disused New Engine Mine, 224.773, are visible for many miles. Glebe Mines Ltd has a modern spar-grinding mill here.

Turnpike road. 218.778. Sir William Road has a short disused stretch evocative of the eighteenth-century turnpike.

Small factories. Eyam has a number of small factory buildings. A two-storey building opposite the church has an interesting iron crane; once a boot and shoe factory operated by James & John Bromley, 1857, it now belongs to Wests; the firm also has a boot and shoe factory in the low building, formerly a school, on the bend of the road. At the west end of the village, G. Robinson & Co (Eyam) Ltd make boots and shoes in what was Froggatt's silk-weaving establishment, 1857. This may be the cotton-spinning mill built by Daintry & Ryle of Macclesfield in 1808, housing 100 workers.

Eyam has been well documented by Mr Clarence Daniel.

FENNY BENTLEY—see TISSINGTON

FINDERN

At 311.297 were docks and warehouses on the Trent & Mersey Canal. Here is an interesting long road bridge over canal, railway, and the new railway taking coal to the new power station, which embodies techniques of different ages, from cast-iron beams to reinforced concrete.

FORD—see ECKINGTON

FRITCHLEY

Factory. 357.536. Converted to dwelling houses over a century ago, this is probably late eighteenth century and is known as the Hat Factory.

Tramroad. Fritchley Tramroad passes under the road here, and there is an engine shed of c 1790. There is a tunnel at 358.530 and stone sleepers can be seen. See BULL BRIDGE.

Bobbin factory. 359.532. Remains of Wightman's Bobbin Factory, dam and mill tail can be seen. Built about 1795, the factory was burnt out in 1885 and the firm moved to Bull Bridge. Forty men and boys were employed.

Corn mill. 361.527. A fine gritstone building, now incorporated into a farm.

GLOSSOP

In 1784 there was only one textile mill in Glossop. In c 1809, according to Farey, there were fifty-four cotton spinning mills in this north-west area, out of 109 for the county as a whole. By 1851 the population of Glossop was 28,625, with sixty mills. In 1810 Howard Town had only two families. It grew into New Glossop, which has changed little in appearance since the 1840s. This rapid industrial development is well described in *Small Town Politics* by A. H. Birch

(OUP, 1959), but there remains considerable scope for the industrial archaeologist.

Woollen mill. 040.924. Gnathole Mill at Chunal survived until 1857 at least, but has been converted by the present owner into dwelling houses.

Cotton mills. 029.942. The great complex of Wrens Nest was begun 1815 by Mathew Ellison, agent to Lord Howard. In 1827 his relative Francis Sumner joined him and began the great expansion of the works, in 1948 producing Sumnadale fabrics. The early dam and old buildings stand at the western end of very large spinning mills and weaving sheds of later dates. A Catholic firm, it brought many girls from Ireland to work in the mills. In 1830 John Wood moved from the Water Mill into Howard Town (ie the Glossop of today), initiating the other major establishment which later specialised in Two Cities fabrics. More recently, Wood Brothers Ltd is spinning cotton and rayon. Many new industries have been introduced, eg in crepe rubber, plastic products and animal foods, which occupy parts of these large factories. Old mills at 045.948 were demolished 1965, when the Cowbrook Mill, 049.940, was also in ruins.

At Hadfield, the Waterside Mills, 019.967, were established by the Winterbottom family. The two large gritstone buildings, with large and more recent additions, are today occupied by the Maconachie pickle-manufacturing concern. At Padfield, 032.960, is a smaller building, in ruinous condition, once a cotton-spinning mill.

Calico printworks. 015.947. Here is the extensive works established by Edmund Potter in 1825, on a long narrow plan determined by the topography.

Paper mills. 033.931. Stood until 1965. Started possibly by Thomas Ibbotson, 1837, this became the very large establishment of Olive & Partington. A flued chimney across the A6016 road, high on the western hillside, is a landmark. Nearby, at 035.927, the Dove mill, with a picturesque dam fed by an underground leat, was a wool-carding and fur-blowing establishment, operated by Joseph Bennett in 1857. Later it too became a paper mill.

Ropeworks. 007.931. In 1833 the Holroyd Rope Works was established in Charlesworth. It still claims to make the best fishing cordage in the world, and is operated by the fifth generation of the Jackson family, who founded it.

Railway station. 035.942. This was built 1845 by Lord Howard, at the terminus of a 1 mile spur from the Sheffield & Manchester Railway at Dinting; in gritstone, it has a large stone lion over the main entrance.

Railway viaduct. 018.945. The Dinting Vale Viaduct, of the Sheffield & Manchester Railway, struck 'the beholder with astonishment at the daring of the present generation' in 1845. Originally it had sixteen arches, supported by the existing tall ashlar columns, but today it has been greatly reinforced, which detracts from its appearance.

Gasworks. 031.942. Built 1845, with a dignified office building, it has had three successive generations of gasholders.

Market Hall in High Street West, opened 1845, is a fine example of its period and deserves preservation.

GLUTTON BRIDGE

At 084.666 is a small cheese factory, still working.

GRANGE MILL

Corn mill. 243.577. Pre-1767. It is hardly recognisable as a mill, but the dam, fed by a long leat, still fills in wet weather.

Cheese factory. At the crossroads a two-storey limestone building, with gritstone groins. Its two foundation stones were laid by Teresa C. Chandos Pole Gell, and H. Chandos Pole Gell, of Hopton Hall, on 20 March 1875.

GREAT HUCKLOW

Leadworking. 178.778. Hucklow Players' Theatre occupies a converted lead-smelting mill. Many remains of lead mines are traceable locally. High Rake and Deep Rake on Longstone Edge have vanished recently under the attack of bulldozers for the local fluorspar enter-

Q

prise of Laporte Industries Ltd. At Windmill, on High Rake, 164.777, are traces of an engine house and an unusually large winding shaft, 18 ft × 16 ft 6 in. A gritstone block 8 ft × 4 ft × 20 in, weight about 4 tons, has been part of the engine foundation. Remains of a large crushing circle, 24 ft OD, wheel 64 in OD, 7½ in wide at rim, 11 in at boss, with square hole 1 ft 3 in, and six grooves across the rim for wedging the iron tyre, which is missing. From here, looking westwards, Tideslow Rake gives a fine impression of early workings, dating from the sixteenth century (plate, page 17). Another crushing circle is along this rake at Wash-house Bottom, 161.778.

GRINDLEFORD BRIDGE

Once a busy grindstone-quarrying centre. Stoke Quarry shut down in 1965.

Railway tunnel. 252.788. Dore & Totley Tunnel, Midland Railway, opened 1893, emerges close by the station, with a handsome stone arch.

HACKENTHORPE

Scythe and sickle industry. A centre of scythe and sickle-making for over two centuries. An important survivor is the Severquick Works of Thomas Staniforth & Co Ltd, 418.833. The oldest building dates from 1743. In 1857 Staniforth's was the biggest sickle-maker (30,000 dozen pa) in the United Kingdom. Today old and new techniques are used as appropriate. The sickle grinders work seated on swinging 'horses' (plate, page 35). See ECKINGTON.

HADFIELD—see GLOSSOP

HARTHILL

Leadworking. Many traces of old lead mines and lime kilns survive. A boundary stone (230.644) bearing A for Arkwright and N for Nightingale marks the junction of the lead-mining properties of these two families. At 231.640 are a derelict lead-ore washer, a lime kiln, and nearby a ruined watermill, very old. At Hawley's Bridge, 231.647, is Wheel Rake lead mine, an adit still open by the side of the Lathkill. An old lime kiln is beside the Winster road.

HARTINGTON

Cheese factory. 126.604. Nuttall's Stilton cheese factory was originally established as a co-operative venture by the Duke of Devonshire, c 1900.

HARTSHORNE

Screw mill. 325.214. The water-powered screw mill, 1776, belonged in 1827 to Smith, Port, Wood & Co. It made woodscrews of all sizes from $\frac{1}{2}$ oz the gross to 30 lb the gross. Derelict. See page 124.

HASSOP

Railway station. 217.705. The elegant railway station (1863–7) was built to serve the Duke of Devonshire, who wished to have his own station, as the Duke of Rutland used Bakewell station $1\frac{1}{2}$ miles away. Is now Fearn's depot for agricultural machinery.

HATHERSAGE

Needlemaking. Christopher Schutz is said to have introduced wire-drawing here, c 1560, to make sieves for washing lead ore. Needles were made from 1570–80 until the late 1800s. Robert & David Cook brought their needle business here from Redditch in 1811. Their factory (229.815) was part of the buildings now comprising Thompson's Garage—an imposing stone frontage, clock over entrance arch, remains of older workshops behind.

Wire drawing. The Atlas Works of Crocker & Sons, who drew steel wire for Huntsman, was on the site of the present Catholic School. Samuel Fox began his umbrella-frame wire drawing 'at the bottom of the village', before moving to Stocksbridge.

Button factory. 235.818. Dale Mill is an old button factory, in gritstone, three storeys high, seven bays wide, square stone chimney;

now occupied by light-engineering firms. Upstream is a dam, and another factory stood on the site of today's milk-loading bay.

Leadworking. 234.866. Leadmill Bridge has the tail race of the old mill under the roadway. The mill ruins are now a rockery in an adjacent garden. Below Higger Tor, 253.819, was a lead-smelting cupola, of which disturbed ground is the sole remaining evidence.

Paper mill. At Green's House, near North Lees, an extensive paper mill was worked in the 1840s by Charles Ibbotson to make shop and factors' paper. The dam can be identified.

HAYFIELD

Mills. By the weir in the centre of the village is a very old corn mill, dilapidated. Several important paper mills and calico printworks were established in the first half of the nineteenth century along Kinder Brook and Sett Brook, from Hayfield down to New Mills, including Hayfield Printing Co Ltd, Birch Vale Print Works, with its imposing chimney pedestal, and the Bank Vale Paper Mills of John Slack Ltd (031.874), established in the early 1800s.

At Little Hayfield is the large Clough Mill, 032.883, with extensive ruins of an older mill behind it. This was a cotton-spinning mill, and is now a hen battery, with prospects of becoming a paintworks. Downstream at Primrose Vale, 032.880, all that remains of a buckram mill is a flued chimney on the hill, and a row of substantial houses for the employees.

HAZLEWOOD

Romano-British pottery site. 326.468. Second to third century AD, discovered by S. O. Kay, 1958. Products identified at forts on Hadrians Wall.

HEAGE

Windmill. 366.358. A tower windmill with, unusually, six sails and a nice ogee cap. Its earliest recorded date is 1850. The structure was restored 1967 by Derbyshire County Council.

Ironworks. 380.492. Morley Park Ironworks has a fine pair of cold-blast coke iron furnaces, erected by Francis Hurt 1780 and 1818 and worked later by C. & J. Mold. The older furnace was probably the first of its type in Derbyshire. These square pyramids in gritstone, about 36 ft high, were built against a hill to facilitate loading. They were formerly surmounted by cupolas. In 1846 the works had 400 employees and 300 hp; it was last in blast about 1875. Protected by Stanton Ironworks at the instigation of Sir Frederick Scopes, but urgently in need of preservation (plate, page 35).

Coal mining. In the adjacent Engine Shaft is the broken spear of a beam pumping engine, and a rising main; reputedly used for draining nearby collieries until the 1920s. This site has been worked for coal and ironstone since 1372, when coal was won by opencast working, as it was again in the 1940s.

HEANOR

Much coal mining. An old brickworks at Loscoe, probably c 1800 or earlier, is still producing at 426.472.

Railway bridge. The bridge carrying the Erewash branch of the Midland Railway over Station Road at Langley Mill has long straight cast-iron girders, now with steel reinforcement. Built probably 1847.

Lace factory. The oldest lace-making firm is Geo H. Fletcher & Sons Ltd, established c 1840. Present works are c 1900 and unremarkable.

Knitwear factory. I. & R. Morley Ltd has a large factory, interesting for its time, 1874, making knitwear and hosiery.

HIGHAM

Corn mill. 1750, with 16 ft waterwheel; also a cheese-factory building and the ruins of a 'bump' (ie candlewick) mill, at Dairy Farm, 388.583.

HILTON

Mill. 243.305. An old red-brick watermill with a chimney of later date, and older buildings adjacent; now derelict. Site shown on Burdett's map, 1797. In 1895 T. C. Greensmith & Co milled flour and baked 'the celebrated Derby dog biscuits'. More information is needed.

HOLBROOK

Romano-British pottery sites. 360.445. Excavated by members of Derbyshire Archaeological Society, 1960. One kiln in good state of preservation.

Stockingers' workshops. 364.449 and 364.448. Small two-storey brick buildings on an older stone base. Dilapidated.

HOPE—see BROUGH and BRADWELL

HOPTON

Railway incline. 255.546. The steepest incline climbed by locomotives in the UK, on the C & HPR. Maximum gradient 1 in 14. Last used 1967.

ILKESTON

Brickworks. 460.412. Oakwell Brickworks (now Stanton & Staveley) has a Hoffmann kiln about ninety years old, reconditioned since world war II but abandoned 1966.

Erewash Canal. 463.453. At Shipley Gate are locks and warehouse buildings. A small arched stone aqueduct over the Erewash, on the county boundary, 1779, is a miniature of Brindley's Monks Bridge of 1766; see page 145.

Warp-knitting establishments. W. Beardsley & Sons Ltd, today producing warp-knitted goods in most fibres, since c 1820 has had an old works, probably original, at Primrose Street. Two storeys, with stilted-arched cast-iron windows. Contemporary cottages in factory courtyard. W. Ball & Son Ltd, manufacturing pure silk milanese warp and glove piece goods since 1825–30, has a plain works of pleasing appearance in Burr Lane. Small-paned rectangular cast-iron windows in a four-storey, nine-bay building with pediment and clock suggest an early date.

Behind the Co-operative Stores is an old brick building of three storeys, now the ICS shoe-repairing department, with a slender cast-iron swivelling hoist arm at the top storey. Early purpose of building not known.

IRONVILLE—see ALFRETON, RIDDINGS

LANGLEY MILL—see HEANOR

LITTLE EATON

Paper mills. 354.423. Peckwash Mill on the Derwent has been fully documented by Hickling. Site references date from 1425. Rights exist to take 800 hp from the Derwent. A broken weir and burnt-out buildings remain, with marks of waterwheels visible. Smoke from chimney erected 1895 offended local residents; see page 206. Brook Mill, 363.413, in the village, mid-nineteenth century, is still in operation, worked by Dowdings.

Railway and turnpike. The embankment of the spur from the Midland Railway which crossed the Derwent to Peckwash Mill is still visible, but the wooden pile bridge has gone. At the west end of the embankment are the stone posts of the turnpike which was situated in the Derby road; they were placed here in 1875 for preservation. The MR branch railway to Ripley, 1856, now carries minerals only; a 'parachute' water crane stands south of the level crossing.

Brewery. 361.413. Gritstone buildings now incorporated in farm buildings. John Tatham was maltster in 1835.

Canal wharf. 363.410. On the Derby Canal, but now filled in and occupied by a garage. The clock house, 1793, still stands. The track of the Gangroad to Denby can be traced, stone sleepers being seen occasionally in walls of buildings.

Quarries. 366.429. These produced scythe whetstones—'spoilers' are still to be found, although according to Farey only 3 in 120 were broken in the making. They sold in 1809 at 10s per long 100 (120). *Industrial housing*. 357.425. Blue Mountain Cottages were built by Tempests of Peckwash Mill, 1820 onwards. Note the steep footpath down to the mill.

Waterworks. 364.407. Derby Waterworks building is in pseudo-Gothic style, 1848. Beam engines of 1875 were removed 1948; see page 212.

LONG EATON

Railway sheet stores. 488.321. Best seen from the train, this was established 1845 onwards, first as a coke warehouse, then for the manufacture of the tarpaulin sheets required in large numbers to cover goods in open wagons. Interesting developments of different buildings from ventilation by open top-storey windows, to vented lantern roof. Variety of fancy cast-iron windows. Large dock of Erewash Canal. Narrow-gauge railway with cast-iron junction plates passes under main line.

Railway station. 496.322. Trent station, Midland Railway, opened 1 May 1862; an important junction for the London, Derby & Nottingham lines, but remote from the town. Imposing buildings with gables and decorative barge-boards, pent glazed platform roof on cast-iron columns. Old MR water crane, and terraces of employees' dwellings. In 1968 efforts to keep the station open were unsuccessful. Now demolished.

Mills. 488.337. The large three- and four-storey tenement lace factories are notable for their great length. Brick, with large staircase turrets containing cat heads and loading bays. West End Mill 1887, Harrington Mills 1888.

Bridge. 472.312. Harrington Bridge at Sawley carries the A453 over the Trent; built 1790, rebuilt 1905–6.

Canal. 487.330. The Erewash (Grand Union) Canal is easily visible alongside the A453 road. It joins the Trent at Trent Lock, 491.312, an unchanged area with locks and keepers' cottages.

LONGFORD

Corn mill. 220.375. A fine building in mellow brick, with leaded windows simulating domestic architecture. Hoist platform with cast-iron scroll brackets. Date 'F.G. 18–7' on sandstone plaque, partly obliterated by scuffing of corn sacks: probably read 1837. A mill here 1767. Grinding chicory until recently. Now disused. Worthy of preservation.

Road bridges. Two simple three-arched brick bridges over stream and mill-tail, with plaque 'These county bridges were erected at the sole expense of Thomas William, Earl of Leicester. AD MDCCCXLII'. (Thomas William Coke, d 1842, first Earl of Leicester.)

Cheese factory. A low wooden building, bears on a plaque 'The first cheese factory built in England. Opened 4 May 1870, under the management of Cornelius Schermerhorn'. The cheese was made on the American system of quantity production by the Longford Dairy Association of local farmers, who processed the milk from 600 cows. See page 210.

LUMSDALE—see TANSLEY

LINGS—see CLAY CROSS

LITTON

Cotton mill. 160.730. The original cotton mill started by Needham, Frith & Co about 1782, was made notorious by the Robert Blincoe story of the ill-treated London orphan apprentice, 1810–20. Few traces remain of the original buildings. The iron-capped gateposts to the now-vanished bridge over the stream to the site of the Apprentice House still stand, as do the waterwheel sluice controls. The present mill was built 1874 after a fire.

LONGCLIFFE—see BRASSINGTON

MAKENEY

Old forge site. 351.449. By lower weir. Later Hampshire's chemical factory. Walter Mather came here in 1783, and started to operate at Staveley the same year. This is possibly the site of the works of Zouch, where he used the inventions of Christopher Schutz for wire drawing (see page 51), and of Burkhard Cranich's lead-ore stamping mill, of the 1560s. See page 31.

Turnpike Road. By Holly Bush Inn at 353.446 is a stone marked 'Derby Coach Road, 1739'.

MARPLE BRIDGE

When the works described below were carried out, the parish of Glossop was bounded by the Etherow and the Goyt, and included Marple Bridge, then in Derbyshire.

Canal. SJ.98.961.885. Just over the old county boundary the Peak Forest Canal has a fine stair of locks with a horse tunnel, and an old warehouse reputedly built by Arkwright, 1794–1800. The aqueduct carrying the canal over the Goyt, SJ.99.955.901, was in 1793 'one of the most considerable works of its kind'; three 60 ft-span arches, 78 ft high.

Lime kilns. SJ.98.963.882. Built by Samuel Oldknow, 1790s, employing Derbyshire lead miners as masons. The kilns impressed Farey as 'the most complete he had ever seen', 36 ft deep, $13\frac{1}{2}$ ft diameter at top, $14\frac{1}{2}$ ft diameter at belly, $3\frac{1}{2}$ ft at bottom. False front to simulate an ancient castle (plate, page 54). Now threatened by encroaching housing development.

See MELLOR.

MATLOCK

Identified as Metesforde, and thought possibly to be Lutodarum, the Roman lead-smelting centre.

Leadworking. 309.607. By Hurst Farm were the Lumb smelting mills, held by George White in 1768. A grass-grown mound and slag-coated stones in neighbouring walls are the sole remains. At 296.588 was a lead mine; in 1769 John Barber, gent, and George Goodwin, miner, erected waterwheels on the east side of the Derwent under High Tor. An 80 hp wheel remained intact until destroyed by fire in 1896. It was repaired and in use in 1903. Now a colour works.

Textile mills. John Smedley of Lea erected extensive mills, and in 1857 the Hydro, now the headquarters of Derbyshire County Council.

Railway station. By Paxton, it was completed in 1850 (see page 165). North of the station is an old cross-bar signal of the Midland Railway. Station-master's house also by Paxton.

Street tramroad. At the top of Rutland Street is the gritstone engine house and depot of the Matlock Cable Tramway, opened 1893, closed 1927. See page 169. In the gardens by the Derwent bridge is the decorated iron tram shelter, moved here from Crown Square.

MATLOCK BATH

George White, who held Lumb smelting mills 1768 (see page 188), obtained a lease to build mills and erect wheels at the Masson, 294.573, for ninety-nine years at £1 pa. In 1772 a grant was made to George White and Robert Shore to convey water to a paper mill for twenty-one years. This is the south weir at Matlock Bath, and was adjacent to Arkwright's Masson Mill (see CROMFORD). In 1788 Shore, White and Swetnham were working the prosperous Llwyn Llwyd lead mine in Cardiganshire, visited by Francis Thompson of Ashover.

Railway station. In the style of a Swiss chalet; c 1849.

MELBOURNE

Mills. The firm of Thomas Haimes & Co Ltd was established 1812 by William Haimes, producing knitted goods ornamented with floral patterns. Castle Mills was erected 1857, the present frontage dating from 1933; see page 179.

Ironworking. 381.243. An eighteenth-century charcoal iron furnace has been excavated by Mr W. H. Bailey of Hathersage. The site is now under a reservoir. See page 55.

MELLOR

Cotton mill. SJ.98.967.885. In 1792 Samuel Oldknow designed and built a large cotton-spinning mill on the Goyt, helped financially by Richard Arkwright. It was burnt down in the 1890s, but a contemporary painting shows a resemblance to the frontage of Willersley Castle (plate, page 144); 120 hp water power, of which the tunnel leats can be traced in the ruins. In 1857 it had combined steam and water power of 300 hp. The dams are now the Roman Lakes. After considering the use of iron, Oldknow built the elegant single-arched bridge over the Goyt in stone. On Oldknow's death the mill was taken over by Arkwright II. It remained in use until the fire. Bottom's Hall, now a farm, was reputedly the Apprentices' House.

MIDDLETON BY WIRKSWORTH

Anciently an important lead-mining area, with many interestingly named mines still productive in 1857.

Stoneworks. 276.555. Established over a century, it now obtains limestone of high purity from a stone mine.

Railway. 279.552. At Rise End is a bridge carrying the Cromford & High Peak Railway over the road, with cast-iron beams similar to those by Butterley at Longcliffe. The Middleton Incline of the C & HPR crosses the road from Wirksworth, 677 yd long, gradient 1 in 8¼. At 275.552 is the Middleton winding engine built by Butterley, 1825, 25 in bore × 60 in stroke, 5 psi. The fate of this engine is not yet decided, but there are grounds for hope that it will be preserved.

MILFORD

Mills. 351.452. On either side of the stone bridge over the Derwent in 1790 were the extensive cotton-spinning, bleaching and dyeing mills built by Jedediah Strutt from 1780 onwards. The fine old mills south of the bridge were demolished 1964. Fortunately they were fully documented by Johnson and Skempton. Stone from Hopping Hill Quarry, 352.453, was used for the mills. It was exceptionally difficult to work but was beautifully dressed, and the buildings were difficult to demolish. Examples of William Strutt's fireproof design, with cast-iron stanchions and beams, hollow earthenware pots and plaster flooring, have been preserved locally and in the Science Museum. The mills were light, airy and warm.

Foundry. 348.455. Upstream of the mills, the Glow Worm Foundry is on the site of an early one worked by Strutt in the 1780s to produce much of his ironwork for buildings and waterwheels. There was a large weir here in 1745. The copings of the drystone wall by the mill tail of the cotton mills are 'skulls' from ladles of cast iron, presumably from this foundry.

Industrial housing. Large numbers of substantial houses were built in ascending terraces up the side of Hopping Hill, and across the river at Bank Buildings, 347.454. Still occupied. In 1842 a Wesleyan chapel was provided, in 1849 a Baptist chapel and a Lancasterian school. All are still standing.

Strutt's Farm. 346.444. Moscow Farm, in the same substantial style as the mills, was built by the Strutts to provide fresh milk and vegetables for their employees. Thought to have been completed 1812, the year of Napoleon's retreat from Moscow.

See BELPER, MAKENEY.

MILLERS DALE

Mills. Dakin's Mill or Tideswell Mill, a corn mill at 138.733, is dilapidated but contains fine wooden machinery and a wheel of 12 ft diameter × 6 ft wide. Deserves restoration. Nearby another corn mill of 1860, in limestone with gritstone quoins, is used by Staffordshire Farmers.

Railway. There are two high railway viaducts, one 1863, the later one built with ironwork from Butterley in 1903. The railway station,

1863, now closed, was unusual in having a post office on the platform.

MONYASH

The Barmote Court of High Peak Hundred meets when necessary at the Bull's Head Inn.

Lime kiln. 155.615. A primitive lime kiln has been excavated and recorded by Mr P. F. Dagger and others. A model has been deposited in the Derby Borough Museum.

MONSAL DALE

Railway. The fine stone viaduct of the Midland Railway, 1862–3, roused the ire of Ruskin, although to modern eyes it blends well with the landscape.

MORLEY PARK—see HEAGE

MORTON

Coal mining. 414.602. Clay Cross No 5 shaft was sunk 300 yd deep in 1865. A two-cylinder winding engine designed by William Howe, and using his Link Motion, built by Andrew Handyside, Derby, was still running in 1965. Cast-iron roof beams in engine house. Engine to be preserved at Leicester Museum of Technology; see page 118.

NEW MILLS

So-called because c 1500 a new corn mill was set up on the site of the King's Mill; the site, at 002.858, was later occupied by Salem Mill, for cotton spinning and weaving. Salem Mill is probably c 1800 or earlier, and is now used by a sheet-metal firm. The streams in this region form the strings of a necklace of corn, textile and paper mills connecting Hayfield, Newmills, Chinley and Whaley Bridge. In 1846 there were four calico printers, eight cotton spinners, four candlewick manufacturers and two dyers, at Grove Mill, Rock Mill, Strines Works, Torr & Torr Top Mill, all on the Goyt; Beard Mill, Garrison Side Works, London Place, Marsh Mill, St George's Works, on the Kinder. The CPA Ltd owns several of these mills. There are interesting dams and water works, and industrial housing, at locations all down the valley from Hayfield, qv. The large Birch Vale Print Works has two very large dams and an imposing gateway. Adjacent is an interesting curved row of workers' cottages, and a primitive wooden railway station of the Marple, New Mills & Hayfield Junction Railway, 1865, still in use in 1966.

At SJ.98.996.848, see Newtown Buildings, a row of substantially built cottages, 1857; the Albion Mill, 1859, and the Brunswick Mill, rebuilt 1883.

OAKERTHORPE

Coal mine. 392.551. The ruins of Speedwell Mine's beautiful beam-engine house in golden sandstone still stand, with tall round-arch windows framed with shaped freestone. This housed Francis Thompson's atmospheric engine of 1791, which was removed to Pentrich Colliery in 1841, and to the Science Museum in 1917. See plate, page 72, and page 115. Inside dimensions 30 ft × 17 ft 6 in; walls 2 ft thick; maximum height about 30 ft. Tall narrow windows at east end 5 ft 3 in wide, 16 ft high, stone framing 8 in × 9 in cross-section. Window at west end 8 ft wide × 19 ft high. Adjacent are a broken winding-pulley wheel and valve bodies. A small circular brick building, with no windows, may have been a powder magazine. Nearby, at 399.548, are the ruins of a later colliery, with brick buildings. A wagon boiler, 4 ft diameter, has forty-five $2\frac{1}{2}$ in-bore fire tubes.

OVER HADDON

Lead mine. 196.662. Imposing ruins of Mandale Mine's beam-engine house are in the care of the Peak District Mines Historical Society. The flued chimney up the hillside was for the boiler furnace. A waterwheel in the pit on the west side of the engine was fed by water carried by a leat running above and alongside the Lathkill for $\frac{3}{4}$ mile from Carter's Mill, and crossing the river by a launder supported by stone columns, ruins of which still stand. Sanderson's map of 1834 shows a 52 ft-diameter waterwheel. This is reputed to be one of the oldest lead mines in Derbyshire.

Corn mill. 203.662. By Lathkill Lodge is an old mill containing fine wooden machinery, with beautifully worked framing. The wheel has gone.

PARSLEY HAY

Railway. This was an important station on the Cromford & High Peak Railway, 147.636. Wharves and warehouses can be seen, and a handsome tunnel at 151.629, under the main A515 road from Ashbourne to Buxton, with interesting medallions of the railway company, in limestone.

PEAK FOREST—see BUXTON

PENTRICH

Coal mining. The huge red spoil heaps of Haslam's Colliery (where Francis Thompson's 1791 engine was recognised and rescued by W. T. Anderson in 1917) are being cleared and all traces of the establishment will disappear. This was an important enterprise and had mineral railways with massively built masonry tunnels and bridges now disused.

Canal. 394.518. The western entrance of the longest tunnel of the Cromford Canal is clearly visible, but it is closed by mining subsidence.

See RIPLEY.

PINXTON

Coal mining. 449.543. An old colliery engine house remains, with stone beam-bearing supports inserted in side walls of brick.

Canal. Branch of Cromford Canal, from Codnor Park via Pye Bridge, 1793, was in use until c 1914, now derelict. Bridges have flatter arches than usual on this canal. Traces only remain of pottery and canal wharves, 453.543. Examples of the ware can be seen in the Derby Borough Museum.

PINXTON GREEN

Beam-engine house and horse gins. 465.553. Until 1965 a ruined beam pumping-engine house in brick, a barrel-type horse gin and a geared horse gin, with wooden horse harness, stood just over the county boundary. These being in the line of the M1, the NCB agreed to remove the gins to the apprentices' school at the Bentinck Colliery. A model of the barrel gin is in the Derby Borough Museum.

PLEASLEY VALE

This lovely but little-known valley (518.649) in magnesian limestone, on the county boundary, had a corn mill in 1255, iron forges from 1660 to 1770, and textile mills since 1784. The mills of William Hollins & Co Ltd, in the warm-coloured local magnesian limestone, and their dams, now dominate the valley. The present buildings date from 1840-4. See page 194.

RENISHAW—see ECKINGTON

RIDDINGS—see ALFRETON

RIDGEWAY—see ECKINGTON

RIPLEY

Canal tunnel. 406.515. The Butterley Tunnel on the Cromford Canal was driven in 1792, a task made difficult by soft shale. Lined with brick for much of the 2,966 yd, at a cost of £7 per yd, it is 9 ft wide, 8 ft high. It collapsed in 1889 through mining for coal beneath it, and again in 1900, finally cutting the canal. A large reservoir is at the west end, and another in Golden Valley.

Butterley Works. 401.517. Established 1790 by Benjamin Outram et al. See page 59. Quaint Butterley Post Office at entrance.

R

Railway station. 402.519. On Ambergate, Nottingham, Boston & Eastern Junction Railway, 1852, now disued and deteriorating. With its simple, pleasing design it deserves a better fate.

Parish church. The clock was designed and made by Sir John Alleyne, whose inventions made possible the production of large plates and sections in wrought iron, such as were used in the roof structure of St Pancras station. See page 60.

ROWSLEY

Railway station. 258.660. The original terminal railway station of the Manchester, Buxton, Matlock & Midlands Junction Railway, 1849. A simple stone building, designed by Sir Joseph Paxton, it is now an office in the road-transport yard. The present station was built in 1863 when the line was continued to Buxton: a stone building with decorative stone columns and pediments, and glass canopy with decorative cast-iron columns. Midland Cottages is a uniform row of railway employees' houses, on the Chatsworth Road; two pairs of these are thought to be by Paxton.

SANDIACRE

Starch factory. 481.372. A large brick three-storey building erected 1837 by Lawrence Hall, for £5,000, with a 12 hp steam engine.

Lace factory. 481.365. A large and imposing tenement lace factory, built 1888 by Terah Hooley, whose monogram appears on large numbers of cast-iron tie plates on the front of the building. It is of four storeys, with forty-one bays, with unusually large cast-iron windows, a frontage of about 350 ft, and a gabled centre with a clock. At the rear are large staircase turrets and an engine house with unusual round cast-iron windows. The engine, with rope drive to all floors, was removed c 1940. The total capacity of the factory was 160 lace machines, and 'when all were running the building shook alarmingly'. Hence all the transverse ties.

Canal. 483.358. A lock-keeper's cottage stands near the Erewash

Canal's junction with the now-derelict Derby Canal. An unusual cast-iron and wooden footbridge is to be seen at 481.367.

SHARDLOW

Under its earlier name of Wilden Ferry, this was an important port on the Trent. Leonard Fosbrooke was a carrier, and in 1684 he built Shardlow Hall, now offices of the Ministry of Agriculture & Fisheries. James Sutton succeeded Fosbrooke as a leading carrier, and took over the Hall. Soresby and Flack also ran fly-boats on the Trent. Subsequently, with the opening of the Trent & Mersey Canal (Brindley 1770), the Suttons and the Soresbys were the main carriers.

Wilden Ferry was replaced by Shardlow Bridge (Act 1758, built 1761), which retained the same high tolls as the ferry; see page 142. These tolls are recorded on a stone preserved at the northern approach to the bridge, which collapsed in the floods of 21 March 1947. The present bridge was opened 1956, having cost £250,000 as compared with £3,333 for the first bridge.

With the opening of the canal, Shardlow became an inland port with an important trade in coal, limestone, freestone, gypsum, bar-iron, lead, pottery (Wedgwood was a partner in the canal company), ale, cheese, deal and pig-iron, flint, chert, malt and barley. Despite the rebuilding of a burnt-out warehouse and the recent establishment of a marina for modern canal craft, the area is still evocative of the late eighteenth century.

Canal wharves and warehouses. Warehouses for the Trent & Mersey's iron, coal, timber, grain and malt traffic still stand, with old cranes and hoists (plate, page 90). The large grain warehouses were taken over by H. E. Stevens during this century. No 1 Mill, 1790, on the west side of the A6 road, shows clearly how these warehouses were built over spurs of the canal, to facilitate loading and unloading of the barges. No 2 Mill bears the date 1780. The large malting of the Shardlow Malt Extract Company dates from about 1790. The Malt Shovel Inn is of later date than the adjoining warehouse of 1799.

Broughton House, now Stevens' offices on the main road, is said to have been built by Capability Brown (1715–83) for Clifford, a partner of Sutton's.

Ropemaking. Men hauled the boats on the Trent & Mersey until about 1785, when horses began to be used. Stables for 100 horses were demolished recently. At 445.503 was the ropewalk of George Henshall, now indicated only by long parallel hedges flanking a hen battery. Barge-masters left their short canal ropes here to be dried and reconditioned, picking up the longer ropes needed for towing along the Trent.

Mileposts. A cast-iron canal milepost, Shardlow–Preston Brook 92 miles, contrasts with an iron road milepost by John Harrison of Derby on the A6 road by an old warehouse.

Canal bridges. Porter's Bridge, 453.306, has an iron bracket which may have been used for a torch or lamp to aid navigation at night. At Derwent Mouth, 459.309, where the canal joins the Trent, a concrete horse-bridge crosses the river, replacing an older wooden bridge a few years ago.

Canal locks. The Trent & Mersey is broad along this stretch, taking boats of 40 tons burden, 13 ft 6 in, as far as Horninglow, near Burton-on-Trent. Shardlow Lock, 442.303, with its keeper's cottage and the Trent close by, is striking.

Workhouse. At 429.305, the large red-brick establishment was the House of Industry, 1821, which became one of the first Union Workhouses (Act of 1834), serving forty-nine parishes.

Church. 438.304. St James' church, built by public subscription 1838, has cast-iron windows simulating Perpendicular tracery.

SHELDON

Lead mine. 173.682. Magpie Mine has the most extensive surface ruins still remaining at any lead mine in the county. The Peak District Mines Historical Society has its field headquarters here and has restored some of the buildings.

SHIRLAND

Colliery winding engine. 398.580. The colliery has a two-cylinder winding engine built 1865 by Thornewill & Wareham of Burton-on-Trent; still working 1965. About 250 hp with a heavy cast-iron segmental drum on an octagonal shaft, fitted with oak non-slip blocks. Should be preserved, like the engine at Morton Colliery.

SMALLEY COMMON

Pottery. 434.422. With one bottle kiln, the Peak Pottery was still in use c 1945. It supplied the hollow earthenware pots used by William Strutt for his fireproof mills at Belper and Milford, 1793 onwards (plate, page 54).

Stainsby House. 403.443. Was the home of John Barber, who took out the first patent for a gas turbine, 1791. Now much enlarged and used as a boys' school.

SOUTH NORMANTON

Railway. 427.578. The very large West Houses railway-engine sheds have three bays, brick, about 240 ft × 100 ft. Tall cast-iron windows, probably 1887.

Windmill. 436.562. The heavy timber framework of the post mill is still standing, but closely surrounded by new houses. The earliest date recorded is 1794, but it was shown on Burdett's map of 1767. According to Mr J. C. Williams, this may be the mill mentioned in 1699.

SOUTH WINGFIELD

Railway station. 385.557. Built 1839-40; the most often quoted example of Francis Thompson's station architecture. A 5 ton crane in the yard, with cast-iron gears and wooden gib, is by Kitson, Thompson & Hewitson, Airedale Foundry, Leeds.

Lace-thread mill. 372.540. Wingfield Park Mill is now ruinous but has been 'of striking appearance, in golden sandstone'. A lace-thread spinning mill in 1816, it had two dams, one now a garden pond.

Corn mills. 379.535. Weir Mill is sometimes incorrectly recorded as Wire Mill. A corn mill on the Amber, recorded by Farey, 1807. Pentrich Mill (377.520), another corn mill, was rebuilt 1878 on an old site. Has been a lace mill. 'French' stones stand near.

SPONDON

British Celanese works. 398.348. Established 1916 by Swiss chemists Henri and Camille Dreyfus, originally to produce cellulose acetate for aeroplane dope. Now 'one of the largest and most complex factories in the world'; 350 acres, 5,000 employees. Tricel fibres, acetate flake, plastic film, chemicals, weaving and warp knitting.

STANTON-BY-DALE

Ironworking. This is an ancient ironworking area, today occupied by Stanton Iron Works, 469.385, established 1840s, now part of Stanton & Staveley, in turn members of Stewart & Lloyds Ltd. The pattern shop and fitting shop are probably the oldest buildings. In 1846 three small blast furnaces were each producing 18–20 tons of pig per day. Today this works is the largest producer of spun-iron pipes, with 6,500 employees. The total output of Stanton & Staveley is 1,000,000 tons per annum of foundry iron, half of which is used by the company.

A triple-expansion vertical steam engine of 1897, by the Glenfield Co Ltd, Kilmarnock, actuates an 80 ton hydraulic accumulator. This operates 10 ton and 20 ton 'jigger' cranes in the casting shop, and a portable one in the yard. Hydraulic jiggers were invented in the mid-nineteenth century; by hydraulic rams they force apart pairs of pulleys, round which chains are passed.

Canal. 467.395. Short stretches of the Nutbrook Canal (1795) remain to give pleasure to anglers.

STAVELEY

Staveley Iron Works. A forge was here in 1608. In 1700 production was 98 tons of iron, in 1750, 200 tons. Mather worked a forge here, and another at Makeney, 1783. Pilkington reproduced an outline sketch of a Staveley blast furnace in 1789. Richard Barrow had four blast furnaces in 1846 producing 250 tons of iron per week, and had sunk Speedwell Colliery 435 ft deep. He met Charles Markham, assistant locomotive superintendent of the Midland Railway at Derby, and they joined forces in 1863, turning the company into the Staveley Coal & Iron Co. Markham was managing director until he died. He married Rosa Paxton, daughter of Joseph Paxton of Chatsworth. One of their sons, Charles Paxton Markham, became a director in 1888, when twenty-three years old. Under his management the firm grew and prospered. He established the huge Devonshire Chemical Works, 425.747, adjacent to the ironworks, 414.747.

Little remains of the old works in today's vast complex, but in June 1966 three very large horizontal single-cylinder gas engines, using blast-furnace gas, ran for the last time. Built by Cockrill of Belgium in 1924–8, these each developed 7,150 bhp, driving three 5,000 kW alternators. Cylinder bore $51\frac{1}{4}$ in, stroke 59 in, $91\frac{1}{2}$ rpm. The IMEP was 75 psi, and cooling-water flow was 50,000 gph. To cope with these duties, the piston rods were $14\frac{1}{2}$ in diameter, and the engines, *Vera*, *Enid* and *Edna*, each weighed approximately 1,000 tons. The engine house itself was remarkable, $238\frac{1}{2}$ ft long × $101\frac{1}{2}$ ft wide, $70\frac{1}{2}$ ft high to the apex of the roof.

Industrial housing. Markham planned workers' houses, most of them with electricity and hot water supplied from the plant. Two housing estates adjacent to the works contrast greatly in style: Poolsbrook, 444.735, probably of the 1890s, consists of parallel ranks of barracks-like houses. These houses have no gardens, springing directly out of the bare earth like those at Arkwright Town. Hollingwood Estate, 415.743, probably about thirty years later, is a model village, each house having its garden and the streets being planned to avoid tedium and uniformity.

STONEY MIDDLETON

Lead and lime working. 213.757. The scene of Chantrey's well-known pictures of lead smelting and lime burning, 1817. The present Cupola Quarry is the site of the first lead condensing flues introduced by Bishop Watson in 1778. Traces of a flue and chimney exist, possibly original and of this time. Several large lime kilns are still to be seen between here and the village.

Tollhouse. 229.755. This is a well-known landmark, built in gritstone, 1840, cost £87 15s.

SWADLINCOTE

Potteries. Coal was being worked in small villages in this area in 1294 and 1567. Today Swadlincote, with Church Gresley and Woodville, forms a large area of collieries and earthenware potteries, which expanded considerably during the early nineteenth century. There are still bottle kilns to be seen here, becoming increasingly rare as they are replaced by tunnel kilns, as has happened with tableware manufacture at Denby and Derby. The pottery industry followed the development of collieries, but local deposits of refractory clay were discovered, suitable for casting pots for founders and steel refiners (1846). See the works of Greens (c 1830) in the centre of Swadlincote, with beehive kilns, Thomas Wragg & Sons Ltd (1872), J. Woodward Ltd (1790).

At Woodville (formerly called Wooden Box), the derelict works of Mansfield Bros Ltd (1879), with many bottle kilns, is opposite the abandoned railway station, 321.191. Mansfields has another pottery opposite the church in Church Gresley. John Knowles & Co (Wooden Box) Ltd, founded 1849 by a contractor to Robert Stephenson, makes drain pipes and refractories. Present premises dated 1884.

TANSLEY AND LUMSDALE

Mills. The area comprises the adjacent valleys of two small streams and is packed with interest. Pilkington, 1789, wrote that a cotton mill had been built 'a few years ago' of the Arkwright type. Farey listed a bleaching house, a candlewick mill, four cotton-spinning mills, a dye house, a flax-spinning mill and a bobbin mill.

The first spinning mill was built by Samuel Unwin of Sutton-in-Ashfield, at 318.599: a gritstone building of three storeys, sixteen bays, with plain rectangular cast-iron windows. A house of later date stands at its western end. Later it was used as a smallware factory, a tape mill, a joinery and now a store. A fine dam. The Top Mill, 320.599, three storeys, eight bays, is also of early date and was owned by the Unwin family. Water led to an overshot wheel (inside the main building) by a cast-iron pipe supported on a three-arched stone wall. Now a joinery. A small bobbin mill at 322.604 was owned by Edward Radford, who had a large spinning and candlewick mill, the Tansleywood Mill, 313.601 (now occupied by F. H. Drabble & Sons Ltd, dyers and finishers) on the adjacent Bentley Brook.

Also on Bentley Brook, at 313.605, are ruins of bleaching mills, and at 309.599 a large tall corn mill of striking appearance, now E. H. Bailey Ltd, formerly Gartons. Of 1799 date (Pevsner).

TICKNALL

Tramroad. 356.250. A round-arched brick bridge over the road carried the tramroad from the lime works to Ashby-de-la-Zouch and Leicester, 1794. The track can be followed, with many stone sleepers in position, and a low tunnel about 120 yd long. Casting the rails absorbed the full capacity of the Butterley foundries for fifteen months.

Pottery. Brown kitchenware recorded 1635. The clay pits form beautiful lakes, and at 361.242 is an ancient rustic open-sided drying shed 81 ft × 18 ft, and a ruined kiln, rectangular, 30 ft × 18 ft, probably early nineteenth century.

Lime quarries. Across the road are remains of extensive lime quarries, many lime kilns, mostly overgrown, and flooded lime pits.

TIDESWELL

Calico-weaving factory. 147.764. The former calico-weaving factory, with flued chimney, is now making magneto-electric components.

TISSINGTON

Turnpike. Spend Lane and Gag Lane, the steep and narrow gated road from the Dog & Partridge Inn, 165.505, to the old tollhouse near the New Inns Hotel at 158.544, is an interesting relic of the old turnpike, c 1760, from Ashbourne to Buxton. It was bypassed by the present direct route from Sandybrook about 1805.

Lace-thread mill. 185.504. Woodeaves Mill and canal, by Fenny Bentley. The mill was established 1784 by Cooper of Hanging Bridge Mill for lace-thread spinning; it closed 1907–8 and was demolished, the site now being hardly distinguishable amongst farm buildings. The arch of the tail race, and the dam, now an ornamental pond, remain. In 1857 it had a 16 hp steam engine. The 'canal', 1802, can be traced upstream for ¾ mile, and was built as a dam for the mill, but was also used to convey limestone from Bradbourne in small boats.

Lime kiln. 156.525. A large lime kiln, by the footpath to Bostern Grange, has an architectural front reminiscent of railway-tunnel portals. The draw hole is 9 ft wide, and the kiln about 11 ft high, 15 ft deep. Worthy of preservation.

TOADHOLE

Mill. 386.584. A three-storey sandstone building, with cast-iron windows. A water mill is mentioned by Farey, and Sanderson's map, 1834, shows it as a bump (candlewick) mill. Now occupied by Fred Turner (Hosiery) Ltd. At other times it has been a corn mill, a mustard factory and a jam factory.

TURNDITCH

Lime working. 294.453. Old lime works, with ruins of kilns, which were 27–33 ft high, 1808.

Ironworking. This area was mined for ironstone at an early date and would repay further study.

UNSTONE

Railway viaduct. 375.768. The high railway viaduct on the Midland Railway line opened 2 February 1870.

Beehive coke ovens. 378.772. The ovens, overgrown, and the footrill of a coal mine of c 1846, were found in a garden, 1956.

Cutlery works. 371.775. Harrison's long-established cutlery works may yet be preserved.

WESTON-ON-TRENT

Canal. The Trent & Mersey Canal runs close to the river Trent near Cliff Inn, once a place of note amongst canal users, now a Ukrainian hostel, 394.274. Here were wharves with cranes to transfer goods from river boats to canal barges. An iron canal mile-post, 'Shardlow 4 miles, Preston Brook 88 miles'. This canal is still in use. Weston Lock and keeper's cottage are at 408.278.

WHALEY BRIDGE

Canal. 012.816. The terminal of the Peak Forest Canal, 1800, and the Cromford & High Peak Railway, 1825. Dock and large gritstone warehouse survive little changed, but railway lines and a horse chain on the incline have been removed recently. A warehouse dated 1832 AD at west end, 1916 AD at eastern extension, is still in use, as a garage. A heavy cast-iron beam 20 ft long forms a lintel over entrance to covered dock. The arched C & HP railway bridge over the Goyt is of interesting composite cast and riveted wrought-iron construction. Houses and stables are of contemporary date. By the canal wharf was a man-operated tippler to empty wagons into barges, remembered locally as in use about fifty years ago. At 006.810 is the Todd Brook dam, to feed the canal.

Mills. Goyt Mills, 1865, a large two-storey cotton-weaving mill in gritstone, was seemingly originally of one storey. The chimney appears to have been heightened twice. Adjacent is the Cepea Fabrics mill, with romanesque windows. A street of substantial houses is contemporary with Goyt Mills.

Railway bridges. At 011.812 and 011.827. Two skew-arched bridges with massive cast-iron arched beams, over the A6 road. Midland Railway, 1864.

WHATSTANDWELL

Leadworking. 326.554. Meerbrook Sough was begun in 1772, to unwater Wirksworth lead mines. A large arched outlet bears the letters 'F.H.' (Francis Hurt). In 1881 the sough was 3 miles long and was being extended. The water is used today by the South Derbyshire Water Board. At 325.553, the remains of Meerbrook lead-smelting works were largely destroyed recently by trenching for the gas-grid main. Ruins of Meerbrook Mine are at 312.553, on the line of the sough.

Railway station. 332.544. The original railway station, 1849, exists as a platform and simple wooden building at the north end of the tunnel, behind the Derwent Hotel. In the railway embankment wall, opposite, is a drinking fountain, presumably to represent the original well, bearing 'Watstandwell, MDCCCLXI'. The present railway station at the south end of the tunnel has an iron footbridge by Andrew Handyside, Derby, 1894.

Quarries. 347.515. Gritstone quarries above Shining Cliff Wood were worked by the Sims family for over a century, producing millstones, exported to Norway, India, USA. Half-finished stones still lie in the quarry.

Brickworks. Adjacent to the old turnpike road, now B5035, are ruins of what was an important brickworks. A ruined beehive kiln can be seen. Coal was obtained nearby.

See ALDERWASLEY.

WHITTINGTON

Mill. 383.243. An old corn mill, thoroughly documented by Mr R. A. Oakley in 1962, now a neglected four-storey gritstone building

50 ft × 35 ft, with one wheel remaining. It had two wheels in 1735, and five pairs of stones.

WINGERWORTH

Ironworking. 383.662. Only faint traces remain of coke iron furnace, 1780. See page 55.
Tramroad. See CLAY CROSS for Butler's Tramroad.

WINSTER

A once important lead-mining town, little changed since the late eighteenth century. At 232.611 was the famous Portway Mine, and at 238.611 the equally well-known Placket Mine.
See BIRCHOVER.

WIRKSWORTH

An ancient town, little changed in the past two centuries. It was originally an important lead centre, possibly a market for lead in 1307. The textile industry, established by Arkwright 1780, and especially the limestone quarrying are still important.
Leadworking. Six or seven soughs run under the town, and everywhere is the disturbed ground of old lead mines, eg Dovegang Mine, 288.557, where in 1615 George Sayers and partners sank an 'engine' shaft 240 ft deep, and Meerbrook Sough Mine, 288.546, with buildings still standing. At Black Rocks, 292.557, are recognisable ruins of a lead-smelting cupola, its hearth 21 ft long × 10 ft wide, with a square stone chimney, formerly with an iron extension. There was a smelter here in 1787, and the smelting works of Joseph Wass, which was discontinued before 1883. In the wall of the south transept of the church is a stone from Bonsall, thought to be of the twelfth century, possibly earlier, bearing the figure of a lead miner, wearing his miner's hat and carrying his pick and kibble (illustrated on page 25).
The Moot Hall was built in 1814, replacing an earlier one of 1773. It houses the standard reference dish for measuring lead ore, of 1513. See page 37.

Mills. Mr F. S. Ottery has identified the Speedwell Mill (cotton), 283.539, as that established by Richard Arkwright in 1780. It appears to have been built in three stages, but to house the 200 employees reported by Pilkington in 1789 it probably reached its present size quite early. It is now a textile-machinery factory; an ancestor of the manager worked it as a tape mill in 1852. Providence Mill, at Gorsey Bank, 290.531, was first recorded in 1823, and is still in use, weaving narrow fabric. A mill leat once ran beneath it. Adjacent houses are of the same period. Willowbath Mill is a low stone building on the main branch of the Ecclesbourne. Mentioned in 1816, it is still producing red tape. Haarlem Mill, 284.526, established by Hackett, was made famous by the story of *Adam Bede*, whose cottage is by the garage opposite. It comprises two buildings, one of brick—possibly a silk mill before 1844. G. H. Wheatcroft & Co produce narrow fabrics. Steam replaced water power in 1900.

Railway. The Midland Railway from Duffield to Wirksworth was opened in 1867. It was intended to drive it through the high hills to Rowsley, if the LNWR terminated the lease of the Ambergate–Rowsley line. It is now only a mineral line. The station was a pleasantly symmetrical building in pink gritstone with yellow stone quoins and sills, with an early instance of a rolled-steel joist lintel, decorated by piercing the web. Demolished recently.

House of Correction. 293.541. A terrace of four houses was the House of Correction, 1791. Exercise yards were at the rear, with male and female inmates segregated. It is now privately occupied.

WOODVILLE—see SWADLINCOTE

YOULGREAVE

Bridge. 213.656. Conksbury Bridge carries the Bakewell–Newhaven turnpike over the river Lathkill. The very steep hill is probably one of Celia Fiennes' 'precipices'.

See ALPORT, OVER HADDON.

References

Abbreviations

Bull PDMHS   *Bulletin* of the Peak District Mines Historical Society
DAJ   *Journal* of the Derbyshire Archaeological Society
DM   *Derbyshire Miscellany.* The Bulletin of the Local History Section
             of the Derbyshire Archaeological Society
LHS DAJ   Local History Section of the Derbyshire Archaeological Society
Proc ICE   *Proceedings* of the Institution of Civil Engineers
Trans NS   *Transactions* of the Newcomen Society for the History of Tech-
             nology
VCH   *Victoria County History*

CHAPTER ONE (*The County of Derby*. Page 15)

1 Glover, Stephen, *The Peak Guide*, 1830.
2 Watson, White, *A Delineation of the Strata of Derbyshire*, 1811.

CHAPTER TWO (*The Exploitation of Mineral Wealth*. Page 23)

1 Tylecote, R. F., *Metallurgy in Archaeology*. Arnold, 1962.
2 Stokes, A. H., *Lead and Lead Mining in Derbyshire*, 1880–3. Reprinted as
   PDMHS Special Publication No 2, 1964.
3 Raistrick, A. and Jennings, B., *A History of Lead Mining in the Pennines*.
   Longmans, 1965.
4 Agricola, Georgius, *De Re Metallica*, 1556. Translated by H. C. and L. H.
   Hoover, *The Mining Magazine*, 1912.
5 Thornhill, R., 'Lead Mining near Calver', *DM* III, No 6, Oct 1965.
6 Ferber, J. J., *Eine Oryktographie von Derbyshire in England*, 1776.
7 Schubert, H. R., 'The First Stamp Mills in English Industry', *Jnl* Iron & Steel
   Institute, Nov 1947.
8 Thompson, Francis, 'Journey into Wales and Back Again', 1788. *DM* III, No 5,
   June 1965.
9 Raistrick and Jennings, op cit.
10 Kirkham, N., 'Ridgeway Level, Whatstandwell', *DM* I, No 6, June 1957.
11 Hooson, *The Miner's Dictionary*, 1747.
12 Cameron, K., *The Place Names of Derbyshire*. CUP, 1959.
13 Lousley, J. E., *Wild Flowers of Chalk and Limestone*. Collins, 1950. Also Linton,
   W. R., *Flora of Derbyshire*, 1903.
14 Raistrick and Jennings, op cit.
15 *VCH* Derbyshire II, p 331a.

16 Stuckey, L. C., 'Lead Mining in Derbyshire', *The Mining Magazine*, Vol XVI, No 1, 1917.

17 Ure, A., *Dictionary of Arts, Manufactures and Mines*, 1839, p 757.

18 Rieuwerts, J. M., 'A List of the Soughs of the Derbyshire Lead Mines', *Bull PDMHS*, Vol 3, No 1, July 1966.

19 Oakley, M., 'A Recent Exploration of Hillcarr Sough', *Bull PDMHS*, Vol 2, No 2, Oct 1963.

20 Kirkham, N., 'The Draining of the Alport Lead Mines', *Trans NS*, XXXIII, 1960–1.

21 Kirkham, N., 'The Tumultuous Course of Dove Gang', *DAJ*, LXXIII, 1953.

22 Sitwell, George R., 'A Picture of the Iron Trade in the Seventeenth Century', *DAJ*, X, 1888.

23 Schubert, H. R., *History of the British Iron & Steel Industry from c 450 BC to AD 1775*. Routledge & Kegan Paul, 1957.

24 Ashton, T. S., *Iron & Steel in the Industrial Revolution*. Manchester UP, 2nd ed, 1951.

25 Robson, M. E., 'The Nailmaking Industry in Belper', *DM*, III, No 2, June 1964.

26 Harbord, F. W., *The Metallurgy of Steel*, 1905.

27 Needham, Joseph, *The Development of Iron and Steel Technology in China*. Newcomen Society, 1958.

28 Strutt, F. and Cox, J. C., 'Duffield Forest in the Sixteenth Century', *DAJ*, XXV, 1903.

29 Mott, R. A., 'Early Iron-making in the Sheffield Area', *Trans NS*, XXVII, 1949–51.

30 Bailey, W. H., *Bulletin No 3*, Historical Metallurgy Group, June 1964.

31 Meade, R., *The Coal and Iron Industry of the United Kingdom*, 1882.

32 Christian, Roy, 'The Handyside Story', *Derbyshire Advertiser*, 7 April 1961.

33 Dearden, J., 'The Centenary of the Steel Rail', *Railway Steel Topics*, Vol IV, No 1, 1957.

34 Report of the Manuscripts of Lord Middleton. HMSO, 1911, p 174.

35 Smith, R. S., 'Huntingdon Beaumont, Adventurer in Coal Mines', *Renaissance and Modern Studies*, 1958, I; and 'England's First Rail: A Reconsideration', *Renaissance and Modern Studies*, 1960, IV.

36 Nef, J. U., *The Rise of the British Coal Industry*, 2 vols. Routledge, 1932.

37 Houghton, Thomas, *A Collection for the Improvement of Husbandry and Trade*, 1692–1703.

38 Tyson, G. J. G., 'Early Use of Coke in Derby', *DAJ*, LIV, 1933.

39 Nixon, F., 'The Early Steam Engine in Derbyshire', *Trans NS*, XXXI, 1957–9.

40 Mott, R. A., *The Triumphs of Coke*. Coke Oven Manufacturers Association, 1965.

41 Mushet, David, *Papers on Iron & Steel*, 1840.

42 Bailey, E. M., 'The Dawn of Petroleum Refinery', *Inst of Petroleum Review*, Vol 2, No 24, Dec 1948.

43 Armstrong, Leslie, 'The Buxton Lime Trade', *Cement, Lime and Gravel*, 1950.

44 Rolt, L. T. C., *Great Engineers*. Bell, 1962.

45 Ford, T. D., 'The Black Marble Mines of Ashford-in-the-Water', *Bull PDMHS*, Vol 2, No 4, Oct 1964.

46 Ford, T. D., 'Inlaid Ashford Marble', *Derbyshire Countryside*, Vol 23, No 5, August/September 1958.

CHAPTER THREE (*The Evolution of Engineering.* Page 93)

1 Keller, A. G., *A Theatre of Machines*. Chapman & Hall, 1964.
2 Strutt, F. and Cox, J. C., 'Duffield Forest in the Sixteenth Century', *DAJ*, XXV, 1903.
3 Williamson, F., 'George Sorocold, of Derby', *DAJ*, LVII, 1936.
4 Jenkins, Rhys, 'George Sorocold: A Chapter in the History of Public Water Supply', *The Engineer*, 18 Oct 1918.
5 Smeaton, John, 'Experimental Engineering Concerning the Natural Powers of Wind and Water', 2nd ed, 1796. (Read before Royal Society, 1758.)
6 Trevithick, F., *Life of Richard Trevithick*, 1872.
7 Kirkham, N., 'The Draining of the Alport Lead Mines', *Trans NS*, XXXIII, 1960–1.
8 Thornhill, R., 'The Arkwright Mill at Bakewell', *DAJ*, LXXIX, 1959. *The Times Review of Industry*, July 1955. *Engineering*, 11 Jan 1958.
9 Nixon, F., 'The Early Steam Engine in Derbyshire', *Trans NS*, Vol XXXI, 1957–9.
10 Kirkham, N., 'Steam Engines in Derbyshire'. Newcomen Society, Feb 1966.
11 Patent No 1833, 1791.
12 Farey, John Jr, *A Treatise on the Steam Engine*, 1827.
13 Fitton, R. S. and Wadsworth, A.P., *The Strutts and the Arkwrights*. Manchester UP, 1958.
14 Anderson, W. T., 'Notes on an old Colliery Pumping Engine, 1791', *Trans* Inst Mining Engineers, LII, 1917.
15 Sidebotham, A. G., 'Winding up a Century', *Edgar Allen News*, April and May 1965. This house journal did good service to the cause of industrial history until its demise in December 1966.
16 *The Pirotechnia of Vanoccio Biringuccio*. Trans Smith and Gnudi. Am Inst Mining & Metallurgical Engineers, 1942.
17 White, W. D., 'Derbyshire Clockmakers before 1850. The Whitehurst Family'. Supplement No 3, *LHS DAJ*, March 1958.
18 Woodbury, R. S., 'History of the Gear-Cutting Machine'. MIT, 1958.
19 Fraser, W., 'Some Derbyshire Water Mills', *Derbyshire Countryside*, Jan–March 1951; and Rolt, L. T. C., *Tools for the Job*. Batsford, 1965.
20 Robinson, P., *The Smiths of Chesterfield*. Robinson & Sons Ltd, 1957.
21 Dickinson, H. W., 'The Diary of John Bodmer, 1816–17', *Trans NS*, X, 1929–30.
22 Rolt, L. T. C., *Tools for the Job*, op cit.
23 *Engineering*, 11 April 1879.
24 'The Midland Railway Carriage and Wagon Works at Derby', *The Railway Engineer*, Dec 1921–May 1922; six instalments.

CHAPTER FOUR (*Communications.* Page 135)

1 Mehew, S., 'Packhorse Bridges in Derbyshire', *DM*, I, p 11.
2 Ford, T. D., 'Faujas de St Fond (1741–1819)', *Bull PDMHS*, Vol 2, Part 5.
3 Twells, H. S., 'The Beginning of a Turnpike Trust', *DAJ*, LXVI, 1942.

S

4   Pecchio, Count Giuseppe, *Italian Exile*, 1833.
5   Castle Donington WEA Group, *Historical Account of the Ancient Kings Mills*, 1960.
6   Hadfield, C., *The Canals of the East Midlands* and *The Canals of the West Midlands*. David & Charles, both 1966.
7   Rolt, L. T. C., *The Great Engineers*, op cit.
8   Smith, R. S., op cit.
9   Lee, C. E., 'The Evolution of Railways', *Railway Gazette*, 1943.
10 Garlic, S. L., 'The Zig-Zag Railway', *DM*, III, No 4, Feb 1965.
11 Baxter, B., 'Early Railways in Derbyshire', *Trans NS*, XXVI, 1947-9.
12 Lindsay, Jean, 'The Butterley Coal & Iron Works, 1792–1816', *DAJ*, LXXXV, 1965.
13 Fryar, Mark, *Some Chapters in the History of Denby*. Privately published, 1934.
14 Pendred, Loughman St L., 'A Note on Brunton's Steam Horse 1813', *Trans NS*, II, 1921-2.
15 Rimmer, A., *The Cromford and High Peak Railway*. Oakwood Press, 1956.
16 Simmons, Jack, *The Railways of Britain*. Routledge Paperback, 1962.
17 Smith, J. Frederick, *Frederick Swanwick*. Printed for private circulation 1888, per Mr C. C. Handford.
18 Coleman, Terry, *The Railway Navvies*. Hutchinson, 1965.
19 *Derby Mercury*, 20 May 1840.
20 Hoult, W. H., 'Fell's Experimental Railway in Derbyshire', *The Railway Magazine*, Jan 1961.
21 Platt, K. P., *The Ashover Light Railway*. Private, 1955.
22 *The Railway Engineer*, op cit.
23 Bryan, B., *Matlock, Manor and Parish*, 1903. Also Hall, C. C., *The Matlock Cable Tramway*. Tramway Museum Society, 1965.
24 Morton, C. W., *A History of Rolls-Royce Motor Cars*, Vol 1, 1903-7. Foulis, 1964.

CHAPTER FIVE (*Textiles*. Page 173)

1   Aspin, C. and Chapman, S. D., *James Hargreaves and the Spinning Jenny*. Helmshore Local History Society, 1964.
2   Fay, C. R., *Great Britain from Adam Smith to the Present Day*. Longmans, 1953.
3   Brown, John, 'A Memoir of Robert Blincoe' (1828). Reprint in Supplement No 10, *LHS DAJ*, 1966.
4   Higgens, C. W., 'The Framework Knitters of Derbyshire', *DAJ*, LXXI, 1951.
5   Williamson, F., 'George Sorocold of Derby', *DAJ*, LVII, 1936. The source work on Sorocold and the silk mills of Cotchett and Lombe.
6   Chapman, S. D., 'The Transition to the Factory System in the Midlands Cotton Spinning Industry', *Economic History Review*, Second Series, Vol XVIII, No 3, 1965.
7   Fitton and Wadsworth, op cit.
8   Aspin and Chapman, op cit.
9   Swindin, K., 'The Arkwright Cotton Mills at Cromford', *Jnl Ind Arch*, Vol 2, No 1, March 1965.

10 Ottrey, F. S., 'Geographical Aspects of the Development of Wirksworth, 1800–1965', MA thesis. Nottingham, 1966.
11 Skempton, A. W. and Johnson, H. R., 'William Strutt's Cotton Mills, 1793–1812', *Trans NS*, XXX, 1955–7.
12 Mackenzie, M. H., 'Calver Mill and its Owners'; Parker, Vanessa, 'The Calver Mill Buildings'; Mackenzie, M. H., 'Calver Mill and its Owners: A Supplement', *DAJ*, LXXXIV, 1964.
13 Pigott, Stanley, *Hollins: A Study of Industry, 1784–1949*. Wm Hollins & Co Ltd, Nottingham, 1949.
14 Ashmore, Owen, 'The Early Textile Industry in the Derwent Valley', *DM*, I, 5, March 1957.
15 Ashmore, Owen, 'The Early Textile Industry in North West Derbyshire', *DM*, I, 9, June 1958.
16 Unwin, George, 'Samuel Oldknow and the Arkwrights'. Manchester, 1924.
17 Felkin, William, History of the Machine-Wrought Hosiery and Lace Manufactures (sic) 1867. Reprinted David & Charles, 1967.

CHAPTER SEVEN (*Other Industries*. Page 205)

1 Shorter, A. H., *Paper Mills and Paper Makers in England, 1495–1800*. Hilversum, 1957.
2 Hickling, G., *Duffield in Appletree*. Privately published 1958.
3 Derby Chamber of Commerce, *Year Book*. 50th Anniversary Commemoration. 1916.
4 Cheke, Val, *The Story of Cheese-Making in Britain*. Routledge & Kegan Paul, 1959.

Bibliographical Notes

GENERAL

Gazetteers and Directories. Stephen Glover's *A History of the County of Derby*, 2 vols, 1829, is valuable. Although Vol I derives much information from Farey, Vol II, a gazetteer of places in alphabetical order up to and including Derby, is useful as mentioning industrial developments and installations. The manuscript of the unpublished third volume may be consulted at the Derby Borough Library. Compilers of gazetteers were great plagiarists, identical paragraphs appearing in different works over periods of twenty years or more. Especial care must be taken with the more recent works, which sometimes retain references to companies long after they have become defunct. Particularly useful amongst earlier works on Derbyshire are J. Pigot, 1828, 1831, 1835, Bagshaw, 1846, Freebody, 1852 and White's *History, Gazetteer and Directory of the County of Derby*, 1857. This last, although it contains much of what appeared in Bagshaw, covers the county as a whole much more thoroughly, and is recommended.

Encyclopaedias. The classic technological encyclopaedia is Rees' *Cyclopaedia of Arts, Sciences and Literature*, 45 vols, 1819, which contains comprehensive articles on all contemporary industrial developments by such authorities as John Farey Senior and Junior. Unfortunately it is not easily available. Another useful work is *Pantalogia*, 14 vols, 1813, to which John Farey Jr contributed. The development of industries during the nineteenth century can be traced through Ure's *Dictionary of Arts, Manufactures and Mines*, 1839, and the later 3-volume editions, eg the 7th of 1878.

Periodicals. Especially useful are the *Journal of the Derbyshire Archaeological Society*, first published 1879, and *Derbyshire Miscellany*, published since 1957 by the Local History Section of the DAS, both of which have many articles on the county's industry; the *Bulletin* of the Peak District Mines Historical Society; the *East Midland Geographer* (Nottingham University); and *Histories of Derbyshire*, a thesis by Mr P. D. Hallsworth, 1956, which may be consulted at the Derbyshire County Library. The *Transactions* of the Newcomen Society for the Study of the History of Engineering and Technology contain much information of fundamental value. The *Bulletin* of the Historical Metallurgy Group is of recent inception but has already covered much useful ground. Old issues of *The Engineer* and of *Engineering* can still be obtained for all dates over the past century. As a guide to current publications the *North Midland Bibliography*, compiled by Mr R. A. H. O'Neal of the Derby & District College of Technology, is extremely useful. The *Derby Red Book*, published annually from 1862 to 1915, contained in many issues a useful review of industrial developments. *Derbyshire Countryside* and *Country Life* often contain articles of historical interest.

Newspapers. Derbyshire is fortunate in having newspaper files covering nearly 250 years. The *Derby Mercury*, 1732–1933, the *Derbyshire Advertiser*, 1832 to the present, and the *Derby and Chesterfield Reporter*, 1832–99, have maintained an interest in industrial developments, as have the current daily and weekly newspapers.

Maps. Much useful information can be obtained from old maps, which may be consulted in the branches of the County Library, the Borough Libraries, and the County Record Office, all of which, incidentally, can give valuable advice. Maps which have been found particularly useful are the map of Derbyshire, Snowden's revised version, 1797, of P. P. Burdett's map of 1767; the *Map of the County of Derby* made by G. Sanderson, 1836, and especially the personal copy of A. H. Stokes, who inscribed upon it the railways, actual and proposed, 1880, which copy was reproduced by the Local History Section of the DAS; W. M. Rogerson's *Plan of the Town of Derby*, 1819.

Local Collections. The Derby Borough Library, the Chesterfield Public Library and the Derbyshire County Libraries and the County Record Office have extensive collections of documents and books of value to the serious worker.

CHAPTER ONE (*The County of Derby*. Page 15)

An excellent introduction to the county and its industry will be found under Geology in Vol I of *VCH Derbyshire*, 1905, and in Industry in Vol II, 1907. Contemporary accounts give useful information, as well as conveying the atmosphere of the times. These include *The Journeys of Celia Fiennes* (1697–8), Cresset Press, 1947 (this intrepid woman took a keen interest in everything novel to her, which included lead mining and Sorocold's waterworks at Derby); Daniel Defoe's *A Tour through England and Wales*, Everyman's Library, 1948; William Bray's *A Sketch of a Tour into Derbyshire and Yorkshire*, 1783; *The Torrington Diaries*, by the Hon John Byng, 4 vols, Eyre & Spottiswoode, 1934–6, which include accounts of journeys into Derbyshire (eg Derby, Cromford, Bakewell) 1781–94; James Pilkington's *A View of the Present State of Derbyshire*, 2 vols, 1789; *An Historical and Descriptive View of Derbyshire*, by D. P. Davies, 1811, contains fairly detailed descriptions of industrial installations and processes.

CHAPTER TWO (*The Exploitation of Mineral Wealth*. Page 23)

John Farey's *View of the Agriculture and Minerals of Derbyshire*, Vol I, 1811, Vol II, 1813, Vol III, 1817, is invaluable. Farey reported on the county's characteristics and achievements in great detail.

The Derbyshire County Library publishes and keeps up to date a bibliography on *Derbyshire Lead and Lead Mining*. W. K. V. Gale's *The British Iron and Steel Industry*, David & Charles, 1967, and *Griffith's Guide to the Iron Trade of Great Britain*, 1873, reprinted by David & Charles 1967, will be found useful, while E. Matheson's *Works in Iron*, 1877, illustrates many of the more important achievements of Handysides. *Mediaeval English Alabasters* by F. W. Cheetham, 1962, published by the City of Nottingham Art Galleries & Museums Committee is a useful reference book. Interesting accounts of the products of the different china enterprises will be found in *Pottery and Porcelain*, by Frederick Litchfield, A. & C. Black, 1925, and in *History and Classification of Derby Porcelain*, by F. Williamson, Derby Museum, 1924.

CHAPTER THREE (*The Evolution of Engineering*. Page 93)

A proper understanding of industrial archaeology and history requires a knowledge of the technologies and of the processes of manufacture, their origins and evolution. An inexpensive and comprehensive work is *A History of Science and Technology*, by R. J. Forbes and E. J. Dijksterhuis, 2 vols, Pelican Books, 1963. An important and readable work, written as a complement to Singer's monumental *A History of Technology*, 5 vols, OUP, 1954–8, is *A Short History of Technology*, by T. K. Derry and T. I. Williams, OUP, 1960. The works of Samuel Smiles are valuable as an introduction to the subject, with much biographical detail. They include *The Lives of the Engineers*, 3 vols, 1861–2, *Industrial Biography*, 1863, both reprinted by David & Charles, 1968, and a number of individual biographies.

CHAPTER FOUR (*Communications*. Page 135)

As far as roads, canals and tramroads are concerned, the works quoted in the References (p 289) will suffice as an introduction. Railways have such an extensive literature that it is not possible to refer to more than *The Midland Railway*, 1876 (reprinted by David & Charles 1968), and *Our Iron Roads*, 1852, 6th ed, 1885, by F. S. Williams, and *The Rise of the Midland Railway, 1844–1874*, by E. G. Barnes, Allen & Unwin, 1966. See especially Chapter VIII, 'Literature and Maps' of Professor Jack Simmons' *The Railways of Britain*, Routledge Paperback, 1965. The Tramway Museum Society can advise on references to the history of street cars.

CHAPTER FIVE (*Textiles*. Page 173)

Those desiring a fuller knowledge of the textile industry should consult E. Baines' *History of the Cotton Manufacture in Great Britain*, 1835, recently reissued by Blackwells of Oxford 1966; W. Felkin's *A History of the Machine-Wrought Hosiery and Lace Manufactures*, 1867, reprinted by David & Charles 1967; and Dr S. D. Chapman's *The Early Factory Masters*, David & Charles, 1967.

Acknowledgments

IN collecting the material for this book so many individuals and companies have been contacted in all parts of the county that it is impossible to acknowledge them all. It must suffice to express here my most grateful thanks to all who have so willingly given help and encouragement, and especially to those who have allowed access to their land and premises. Special mention must be made of Miss Nellie Kirkham, who kindly checked the section on lead mining, and Mr R. W. Clement for helpful criticism of that dealing with the geology of the county.

The editor-in-chief of the series, Dr E. R. R. Green, and my publishers have helped greatly with the co-ordination of a manuscript which has inevitably had to be set aside many times as the demands of an industrial livelihood have intervened. Miss Joan Sinar, the County Archivist, has offered constructive argument, and the unstinting and painstaking assistance given by the staff of the Derby Borough Library's Reference Department has provided essential support to the effort to make the information as accurate and as complete as possible. All this would have been of no avail without the skill and perseverance of Mrs M. M. Butler in deciphering and bringing into excellently typed order a series of hastily scrawled and jumbled notes.

Mr Peter Kirk was of considerable help with the maps and sketches on pages 20, 21, 25, 29, 129 and 162. Mr J. H. Swannell, of the Nottingham Regional College of Technology, kindly had made the print from which the figure on page 47 was made. Ferodo Ltd, who produced the figure on page 104 from their archives, are especially thanked for much useful information.

Index

References to illustrations are printed in italics.